In the Face of Fear

A SHAMBHALA SUN BOOK

In the Face of Fear

Buddhist Wisdom for Challenging Times

Edited by Barry Boyce
and the editors of the *Shambhala Sun*

SHAMBHALA
Boston & London 2009

Shambhala Publications, Inc.
Horticultural Hall
300 Massachusetts Avenue
Boston, Massachusetts 02115
www.shambhala.com

9 8 7 6 5 4

Printed in the United States of America

⊗This edition is printed on acid-free paper that meets the
American National Standards Institute z39.48 Standard.
♻This book is printed on 30% postconsumer recycled paper.
For more information please visit www.shambhala.com.

Distributed in the United States by Random House, Inc.,
and in Canada by Random House of Canada Ltd

Library of Congress Cataloging-in-Publication Data
In the face of fear: Buddhist wisdom for challenging times/edited
by Barry Boyce and the editors of the Shambhala Sun.—1st ed.
p. cm.
ISBN 978-1-59030-757-1 (pbk.: alk. paper)
1. Four Noble Truths. 2. Suffering—Religious aspects—Buddhism.
3. Spiritual life—Buddhism. I. Boyce, Barry Campbell, 1956–
BQ4230.I5 2009
294.3'4442—DC22
2009017721

Contents

PART FOUR

Facing Fear and Other Strong Emotions

PART FIVE

Skillful Means: Money, Work, and Family

Acknowledgments

It's been an honor and a distinct pleasure to put together this anthology, which gave me the opportunity to read such rich, warm, penetrating, and insightful teachings from the principal Buddhist traditions. In my work for the *Shambhala Sun* and *Buddhadharma: The Practitioner's Quarterly*, I've been blessed with the auspicious coincidence of working closely with teachings and teachers from all over the world. We are all fortunate that so many people have dedicated their lives to gaining profound insight, embodying it, and energetically offering it to others.

I want to especially thank my root teacher, Chögyam Trungpa Rinpoche. It is his pioneering spirit and nonsectarian attitude that has inspired me to seek with an open mind teachings from many different traditions and perspectives. May this work repay a small part of my debt to him.

My colleagues at both the *Shambhala Sun* and *Buddhadharma*, Buddhist and non-Buddhist alike, provide me with examples of openness and confidence in the face of many day-to-day challenges. In particular I want to thank Editor-in-Chief Melvin McLeod for his guidance and keen perception throughout the whole process of bringing this book to fruition—and for his very helpful and pithy introduction. My lifelong friend and colleague, Publisher James Gimian has always been available to probe and uncover the next thing that needs to be uncovered. *Buddhadharma* Editor Tynette Deveaux offers a fine example of exercising the care that is needed to bring dharma to a wide audience without dilution. I also want to thank Cecelia Driscoll for being ready to do any task required to make this book happen.

I've benefited for almost forty years from the wonderful output of Shambhala Publications, and I now count many people there as friends. I want to thank Editor Beth Frankl and Assistant Editor Katie Keach for admirably combining patience and persistence. I also appreciate the camaraderie and support of Peter Turner, President of Shambhala, and Vice President Jonathon Green.

Thanks finally to my family: my 95-year-old mom, Mary, who provides an hourly example of wisdom in challenging times, my wife, Judi, and my daughters Anna and Madeline for reminding me of what is important, when, in spite of all the wisdom I'm exposed to, I forget how simple it is to be fully human.

Barry Boyce
Senior Editor
The Shambhala Sun
Buddhadharma: The Practitioner's Quarterly

Introduction

I believe the Buddha's teachings are what we need right now. They are made precisely for times like these. For all of us who are suffering groundlessness, fear, or loss—because of the world's problems or just our own—Buddhist wisdom is the right medicine.

The Buddha is sometimes called the Great Physician. Twenty-five hundred years ago, he made a precise diagnosis of the human condition—our condition. It is as accurate and relevant today as it was then. He diagnosed our problem as *dukkha*, which we generally translate as "suffering." Then he discovered its cause, and he proposed a cure. Today we call this diagnosis and cure the Four Noble Truths.

Famously, the Four Noble Truths describe suffering, the cause of suffering, the cessation of suffering, and a path to the cessation of suffering. But when we say that the Buddha promised an end to suffering, we have to be careful. Buddhist practice does not offer an end to change, loss, or even pain. These are basic facts of life, generally beyond our control. We do not have the power to banish them from our lives.

What we can change is the way we react. The Buddha's great discovery was that most of what we call suffering, dissatisfaction, or unhappiness is really the product of our own reactions, of our own mind. To that suffering he did promise an end.

This book will help you apply the Buddha's wisdom so that you can lessen the suffering of living in difficult times. In the process you may discover resources of love, skillfulness, and happiness you didn't know you had in you.

Life is stressful and insecure for many of us these days. If we haven't actually lost our job or our home, we fear we might. If we run a business, we worry about how to keep it afloat. If we have a family, we are anxious about our children's future. For those of us approaching retirement, we wonder whether our savings will sustain us in our old age.

Beyond the immediate difficulties, we fear for the world's long-term prospects. The relatively peaceful and prosperous life we have enjoyed since the end of the Second World War—long enough to seem all but permanent—seems questionable as we look ahead into the twenty-first century. And to these fears and stresses we add all the normal, inescapable difficulties of everyday life—the profound challenges of sickness, a death in the family, or problems in our relationships.

Much as we'd like to change all this, we probably can't. What we can change—if we're given the right tools—is the way we experience, understand, and deal with these realities. According to the Buddha, that's not just half the battle, it's pretty much the whole battle. We have the freedom to choose how we react to the world, and if we choose wisely, we can find joy, love, and happiness even in difficult times. We can transform our world by transforming how we experience it. In doing so, we benefit ourselves and all those around us.

This book will take you on a journey. It's a practical journey, aimed at helping you deal with whatever difficulties come up. Buddhism is renowned for its array of proven techniques, its skillful means, and you will learn how to apply them in your life. But you will also find that this journey is profound. While this book is not about exalted concepts like "enlightenment," you still might catch a glimpse of that as you work through the daily challenges of life. Buddhism doesn't separate the sacred and the secular; enlightenment is far more ordinary and accessible than you might think, and it's grounded nowhere else but in the gritty realities of life.

The journey this book offers is not an easy or quick one. Any of us who have been practicing Buddhism for years will tell you that it doesn't offer any magic bullets or quick cures. I can tell you that the reality of my own life is proof of that. This journey is a step-by-step path of self-awareness, taming our wild minds, and examining the unstated assumptions we bring to life. It's hard work, and honest self-awareness can be pretty painful sometimes. But any moment of clarity, of opening our hearts, of easing the suffering of ourselves and others, is a better moment. What else we can aspire to in life?

In this anthology, we divide this journey into six parts, or stages. At the same time, while each of the teachings has a particular focus, they by necessity touch on other issues and steps on the journey. So the teachings presented here are interwoven as well as linear.

Like all journeys, this one begins at the beginning—where we really are in our lives, not where we hope or want to be. In part one, "Beyond Denial," we look clearly and courageously at things as they are. We look at some undeniable realities of our lives as human beings, and some fundamental facts about reality as pointed out by the Buddha. Sylvia Boorstein helps us to acknowledge that suffering is not something we alone go through—look around and you see that it is the universal human experience. Jon Kabat-Zinn, the founder of mindfulness-based stress reduction, and His Holiness the Dalai Lama explain that disciplined awareness of mind and body is the great medicine that heals this suffering. The late Zen teacher Shunryu Suzuki Roshi teaches that impermanence and change are the fundamental nature of reality, and his student Zoketsu Norman Fischer, himself a well-known Zen teacher, shows how the best response to change and loss is an open heart.

Beyond these powerful insights, Buddhism's great strength is the wealth of techniques it has developed over the last twenty-five hundred years to help us work with our minds. Generally we call these techniques "meditation," but they are much more than that. Yes, to train our minds we need to sit down in a formal meditation situation and learn how to develop our awareness. But then we bring that awareness into all aspects of our lives.

So we call part two "Tools for a Mindful Life." The beloved American nun and Buddhist teacher Pema Chödrön opens it with a simple and relaxed technique we can use anytime during the day to pause, open our minds, and experience the world around us. Thich Nhat Hanh shows us how simple awareness of the present moment—without judgment or self-criticism—is the refreshing balm that soothes our suffering. The Vipassana teacher Phillip Moffitt presents the very meditation technique taught by the Buddha himself, and the popular teacher Sakyong Mipham tells us how we can start each day with a simple shift in attitude that changes everything. Finally, the Insight Meditation Society cofounder Joseph Goldstein teaches us a loving-kindness meditation we can use to transform our relationships with others.

In part three, "Transforming Difficulty into Awakening," we discover the magic of Buddhist wisdom. Too often we respond to difficulty in habitual, self-destructive ways that only increase our suffering and hurt others, but through the power of awareness, we can transform difficult circumstances into opportunities for awakening and benefit. Is there greater magic than that?

The Dzogchen Ponlop Rinpoche poses the basic challenge: when mistakes and difficulties arise, will we seize the moment as a chance to wake up, or will we sleepwalk through it by falling into our habitual responses? The late Chögyam Trungpa Rinpoche, one of the pioneers of Buddhism in the West, draws upon the Buddhist teachings known as *lojong*, meaning "mind training," to teach us about the fundamental reversal of attitude that transforms suffering into awakening. His student, Pema Chödrön, returns to show us how to break out of the trap of worldly opposites—gain and loss, pleasure and pain, and so forth—that cause us so much suffering. Finally, the psychoanalyst and Buddhist practitioner Polly Young-Eisendrath describes the transformative power of acceptance.

In part four, we come to grips with perhaps our greatest challenge: emotions. Difficult times bring up strong, painful emotions. Conversely, a great many of our problems are caused by our failure to handle strong emotions well. So often the determining factor in the quality of our lives together as human beings—whether as lovers, family members, coworkers, or even nations—is how we work with our emotions.

People are experiencing a lot of fear in these difficult times, whether acutely as panic or chronically as anxiety. More than that, as fragile, mortal beings, fear is at our very core, and how we handle it defines the quality of our lives.

That's why the teachings on fear and fearlessness in this part are among the most important in this book, and why this book is titled as it is. The challenge of fear is central to these difficult times. It is central to how we lead our lives altogether. In "Smile at Fear," Carolyn Rose Gimian presents the unique teachings on fear and fearlessness of Chögyam Trungpa, who more than any other Buddhist teacher emphasized the importance of how we face fear. Dzigar Kongtrül Rinpoche and Tsoknyi Rinpoche teach us about the courage we need to look at life openly and honestly, yet with a sense of humor too. The Zen teacher John Daido Loori gives us advice on working with stress, and the Insight Meditation teacher Jack Kornfield shows us how to transform desire into an appreciation of life's inherent abundance.

In part five, we get specific help on the challenges of difficult economic times, when stress over money, jobs, and the welfare of our families becomes acute. The part is called "Skillful Means," because the Buddha's wisdom helps us to work more skillfully and effectively with our world, benefiting ourselves and all those around us. It turns out the best way to change the world is to change how we relate to it.

The business consultant Michael Carroll advises us on how to handle all the stresses of the workplace. Judy Lief talks about what to do when those we love the most are experiencing difficulty. The Buddhist political thinker David Loy analyzes the false psychology of money, and James Gimian and Barry Boyce (also the editor of this book) explain how understanding the principle of interconnectedness can make us more effective in all our activities. And finally the great Buddhist teacher Thich Nhat Hanh praises the bodhisattva, who is the epitome of skill because he or she is unreservedly devoted to the welfare of all beings.

In easy or hard times, the question is always, How shall we live as human beings? We all want happiness, for ourselves and others, but how do we achieve it? Because the Buddha promised more than just the cessation of suffering. He promised a life of joy, love, and fulfillment, even in the face of difficult times. He could make that promise because of who we really are as human beings.

While much of this book is about changing how we relate to our world, the last part, "True Happiness," reveals that we don't need to change who we are. The true nature of our mind is awareness and wisdom; the true nature of our heart is love and compassion. We suffer because we don't really believe we have these qualities, and we struggle constantly to be someone new, someone better. The cessation of suffering is the cessation of that struggle. Happiness, enlightenment even, is just being who we truly are.

So whether we're living in good times or bad, whether our expectations are met or not, whether our world feels shaky or secure, we have resources of delight, openness, dignity, and, yes, happiness. We can be cheerful even in the face of difficulty, says Sakyong Mipham. We can tap into a deep level of being beyond the ups and downs of life, says the Zen teacher Joan Sutherland. We can learn to rule our life, says Chögyam Trungpa, with dignity and a sense of celebration. And above all, says Dzigar Kongtrül Rinpoche—and indeed every other great Buddhist teacher—we attain true happiness when we put love for others at the center of our being. It is the great, final, counterintuitive secret of life: the key to happiness is putting others first. This is the Buddha's very best medicine.

Melvin McLeod
Editor-in-Chief
The Shambhala Sun
Buddhadharma: The Practitioner's Quarterly

PART ONE

Beyond Denial

Seeing Things as They Really Are

It's All Happening to All of Us, All of the Time

Sylvia Boorstein

We take pain and difficulty very personally. We feel it is happening to us as individuals, as "me" or "I." The Buddha's foremost teaching, says insight meditation teacher Sylvia Boorstein, is that life is difficult— for everyone. Seeing that we are all in this together begins to loosen our focus on our big, special problem, and helps us develop the strength and courage to go forward.

I've been leading a two-hour Wednesday morning class at Spirit Rock Meditation Center for more than fifteen years. Of the seventy or so people there on any given week, there are the folks who have been coming regularly since the beginning, new people coming to see what it's like, and visitors to San Francisco who come because they are in town. I've begun to think of it as our local church. We always begin by greeting newcomers. I then give some meditation instructions and we sit quietly for thirty or forty minutes. In the last minutes of the sitting I remind people that they're welcome to mention the names of people they are particularly thinking of, people facing a special challenge, so that we could, as a group, think of them with shared concern and support. I often start by naming someone I know—"I am thinking of my friend Allison, who is recuperating from surgery for ovarian cancer"—and wait for others to speak. People say a name, a relationship, and a challenge.

"I am thinking of my cousin Joan, who has macular degeneration."

"I am thinking of my daughter-in-law Louise, who just had a miscarriage."

"I am thinking of my brother Tom, whose son just lost his job and his house."

"I am thinking of my friend Michael, who has lung cancer."

". . . my Uncle John, who has emphysema."

". . . my son Tim, just diagnosed bipolar."

". . . my friend Bernie, who lost most of the retirement savings for him and his wife."

". . . my neighbor Virginia, whose daughter died in a car accident last Sunday on her way back to college."

I don't call on people to speak. In random order, from different parts of the room, voices speak out names, and relationships, and special circumstances. Sometimes I recognize a voice, or a name. More often not. Sometimes the naming goes on for what seems a long time. There is always a space between the voices, as if people are reflecting on what they've just heard. I think we share the sense that there is no hurry to get finished, no activity more important to arrive at.

Not all of the special circumstances that people mention are dire, although it seems that sad situations are usually the ones that come up first. Then, in between difficulties, someone will say, "I'm thinking of my daughter Jessica, who has just been accepted into three colleges and needs to choose." Or, "I'm thinking of my son and daughter-in-law, who are on their way to Peru to meet their newly adopted baby daughter." Or, "I'm thinking about my college roommate from Michigan, who has remained my friend for fifty years and who is arriving tonight for a visit."

I don't think I am imagining the communal sigh of relief or

appreciation that follows happy news. Those moments seem like opportunities in which my mind, perhaps everyone's mind, can "catch its breath" and remember the pleasures that punctuate life and make it seem desirable to go on in the face of difficulty.

Sometimes the listing of names and circumstances goes on for some minutes:

". . . my grandson Jason in his second tour of duty in Iraq."

". . . my sister Ruth with breast cancer."

". . . my friend Claire, whose life savings were invested with Bernie Madoff."

". . . my niece Renee, who is nine months pregnant and whose husband just lost his job and their insurance."

". . . my husband's mother, Ruby, who is dying of Alzheimer's disease."

At some point the room becomes quiet again, and we sit a while longer. I say a blessing for all the people we've mentioned, and for all people suffering everywhere, and I ring the bell. Usually, we all just sit there and look at each other for a while. Often, I find myself feeling speechless, stunned both by the array of pains that body and mind are heir to and humbled by our communal courage not only in carrying on in spite of challenges in our lives but in being willing to share them with each other.

What more compelling evidence could there be, apart from personal testimony, of the inevitable difficulties of life? Every week, as we listen to each other and hear about sicknesses of young people and old people, about disappointments and losses at all ages, we directly confirm that it is impossible to be a human being connected by affection to others and not be vulnerable to pains beyond our own. My sense is that hearing the implicit message that most of us carry on in spite of our difficulties builds strength and courage. I'm sure that's true for me, and I think it is for others as well. At the end of each Wednesday I feel remarkably freed of any grievances or ill will I might have had before class. I feel kinder, more connected, through both shared sorrow and joy with the people in the room and, past them, with people everywhere.

Life is difficult, the Buddha taught, for everyone. Suffering, he said, is the demand that experience be different from what it is. Of course we do what we can to address pain. Sometimes illnesses are cured. Sometimes relationships are mended. Sometimes losses are recouped. Sometimes, though, nothing can be done. The Buddha's teaching of liberation was that peace of mind is possible, no matter what the circumstances.

I recall hearing, for the first time, the legend of the young mother rushing with her dead son in her arms to plead with the Buddha, who was known to have miraculous powers to restore her child to life. I knew at once, as you will too if you are new to this story, that when the Buddha responded "I will do it if you bring me a mustard seed from a household in which no one has ever died," the boy would not live. The mother, disconsolate, returns from her quest knowing that everyone dies and that the heart can survive grief. To me, the instruction "bring me a mustard seed" means: "Look around you. You are supported by everyone else in the world." I understand the end of the legend, the mother bowing to the Buddha and becoming his disciple as her miraculous healing.

I feel myself supported by the awareness that everyone struggles. At Spirit Rock on Wednesday mornings, when I hear someone whose voice I don't recognize say "My Aunt Claire, who has Parkinson's disease . . ." I remember my friend Claire, who doesn't have Parkinson's disease but has something else, and Phyllis, who does have Parkinson's disease, and my aunt Miriam who, until her recent death, was the only person left in my family older than I am. A woman's voice saying "I'm thinking of my son Jacob in his second tour of duty in Iraq" reminds me of my cousins, whose son Jonathan is back in Iraq for his third tour, and I think about everyone with sons and daughters in wars all over the world. When I say, in the final dedication of merit at the end of the class, "May all beings be peaceful and happy and come to the end of suffering," I mean it with all my heart.

On one particular Wednesday morning when the list of special circumstances had been especially diverse and the kinship connections unusually wide-ranging, someone said, "Everything happens to everybody." I thought, at the time, that the remark was a response to the vast numbers of complex situations, sorrows, and joys that happen to people. What feels more true to me now is that when I *am* paying enough attention I realize that everything is happening to everyone collectively, and I feel appreciation and compassion for us all.

Dharma

Jon Kabat-Zinn

The founder of mindfulness-based stress reduction tells us that the Buddha was a healer and a revolutionary. The truth, or dharma, he revealed teaches us how the human mind deals with suffering and our quest for happiness. The Buddha's dharma teaches us that if we wish to live at ease, we have no choice but to pay close, intimate attention to what is happening in our body and our mind.

If we wish to know something of who we are, in the spirit of Socrates' injunction to "know thyself" and Yeats's assertion that we don't, there is no way around the need to look deeply into ourselves. If we wish to change the world, perhaps we might do well to tackle change in ourselves alongside change in the world, even and especially in the face of our own resistance and reluctance and blindness to change, even and especially as we are being confronted with the law of impermanence and the inevitability of change, conditions we are subject to as individuals regardless of how much we resist or protest or try to control outcomes. If we wish to make a quantum leap to greater awareness, there is no getting around the need for us to be willing to wake up, and to care deeply about waking up.

In the same vein, if we wish for greater wisdom and kindness in the world, perhaps we could start by inhabiting our own body with some degree of kindness and wisdom, even for one moment just accepting ourselves as we are with kindness and compassion rather than forcing ourselves to conform to some impossible ideal. The world would immediately be different. If we wish to make a true difference in this world, perhaps we must first learn how to stand in relationship to our own lives and our own knowing, or at least learn along the way, which always amounts to the same thing, since the world does not wait for us but is unfolding along with us in intimate reciprocity. And if we wish to grow or change or heal in any way, perhaps to be less strident or acquisitive, or more confident or generous, perhaps we must first taste silence and stillness, and know that drinking deeply at their wells is itself healing and transformative through embracing in awareness itself whatever we find *here* in this moment, including our deeply ingrained and unconscious tendencies.

All of this has been known for centuries. But liberative practices such as meditation were for the most part sequestered for centuries in monasteries under the stewardship of diverse cultural and religious traditions. For various reasons, including the vast distances lying between them geographically and culturally, and because of the distance between themselves as renunciates of the secular world and that world, these monasteries tended to be isolated, sometimes secretive about their practices, and perhaps in some cases parochial and exclusive rather than universal. At least until now.

Now, in this era, everything that has ever been discovered by human beings is out there for our investigation as it has never been before. In particular, Buddhist meditation and its associated wisdom tradition, known variously as Buddhadharma, or simply the dharma, is available to us now as never before and is touching the lives of millions of Americans and other Westerners in ways that would have been unimaginable forty or fifty years ago.

What the Buddhists call the dharma is an ancient force in this world, much like the Gospels, except that it has nothing to do in essence with religious conversion—or with organized religion, for that matter, or even with Buddhism per se, if one wants to think of Buddhism as a religion at all. But like the Gospels, it is literally good news.

The very word "dharma," which means variously the teachings of the Buddha, the lawfulness of the universe, and "the way things are," has found its way into our language in the past century through Jack Kerouac's famous characterization of himself and his beat friends as "dharma bums," through the poet Allen Ginsberg's appellation as the "Dharma Lion," and through the more recent marketing of "Dharma" as a novel woman's name in a television show, for a time displayed prominently in subway stations and on the side of buses, as happens so often in America.

The dharma was originally articulated by the Buddha in what he called the Four Noble Truths. It was elaborated on throughout his lifetime of teaching, and passed down to this day in unbroken lineages and streams within the various Buddhist traditions. In some ways it is appropriate to characterize dharma as resembling scientific knowledge: ever growing, ever changing, yet with a core body of methods, observations, and natural laws distilled from thousands of years of inner exploration through highly disciplined self-observation and self-inquiry, a careful and precise recording and mapping of experiences encountered in investigating the nature of the mind, and direct empirical testing and confirming of the results.

However, the lawfulness of the dharma is such that, in order for it to be dharma, it cannot be exclusively Buddhist, any more than the law of gravity is English because of Newton or Italian because of Galileo, or the laws of thermodynamics are Austrian because of Boltzmann. The contributions of these and other scientists who discovered and described natural laws always transcend their particular cultures, because they concern nature pure and simple, and nature is one seamless whole.

The Buddha's elaboration of the lawfulness of the dharma transcends his particular time and culture of origin in the same way, even though a religion grew out of it, albeit a peculiar one from the

Western point of view, as it is not based on worshiping a supreme deity. Mindfulness and dharma are best thought of as universal descriptions of the functioning of the human mind regarding the quality of one's attention in relationship to the experience of suffering and the potential for happiness. They apply equally wherever there are human minds, just as the laws of physics apply equally everywhere in our universe (as far as we know), or Noam Chomsky's universal generative grammar is applicable across all languages in the elaboration of human speech.

And from the point of view of the universality of dharma, it is helpful to recall that the Buddha himself was not a Buddhist. He was a healer and a revolutionary, albeit a quiet and inward one. He diagnosed our collective human dis-ease and prescribed a benevolent medicine for sanity and well-being. Given this, one might say that in order for Buddhism to be maximally effective as a dharma vehicle at this stage in the evolution of the planet, and for its sorely needed medicine to be maximally effective, it may have to give up being Buddhism in any formal religious sense or, at least, give up any attachment to it in name or form. Since dharma is ultimately about non-duality, distinctions between Buddhadharma and universal dharma, or between Buddhists and non-Buddhists, cannot be fundamental. From this perspective, the particular traditions and forms in which dharma manifests are alive and vibrant, multiple, and continually evolving; at the same time, the essence remains, as always, formless, limitless, and one without distinction.

In fact, even the word "Buddhism" is not Buddhist in origin. Apparently it was coined by European ethnologists, philologists, and religious scholars in the seventeenth and eighteenth centuries who were trying to fathom from the outside, through their own religious and cultural lenses and tacit assumptions, an exotic world that was largely opaque to them. For more than two thousand years, those who practiced the teachings of the Buddha, in whatever lineage (and there were many lineages, even within individual countries, all holding somewhat different interpretations of the original teachings), apparently simply referred to themselves as "followers of the Way" or "followers of the dharma." They did not describe themselves as "Buddhists."

Coming back to "dharma" as the teachings of the Buddha, the first of the Four Noble Truths he articulated after his intensive inquiry into the nature of mind was the universal prevalence of *dukkha*, the fundamental dis-ease of the human condition. The second was the cause of dukkha, which the Buddha attributed directly to attachment, clinging, and unexamined desire. The third was the assertion, based on his experience as the experimenter in the laboratory of his own meditation practice, that cessation of dukkha is possible—in other words, that it is possible to be completely cured of the dis-ease caused by attachment and clinging. And the fourth Noble Truth outlines a systematic approach, known as the Noble Eightfold Path, to the cessation of dukkha, the dispelling of ignorance, and, thus, to liberation.

Mindfulness is one of the eight practices along this path, the one unifying and informing all the others. All together, the eight practices are known as wise or "right" view, wise thinking, wise speech, wise action, wise livelihood, wise effort, wise mindfulness, and wise concentration. Each of these contains all the others. They are different aspects of one seamless whole. Thich Nhat Hanh puts it this way:

> *When Right Mindfulness is present, the Four Noble Truths and the seven other elements of the Eightfold Path are also present.*

Looking Deeply at Despair

His Holiness the Dalai Lama

His Holiness the Dalai Lama counsels that, as much as we would like to avoid or deny suffering and difficulty, it is essential to do just the opposite: wholeheartedly concentrate on and investigate deeply.

As people begin to act, for whatever cause, they often discover that people's despair, and the general level of suffering, is even greater than they had expected. The attitude we have toward the suffering matters a lot. If we look at it from too close up, we may feel overwhelmed, so that on top of the suffering itself, we also have depression and anxiety. But if we look at the same situation from a different perspective, we may be able to see that although it is truly tragic, it could be worse. Looking in this way reduces the level of our anxiety and suffering. In each event, there are a number of aspects. If we look at just one negative aspect, we will think only about that, and we may be overwhelmed.

In Buddhism, we do not deny or avoid despair and suffering. Instead, we concentrate on it, using a kind of analytical meditation. For example, if someone harms us, if we look at that person only as someone who has caused us harm, our anger may be overwhelming.

But if we look at her from the angle of something wonderful she did in the past, we will have another perspective, and it will not be too difficult to practice patience and develop the inner strength needed to overcome our negative feeling. That unfortunate event can actually help us increase our own inner strength, and seeing that can reduce our feeling of negativity toward the other person.

Analyzing the situation in this way is called "penetrating it." If you want to deny or avoid something and have a picnic or a vacation instead, you may feel some short-term relief, but the problem will remain. So instead of doing that, if you penetrate into the suffering or the tragedy and see its nature with some perspective, your mental attitude will improve, and you will have a real chance of resolving the problem.

If you want to lessen some suffering, you can withdraw your mind from it, or you can investigate and penetrate it. From the Buddhist point of view, all sentient beings—beings who have feelings, experiences, and sensations—are regarded as equal, so the idea of gaining benefit for one living being by sacrificing another is not something we can condone.

There is a quotation in a Buddhist sutra that says, "Reflect on your own feelings and sensations, and then see others as the same." Basically, every being is the same. Every being has the right to be happy and to overcome suffering. There is a close connection between oneself and others. Our own survival depends entirely on others. Therefore, showing concern for others ultimately brings benefit to us.

In reality, we have to live together. We cannot destroy all the other beings. Even if we do not like our neighbor, we have to live together. In the field of economics, also, we have to depend on others, even hostile nations. That is a reality. Under these circumstances, it is always better to live harmoniously, in a friendly way, than to maintain a negative attitude. The globe is becoming much smaller and more interdependent. Empathy and altruism are the keys for true happiness.

Altruism is more than just a feeling of sympathy. It includes a sense of responsibility, of taking care of one another. When we consider the other as someone precious and respected, it is natural that we will help them and share with them as expressions of our love. According to many scientists, we need affection for our brains to develop properly. This shows that our very nature is involved with affection, love, and compassion.

Through education, media, family life, and other means, we must introduce and bring to deeper awareness—if not for our present generation, for the future generations—the necessity of this altruistic mind and attitude. In order to awaken future generations' minds to these issues, it is important to present them as questions of survival, not as matters of religion or morality. Pain is unfortunate, but sometimes it can be an important factor to help people wake up, to realize that something is wrong.

As we gain insight into impermanence, or the passing nature of suffering, we do not become apathetic, feeling that nothing matters. We recognize suffering as suffering, and we allow that recognition to give rise to an aspiration to gain liberation from it. This doesn't make us apathetic. But we also realize that it is fruitless to get into turmoil or become anxious about our suffering. We can abandon the habit of becoming anxious about suffering and simply recognize it and allow that recognition to give rise to a desire for liberation.

Transiency

Shunryu Suzuki

*Nothing lasts. There is no truth so simple—nor so hard to accept.
One of the founding teachers of Zen in America, Shunryu Suzuki,
talks about how this basic tenet of Buddhism teaches us how to live
in the world.*

The basic teaching of Buddhism is the teaching of transiency, or change. That everything changes is the basic truth for each existence. No one can deny this truth, and all the teaching of Buddhism is condensed within it. This is the teaching for all of us. Wherever we go this teaching is true. This teaching is also understood as the teaching of selflessness. Because each existence is in constant change, there is no abiding self. In fact, the self-nature of each existence is nothing but change itself, the self-nature of all existence. There is no special, separate self-nature for each existence. This is also called the teaching of Nirvana. When we realize the everlasting truth of "everything changes" and find our composure in it, we find ourselves in Nirvana.

Without accepting the fact that everything changes, we cannot find perfect composure. But unfortunately, although it is true, it is difficult for us to accept it. Because we cannot accept the truth of transiency, we suffer. So the cause of suffering is our non-acceptance of this truth. The teaching of the cause of suffering and the teaching that everything changes are thus two sides of one coin. But subjectively, transiency is the cause of our suffering. Objectively this teaching is simply the basic truth that everything changes. Dogen-zenji said, "Teaching which does not sound as if it is forcing something on you is not true teaching." The teaching itself is true, and in itself does not force anything upon us, but because of our human tendency we receive the teaching as if something was being forced on us. But whether we feel good or bad about it, this truth exists. If nothing exists, this truth does not exist. Buddhism exists because of each particular existence. We should find perfect existence through imperfect existence.

We should find perfection in imperfection. For us, complete perfection is not different from imperfection. The eternal exists because of non-eternal existence. In Buddhism it is a heretical view to expect something outside this world. We do not seek for something besides ourselves. We should find the truth in this world, through our difficulties, through our suffering. This is the basic teaching of Buddhism. Pleasure is not different from difficulty. Good is not different from bad. Bad is good; good is bad. They are two sides of one coin. So enlightenment should be in practice. That is the right understanding of practice, and the right understanding of our life. So to find pleasure in suffering is the only way to accept the truth of transiency. Without realizing how to accept this truth you cannot live in this world. Even though you try to escape from it, your effort will be in vain. If you think there is some other way to accept the eternal truth that everything changes, that is your delusion. This is the basic teaching of how to live in this world. Whatever you may feel about it, you have to accept it. You have to make this kind of effort.

So until we become strong enough to accept difficulty as pleasure, we have to continue this effort. Actually, if you become honest enough, or straightforward enough, it is not so difficult to accept this truth. You can change your way of thinking a little bit. It is difficult, but this difficulty will not always be the same. Sometimes it will be difficult, and sometimes it will not be so difficult. If you are suffering, you will have some pleasure in the teaching that every-thing changes. When you are in trouble, it is quite easy to accept the teaching. So why not accept it at other times? It is the same thing. Sometimes you may laugh at yourself, discovering how selfish you are. But no matter how you feel about this teaching, it is very impor-tant for you to change your way of thinking and accept the truth of transiency.

Hard Times, Simple Times

Norman Fischer

When we lose what we cherish, whether it's a person or the way of life we've become accustomed to, it hurts deeply. The wound to our heart and mind that results is not something to be removed or covered over. The leader of the Everyday Zen community, Norman Fischer, shares his discovery of the possibilities that arise from letting that raw and tender soft spot remain open.

One day in January, feeling expansive and cheerfully open to being interrupted, I answered the phone in my study. Sherril was on the line. "Alan just died in Baltimore," she said. "Can you come over right now?"

Alan is Sherril's husband and my closest friend. We'd known each other forty years, since our days as students at the University of Iowa Writers' Workshop, through years of Zen practice, through Alan's becoming a rabbi and my ordination as a Zen priest, through our establishing a Jewish meditation center together, through retreats, teaching sessions, workshops, marriages, divorces, children, grandchildren. We had shared so much for so long that we took each other's presence in the world as basic.

I got in the car and drove to San Francisco in a daze—a daze I may never recover from.

Our first response to loss, difficulty, or pain is *not* surrendering to what has happened. It seems so negative, so wrong, and we don't want to give in to it. Yet we can't help thinking and feeling differently, and it is the thinking and the feeling—so unpleasant and painful—that is the real cause of our suffering. These days many of us experience troubled thinking and feeling because times are tough. So many are losing jobs, savings, homes, expectations. And if we are not losing these things ourselves, we are receiving at close range the suffering of others who are losing them, and we are reading and hearing about all this in the media and on the Web, which daily depict the effects of economic anxiety all over the world. We are all breathing in the atmosphere of fear and loss.

In one of our last conversations, Alan shared with me an odd and funny teaching about death. He had a sense of humor, and his spiritual teachings were often odd and funny, sometimes even ridiculous, which made their profundity all the more pungent. This teaching involved his fountain pen collection, which was extensive, and worth a lot of money. He had sold several thousand dollars worth of pens to a man he'd contacted online. Before payment was mailed, the man, some years younger than Alan, suddenly died. Since there was no good record of the transaction, the attorney who was handling the estate for the widow said he would not pay. Alan could have hired his own attorney to recover the money, but it wasn't worth the trouble and expense, so he ate the loss. "But I didn't mind," he said, "because I learned something that I should have known and thought I knew but actually I didn't know: when you're dead you can't do anything." He told me this with great earnestness. As if it had actually never occurred to him before that when you're dead you can't do anything anymore.

In a memorial retreat we held a few days after Alan's death, a retreat full of love and sorrow, I repeated this story. I said that since Alan was now dead and couldn't do anything, we would now have to do something because we were still alive. What that something was,

I didn't know. I only knew that somehow, in the face of a great loss, one does something different than one would otherwise have done. So this is what I learned (with Alan's help) about the meaning of loss: that love rushes into the absence that is loss, and that love brings inspired action. If we are able to give ourselves to the loss, to move toward it rather than away in an effort to escape or deny or distract or obscure, our wounded hearts become full, and out of that fullness we will do things differently and we will do different things.

The Tibetan Buddhist master Chögyam Trungpa talks about a soft spot, a raw spot, a wounded spot on the body or in the heart. A spot that is painful and sore. A spot that may emerge in the face of a loss. We hate such spots, so we try to prevent them. And if we can't prevent them we try to cover them up, so we won't absentmindedly rub them or pour hot or cold water on them. A sore spot is no fun. Yet it is valuable. Trungpa calls the sore spot embryonic compassion, potential compassion. Our loss, our wound, is precious to us because it can wake us up to love, and to loving action.

When sudden loss or trouble occurs, we feel shock and bewilderment, as I did when Alan died. We wonder: what just happened? For so long we expected things to be as they have been, had taken this as much for granted as the air we breathe. And suddenly it is not so. Maybe tomorrow, we think, we will wake up to discover that this devastating change was all just a temporary mistake and that things are back to normal. (After Alan's death I had some dreams that he hadn't actually died, that it had all been some sort of correctable slipup). After the shock passes, fear and despair arrive. We are anxious about our uncertain future, over which we have so little control. It's easy to fall into the paralysis of despair, caroming back to our childish default position of feeling completely vulnerable and unprepared in a harsh and hostile world. This fearful feeling of self-diminishment may darken our view to such an extent that we find ourselves wondering whether we are worthwhile people, whether we're capable of surviving in this tough world, whether we deserve to survive, whether our lives matter, whether there is any point in trying to do anything at all.

This is what it feels like when the raw spot is rubbed. The sense of loss, the despair, the fear, is terrible and we hate it, but it is exactly what we need. It is the embryo of compassion stirring to be born. Birth is painful.

All too many people in times like these just don't have the heart to do spiritual practice. But these are the best times for practice, because motivation is so clear. Practice is not simply a lifestyle choice or a refinement. There is no choice. It's a matter of survival. The tremendous benefit of simple meditation practice is most salient in these moments. Having exhausted all avenues of activity that might change your outward circumstances, and given up on other means of finding inner relief for your raging or sinking mind, there is nothing better to do than to sit down on a chair or cushion and just be present with your situation. There you sit, feeling your body. You try to sit up straight, with some basic human dignity. You notice you are breathing. You also notice that troubling thoughts and feelings are present in the mind. You are not here to make them go away or to cover them up with pleasant and encouraging spiritual slogans. There they are, all your demons, your repetitive negative themes. Your mind is (to borrow a phrase from the poet Michael Palmer) a museum of negativity. And you are sitting there quietly breathing inside that museum. There is nothing else to do. You can't fix anything—the situation is beyond that. Gradually it dawns on you that these dark thoughts and anxious feelings are just that—thinking, feeling. They are exhibits in the museum of negativity, but not necessarily realities of the outside world. This simple insight—that thoughts and feelings are thoughts and feelings—is slight, but it makes all the difference. You continue to sit, continue to pay attention to body and breath, and you label everything else, "thinking, thinking; feeling, feeling." Eventually you are able to pick up your coat from the coat check and walk out of the museum into the sunlight.

Confronting, accepting, being with negative thinking and feeling, knowing that they are not the whole of reality and not you, is the most fruitful and beneficial of all spiritual practices—better even than experiencing bliss or Oneness. You can practice it on the meditation cushion in the simple way I have described, but you can also practice it in other ways.

Journaling practice can be a big help. Keep a small notebook handy during the day and jot down an arresting word or phrase when you read or hear one. From time to time look at these words or phrases (they need not be uplifting or even sensible; they can be quite odd or random) and select the ones that attract you. These become your list of journaling prompts. When you have time, sit down with your notebook (doing this in a disciplined way, at a certain time each day, is best), choose a prompt, and write rapidly and spontaneously for ten to fifteen minutes, pen never leaving the paper, whatever comes to mind, no matter how nonsensical or irrelevant it may seem. In this way you empty out your swirling mind. You curate your own exhibition of negativity. It can be quite entertaining and even instructive.

Another way to reorient yourself with your thoughts and feelings is to share them with others. If you are feeling fear or despair these days, you can be sure that you are not alone in this. No doubt many of your friends and family members are feeling this as well. Rather than ignoring your anxieties—which tend to proliferate like mushrooms in the dark room of your closeted mind—or complaining obsessively about them to everyone you meet, which also increases the misery, you can undertake the spiritual discipline of speaking to others.

Taking a topic or a prompt from your notebook, or cueing off something you've read or written, or simply distilling what you have been thinking or feeling into a coherent thought, you can speak to one or more people in a structured way. Bring a few friends together. Divide yourselves into groups of three or four. After five minutes of silence to collect your thoughts, have each person speak as spontaneously as possible for five to seven minutes on the chosen topic. The others just listen, no questions, no comments. If it seems useful, one person can give feedback to the speaker. Not advice (it is a much better practice if advice and commentary are outlawed), but simply reviewing for the speaker, in your own words, what you have heard him or her say. Listening to what you have said repeated back to you in another's voice can be extremely illuminating. And forgetting about your own trouble long enough to actually listen to another is a great relief. It is likely to cause you to feel sympathy, even love. There is no better medicine than thinking of others, even if for only five minutes.

Working with these practices, you'll get a grip on the kinds of thinking and feeling that arise when conditions are difficult. The goal is not to make the thoughts and feelings go away: when there is loss or trouble, it is normal to feel sorrow, fear, despair, confusion, discouragement, and so on. These feelings connect us to others, who feel them as we do, so we don't want to eliminate them. But it would be good to have some perspective—and occasional relief—so these thoughts don't get the best of us and become full-blown demons pushing us around.

Having considered some extensions of meditation practice, let's return to the basic practice. When you sit, noticing the breath and the body on the chair or cushion, noticing the thoughts and feelings in the mind and heart and perhaps also the sounds in the room and the stillness, something else also begins to come into view. You notice the most fundamental of all facts: you are alive. You are a living, breathing, embodied, human being. You can actually feel this—feel the feeling of being alive. You can rest in this basic feeling, the nature of life, of consciousness, the underlying basis of everything you will ever experience—even the negativity. Sitting there with this basic feeling of being alive, you will feel gratitude. After all, you didn't ask for this; you didn't earn it. It is just there, a gift to you. It won't last forever, but for now, in this moment, here it is, perfect, complete. And you are sharing it with everything else that exists in this stark, basic, and beautiful way. Whatever your problems and challenges, you *are*, you exist in this bright world with others, with trees, sky, water, stars, sun, and moon. If you sit there long enough and regularly enough you will feel this, even in your darkest moments.

And based on this experience, you will reflect differently on your life. What is really important? How much do your expectations and social constructs really matter? What really counts? What is the bottom line for a human life?

To be alive. Well, you are alive.

To love others and be loved by others. Well, you do love, and it is within your power to love more deeply. And if you do, it is guaranteed that others will respond to you with more love.

To be kind to others and to receive kindness is also within your power, regardless of expectations, losses, and circumstances.

You need to eat every day, it is true. You need a good place to sleep at night. You need some sort of work to do, but probably you have these things, and if you do you can offer them to others. Once you overcome the sting and virulence of your naturally arising negativity, and return to the feeling of being alive, you will think more clearly about what matters more and what matters less in your life.

You will see that regardless of your conditions you can participate in what matters most. You will see that in the big picture of things, you have what you need and there is plenty to be grateful for—and plenty to do based on this gratitude. You may not have as many impressive appointments to keep as you did when you were busy with your high-powered job. But you have more time to keep up with friends and family—to call and say hello, how did your day go, happy birthday, happy anniversary, happy holiday, and oh yes, I love you and am glad you are in my life.

You may not be able to afford the fancy gourmet meal or the person who comes in to clean the house, but you can prepare with great care some steamed greens with olive oil and lemon and find someone you love to eat it with, and clean up the house yourself, noticing, maybe for the first time, how good the workmanship is on this dining room chair as you dust and polish its legs. Living more slowly and simply—although this may not be what you wanted or expected—may not turn out to be so bad after all.

My own personal reference point for material happiness is a memory I have of my days at the Tassajara Zen monastery, where I lived for five years when I was young. Tassajara is in a narrow mountain canyon that can get pretty cold in the winter months, when very little sun gets in. Our rooms in those days were unheated, so the cold really mattered.

I remember winter mornings standing at a certain spot in the center of the compound, where the first rays of the day's warm sunlight would come. So far, no material luxury I have encountered surpasses this, and I feel it again every time I feel the sun's warmth.

Hard times are painful and no rational person would ever think to intentionally bring them on. Quite the contrary, ordinary human day-to-day life is mostly about trying to avoid the financial, health, romantic, and psychological disasters that seem to be lurking around every corner. So we do not valorize or seek out what is hard or unpleasant. Yet disasters are inevitable in a human lifetime, and it is highly impractical not to welcome them when they come.

Hard times remind us of what's important, what's basic, beautiful, and worthwhile, about being alive. The worst of times bring out the best in us. Abundance and an excess of success and good fortune inevitably bring complications and elaborations that fill our lives with more discrimination and choice. We like this, and seek it, but the truth is it reduces joy. We are less appreciative of what we have. Our critical capacities grow very acute, and we are always somewhat skeptical of whatever excellence we are currently enjoying, ready to reject it in a moment, as soon as something we recognize as superior comes along, whether it's a new phone or a new spouse. When there's less, there's more appreciation, more openness to wonder and joy, more capacity to soften critical judgment and simply celebrate what happens to be there, even if it is not the best—even if it is not so good. It *is*, and there's a virtue merely in that. The sun in the morning and the moon at night.

I remember my good friend Gil, like Alan also gone now, who went to India to relieve the misery of poverty-stricken villagers by offering them the expert eye care he had been so well trained to deliver. He was shocked to gradually realize that these destitute, illschooled villagers were happier and wiser than he and his prosperous, well-educated friends in San Francisco. This is when Gil began his spiritual practice.

In retrospect we can see that the last fifty years or so of ever-increasing prosperity and opportunity have been based on an enthusiastic, exuberant, and naive lust for material goods—as if the goods themselves, and not our satisfaction in them, were the source of our happiness. That lust so raised the bar on what we expect to possess—the houses, cars, vacations, gadgets, information—that we have lost all sense of proportion and have forgotten almost entirely how our ancestors lived and how most of the world still lives. The various economic bubbles produced by that exuberance have proved to be much shakier than they had seemed when we were in the midst of them.

Most experts on the economy predict a slow period of at least a year, to be followed, inevitably, by a return to the upward-reaching growth economy we have come to feel is as reliable as a law of nature. But suppose they are not correct. Suppose we are reaching limits on a limited planet, and that we are in for a very long period of reduced circumstances. What if in the future we won't have top-notch medical care, high-performance cars, automatic houses, and abundant energy? Such an eventuality might cause such a crisis of despair due to dashed expectations that it might usher in a terrible period of the sort of dystopian nightmares we've seen in movies or novels, with chaos and violence everywhere. Or it could bring the opposite—more happiness, more sharing, more wisdom, bigger hearts. More people growing gardens, cooking food, working on farms, taking care of others. A slower, more heartfelt and realistic style of living, and a move toward dying at home surrounded by friends and spiritual supporters rather than in high-tech hospitals hooked into alienating machines run by busy professionals.

This probably won't be the case; the economists are probably right that things will return to what we have come to call normal after a while, maybe after only a year or two. But even so, it would be a healthy exercise to visualize and celebrate this simpler, sparer life—and maybe even to live it.

Coming Back to Where We Are

Ezra Bayda

The longtime meditation teacher Ezra Bayda presents five questions we can ask ourselves to counteract our resistance to remaining present when our mind is shocked by sudden change. The very act of questioning snaps our mind back to present-moment awareness, which is the most helpful place to be to deal with change creatively.

On a recent trip to Alcatraz prison I had the fascinating experience of walking through the halls, standing in the cells, and imagining what it would be like to be confined there. Before Alcatraz was closed as a functioning prison, it was unique in that it kept all of its prisoners isolated in solitary cells. I heard the story of one prisoner who, when put into a pitch-black solitary cell as punishment, ripped a button off his shirt and threw it into the air. He would then get on his knees and look for it, then throw it again—just to avoid going crazy in the dark.

This example may sound like it has nothing to do with us, but the fact is we all have our own ways of avoiding the dark and our own strategies for throwing buttons. They may look more sane and more productive, but they're still attempts to push away our difficulties.

Trying to avoid what's unpleasant seems to be deeply ingrained in the human psyche. After all, when life feels out of sync we naturally seek comfort and relief. But the feeling that life is out of sync is hardly new. As Buddha pointed out over twenty-five hundred years ago, we'll always have to deal with the fact that life entails discomfort and disappointment. We will always have our many problems—concerns about financial security, relationship difficulties, fears about our health, anxious striving toward success and acceptance, and so on. Yet, perhaps the most basic problem is that we don't really want to have any problems; perhaps that's what, in part, makes our current time seem so full of distress.

Many people come to meditation practice with the expectation that it will calm them and relieve the feelings of distress. Certainly meditation can do this to some extent; however, when we're knee-deep in emotional distress, we're fortunate if we can remember these tools. Even if we could remember to meditate, simply sitting down to follow the breath, without directly addressing our difficulties, is unlikely to bring a deep or lasting peace of mind. The difficulties still remain.

Sometimes, when emotions are particularly intense, when we feel the very uncomfortable feelings of groundlessness and helplessness, it is especially difficult to remember what we know. And there's a good reason for this. When we're distressed, the "new" or conceptual brain tends to stop working. This is called "cognitive shock," which turns off the cognitive mind's basic ability to function. When the thinking brain is on temporary sabbatical, we simply can't think clearly. During cognitive shock, the "old" brain, which is based on survival and defense, takes over. At this point we're likely to attack, withdraw, or go numb, none of which are conducive to awareness. To be honest, when caught in cognitive shock, we're fortunate if we can even remember that we want to be awake.

When clarity becomes obscured by the dark and swirling energy of emotional distress, it is useful to have some concise reminders to bring us back to reality. The real question is: what helps us awaken? The answer to this overarching question can be broken down into five very straightforward and specific smaller questions, each of which points us in the direction of clarity.

1. The first question—"What is going on right now?"—simply requires honestly acknowledging the objective situation. But to do this we have to be able to see the difference between our view of what is happening and the actual facts of the situation.

For instance, when we experience the panic of losing our job or seeing our investments disappear overnight, it is easy to get so caught up in our fears that we lose all sense of perspective. But what is actually happening in the present moment? Aren't we usually hijacked by the thoughts we've added of the impending doom of homelessness or hunger, rather than actually experiencing homelessness or hunger? Clearly seeing our believed thoughts—often based in negative imaginings about the future—allows us to come back to the objective reality of what is happening.

Another example: when we're caught in the swirl of emotional distress, we almost always add the thought "something is wrong"—either wrong in general, or, more likely, wrong with another person or with ourselves. In addition, we will almost always think about how to escape from the distress—through trying to fix the situation or through blaming or analyzing. In short, working effectively with our emotional difficulties requires that we first see clearly not only what is actually happening, but also what we're adding to the situation, through our detours, escapes, and judgments.

How much of our distress is rooted in the stories we weave around our experiences? Dropping our story line is critical in being aware of what is actually happening in the present moment. We need to see the story line for what it is and stop rehashing it over and over with our believed thoughts, since all they do is sustain and solidify our painful experiences. This is especially true when we are self-justifying and blaming. Asking the first practice question—

"What is going on right now?"—can help us get out of the poisonous loop of our stories.

2. The second, and crucial, question is: "Can I see this as my path?" If we don't ask this question, we're unlikely even to remember that this is our opportunity to awaken. Yet, it is essential that we understand that our distressful situation is exactly what we need to work with in order to be free. For example, the person we find most irritating becomes a mirror—you could call this person "irritating Buddha"—reflecting back to us exactly where we're stuck. After all, the irritation is what we add.

It is absolutely fundamental that we learn that when difficult situations and feelings arise they are not obstacles to be avoided, but rather these very difficulties are, in fact, the path itself. They're our opportunity to wake up out of our little protected world; they're our opportunity to awaken into a more genuine way of living. This point can't be overemphasized.

Of course, you may have heard this idea before—that our difficulties are our path. But it's a lot easier to understand this intellectually than it is to remember it when we're in the middle of the muddiness of life. Why? Because, again, we instinctively want a life that is problem free. So we usually continue seeking comfort and safety until, at some point, if we're fortunate, we get disappointed enough by life's blows to realize that our strategies—control, trying harder, withdrawing, blaming, whatever they are—will never give us the quality in life that all of us want. At that point—with life's disappointments as our teacher—we can start to use our difficulties as our path to awakening. Remembering the importance of this allows us to make the critical practice step where we can welcome our distress, because we understand that as long as we continue to resist our experience we will stay stuck.

3. The third key question—"What is my most believed thought?"—is like taking a snapshot of the mind. This question is

tempting to skip over, especially since we often take our opinions as Truth, and it can be difficult to see what we're really believing. Even though observation of the mind allows us to see our superficial or surface thoughts with clarity, the deepest beliefs often stay below the surface. Thus, these deep-seated beliefs often dictate how we feel and act, and they continue to run almost unconsciously.

For example, our deeply believed thoughts of personal insecurity may not be at all on the surface in a given situation; truthfully, we're often unaware of their presence. But their poisonous footprint often manifests itself in our anger, blame, depression, and shame. These deeply believed and well-hidden thoughts of insecurity thus act like radar, and we often seek out experiences that confirm that our beliefs are true—the classic self-fulfilling prophecy. For example, if you believe that life is not safe, all you have to do is get a bill that's a little bigger than you expected, and your mind will start weaving scenarios of doom.

We have to know where we get stuck in our particular radar-like beliefs. And we have to know how to work with them. Again, the process begins with asking yourself, "What is my most believed thought?" However, if the answer doesn't come, you drop it, and return to your physical experience, rather than trying to figure it out with the mind. Then, a little while later, you ask the question again. Sooner or later, with perseverance, the answer will present itself, sometimes with an "aha!" quality.

For instance, your surface thought may be, "No one should have to put up with this." This thought expresses the protective voice of anger and frustration. But when we go deeper, a more strongly held thought, like "I can't do this," may be revealed with the "aha" of discovery. Then, as we get to know ourselves, there may also be an "of course" quality. Haven't we seen this belief many times before? It's at this point that we begin to remove some of our investment in our deeply seated negative beliefs about ourselves. But to get to this place, first we must inquire into what our most believed thoughts are.

4. The fourth question, which is perhaps the most important, is: "What is this?" This question is actually a Zen koan, in that it can't be answered by the thinking mind. The only answer comes from entering directly into the immediate, physical experience of the present moment. Right now, ask yourself, "What is this?" Even if you don't feel any distress, this question can apply to whatever the present moment holds. Become aware of your physical posture. Feel the overall quality of physical sensations in the body. Feel the tension in the face, chest, and stomach. Include awareness of the environment—the temperature, the quality of light, the surrounding sounds. Feel the body breathing in and out as you take in this felt sense of the moment. Feel the energy in the body as you focus on the "whatness" (rather than the "whyness") of your experience. Only by doing this will you answer the question "What is this?"

Admittedly, it is difficult to maintain awareness in the present moment in the midst of distress, because to truly experience the present as it is means we have to refrain from our most habitual defenses, such as justifying, trying to get control, going numb, seeking diversions, and so on. The sole purpose of these strategies is to protect us from feeling the pain that we don't want to feel. But until we can refrain from these defenses, and feel the physical experience directly, we will stay stuck in the story line of "me," unaware of what life really is in the moment.

For example, if we feel anxiety, it's natural to want to avoid feeling it. We may get busy to occupy ourselves, or try harder, or try to figure it out. But if we can ask ourselves "What is this?" the only important and real answer comes from the actual physical experience of anxiety in the present moment. Remember, we're not asking what it's about, which is analyzing—the opposite of being physically present. We're simply asking what it actually is.

Asking the question-koan "What is this?" is the essence of awakening the quality of curiosity, in that the only "answer" comes from being open to actually experiencing the truth of each moment. Curiosity means that we're willing to explore unknown territory—the places the ego doesn't want to go. Curiosity allows us to take a step at our edge, toward our deepest fears. Being truly curious means we're willing to say "yes" to our experience, even the hard parts, instead of indulging the "no" of our habitual resistance.

Saying "yes" doesn't mean we like our experience or that we necessarily feel accepting. It doesn't even mean that we override the "no." Saying yes simply means that we pay attention—meticulous attention—to the no. It means we're no longer resisting the people, things, and fears that we don't like; instead we're learning to open to them, to invite them in, to welcome them with curiosity, in order to experience what's actually going on.

Yet, sometimes, when the mind is reeling in the panic of self-doubt and confusion, it is particularly difficult to come back to the heart that seeks to awaken. In these moments, how can we find the willingness to stay present with our own fears—the fears that will always limit our ability to love? When everything seems dark and unworkable, when we've even lost touch with the desire to move toward the light, the one thing we can do is take a deep breath into the center of the chest, on the in-breath, and on the out-breath extend to ourselves the same warmth and compassion we would to a friend or child in distress. Breathing into the heart, physically connecting with the center of our being, is a way to extend loving-kindness to ourselves even when there appears to be no loving-kindness in sight.

While remembering that our distress is also our path, and breathing the distressful sensations into the center of the chest, we can learn to stay with the actual sensations of distress. It's important to understand that being able to ask "What is this?"—and truly reside with what we find there—takes a great deal of patience and courage. Maybe we can only do it a little. But we persevere—even if it's just three breaths at a time. Ultimately, it's awareness that heals. It's awareness that allows us to reconnect with the heart, the heart that is the essence of our being.

Recently I was told I had to have a medical procedure to determine whether or not I had prostate cancer. Combined with the fear around the thought of having prostate cancer were the memories of painful experiences of prior similar medical procedures, leading to a feeling of dread and morbidity. Over the years I've become free of many of my fears and attachments, but each of us has our own particular edge—that place beyond which fear tells us not to go—so even though I had extensive experience practicing with illness and pain, there was no doubt that this particular set of circumstances put me at my own personal edge.

It was helpful to answer the first question—"What is going on right now?"—because I could see that there was actually no physical discomfort other than the discomfort triggered by believing in my fear-based thoughts. It was also helpful to ask myself, "Can I see this situation as my path?"—pointing to the opportunity to work with my own particular attachments and fears. As well, asking "What are my most believed thoughts?" allowed me to see that thoughts like "This is too much" and "I can't do this" were just thoughts—thoughts that were not the truth, no matter how true they felt in the moment.

But the real key to working with the panic and dread came from answering the koan-question "What is this?" The answer was to come back again and again to the physical experience of the present moment, such as the sensations of tightness in the chest and queasiness in the stomach. Sometimes I could only stay with it for the duration of three breaths. Sometimes the experience was so strong all I could do was breathe the sensations into the center of the chest, while remembering all those others who were suffering from the same or similar distress and wishing compassion to all of us.

Staying with the question "What is this?" eventually allowed the self-imposed prison wall of fear to begin to dissolve, and I was able to experience the grace and freedom of surrender. When we can viscerally enter into the question "What is this?" we will see that our experience, however unpleasant, is constantly changing and that, at bottom, it is just a combination of believed thoughts, physical sensations, and old memories. Once we see this, the experience of distress begins to unravel into its individual aggregates, rather than seeming so solid. Again, it's awareness that heals.

5. This leads right into the fifth key question: "Can I let this experience just be?" This is not so easy to do, because our human compulsion toward comfort drives us to want to fix or get rid of our unpleasant experiences. To allow our experience to just be usually becomes possible only after we've become disappointed by the futility of trying to fix ourselves (and others). We have to realize that trying to change or let go of the feelings we don't want to feel simply doesn't work. Allowing our experience to just be requires a critical understanding: that it's more painful to try to push away our own pain than it is to feel it. This understanding is not intellectual but something that eventually takes root in the core of our being.

Once we can really let our experience be as it is, awareness becomes a more spacious container, within which distress begins to dismantle on its own. Sometimes it helps to widen the container of awareness by intentionally including the awareness of air and sounds, or whatever we can connect with that is outside of the skin boundary. Within this wider and more spacious container, the distress may even transform from something heavy and somber into pure, nondescript energy, which is more porous and light. The energy may then release on its own, without any need to try to get rid of it.

This final question—"Can I let this experience just be?"—also allows the quality of mercy or loving-kindness to come forth, because we're no longer judging ourselves or our experience as defective. We're finally willing to experience our life within the spaciousness of the heart, rather than through the self-limiting judgments of the mind.

These five questions—"What is going on right now?"; "Can I welcome this as my path?"; "What is my most believed thought?"; "What is this?"; and "Can I let this experience just be?"—remind us of the key steps needed to work with our emotional distress. Some students carry little laminated cards with the five questions in their pockets for times when "cognitive shock" takes hold, when everything we know is temporarily forgotten.

Remember, though, these questions are just pointers; it's important not to get lost in the technique. In the bigger picture, we ask these questions because when we have emotional distress, we are usually caught in our own self-imposed prison walls—of anger, fear, and confusion. But when our self-imposed prison walls come down, all that remains is the connectedness that we are.

PART TWO

Tools for a Mindful Life

Waking Up to Your World

Pema Chödrön

When the gathering storm of our entanglements causes us to become self-absorbed and small-minded, we can use "pause practice," says the renowned teacher Pema Chödrön. The simple act of pausing for three conscious breaths can break the internal momentum and open us to how big our mind really is. And then we can do it again next time.

One of my favorite subjects of contemplation is this question: "Since death is certain, but the time of death is uncertain, what is the most important thing?" You know you will die, but you really don't know how long you have to wake up from the cocoon of your habitual patterns. You don't know how much time you have left to fulfill the potential of your precious human birth. Given this, what is the most important thing?

Every day of your life, every morning of your life, you could ask yourself, "As I go into this day, what is the most important thing? What is the best use of this day?" At my age, it's kind of scary when I go to bed at night and I look back at the day, and it seems like it passed in the snap of a finger. That was a whole day? What did I do with it? Did I move any closer to being more compassionate, loving, and caring—to being fully awake? Is my mind more open? What did I actually do? I feel how little time there is and how important it is how we spend our time.

What is the best use of each day of our lives? In one very short day, each of us could become more sane, more compassionate, more tender, more in touch with the dream-like quality of reality. Or we could bury all these qualities more deeply and get more in touch with solid mind, retreating more into our own cocoon.

Every time a habitual pattern gets strong, every time we feel caught up or on automatic pilot, we could see it as an opportunity to burn up negative karma. Rather than as a problem, we could see it as our karma ripening, which gives us an opportunity to burn up karma, or at least weaken our karmic propensities. But that's hard to do. When we realize that we are hooked, that we're on automatic pilot, what do we do next? That is a central question for the practitioner.

One of the most effective means for working with that moment when we see the gathering storm of our habitual tendencies is the practice of pausing, or creating a gap. We can stop and take three conscious breaths, and the world has a chance to open up to us in that gap. We can allow space into our state of mind.

Before I talk more about consciously pausing or creating a gap, it might be helpful to appreciate the gap that already exists in our environment. Awakened mind exists in our surroundings—in the air and the wind, in the sea, in the land, in the animals—but how often are we actually touching in with it? Are we poking our heads out of our cocoons long enough to actually taste it, experience it, let it shift something in us, let it penetrate our conventional way of looking at things?

If you take some time to formally practice meditation, perhaps in the early morning, there is a lot of silence and space. Meditation practice itself is a way to create gaps. Every time you realize you are thinking and you let your thoughts go, you are creating a gap. Every time the breath goes out, you are creating a gap. You may not always experience it that way, but the basic meditation instruction is designed to be full of gaps. If you don't fill up your practice time with your discursive mind, with your worrying and obsessing and all that kind of thing, you have time to experience the blessing of your surroundings. You can just sit there quietly. Then maybe silence will dawn on you, and the sacredness of the space will penetrate.

Or maybe not. Maybe you are already caught up in the work you have to do that day, the projects you haven't finished from the day before. Maybe you worry about something that has to be done, or hasn't been done, or a letter that you just received. Maybe you are caught up in busy mind, caught up in hesitation or fear, depression or discouragement. In other words, you've gone into your cocoon.

For all of us, the experience of our entanglement differs from day to day. Nevertheless, if you connect with the blessings of your surroundings—the stillness, the magic, and the power—maybe that feeling can stay with you and you can go into your day with it. Whatever it is you are doing—the magic, the sacredness, the expansiveness, the stillness—stays with you. When you are in touch with that larger environment, it can cut through your cocoon mentality.

On the other hand, I know from personal experience how strong the habitual mind is. The discursive mind, the busy, worried, caught-up, spaced-out mind, is powerful. That's all the more reason to do the most important thing—to realize what a strong opportunity every day is, and how easy it is to waste it. If you don't allow your mind to open and to connect with where you are, with the immediacy of your experience, you could easily become completely submerged. You could be completely caught up and distracted by the details of your life, from the moment you get up in the morning until you fall asleep at night.

You get so caught up in the content of your life, the minutiae that make up a day, so self-absorbed in the big project you have to do, that the blessings, the magic, the stillness, and the vastness escape you. You never emerge from your cocoon, except for when there's a noise that's so loud you can't help but notice it, or something shocks you, or captures your eye. Then for a moment you stick your head out and realize: Wow! Look at that sky! Look at that squirrel! Look at that person!

The great fourteenth-century Tibetan teacher Longchenpa talked about our useless and meaningless focus on the details, getting so caught up we don't see what is in front of our nose. He said that this useless focus extends moment by moment into a continuum, and days, months, and even whole lives go by. Do you spend your whole time just thinking about things, distracting yourself with your own mind, completely lost in thought? I know this habit so well myself. It is the human predicament. It is what the Buddha recognized and what all the living teachers since then have recognized. This is what we are up against.

"Yes, but . . . ," we say. Yes, but I have a job to do, there is a deadline, there is an endless amount of e-mail I have to deal with, I have cooking and cleaning and errands. How are we supposed to juggle all that we have to do in a day, in a week, in a month, without missing our precious opportunity to experience who we really are? Not only do we have a precious human life, but that precious human life is made up of precious human days, and those precious human days are made up of precious human moments. How we spend them is really important. Yes, we do have jobs to do; we don't just sit around meditating all day, even at a retreat center. We have the real nitty-gritty of relationships—how we live together, how we rub up against each other. Going off by ourselves, getting away from the people we think are distracting us, won't solve everything. Part of our karma, part of our dilemma, is learning to work with the feelings that relationships bring up. They provide opportunities to do the most important thing, too.

If you have spent the morning lost in thought worrying about what you have to do in the afternoon, already working on it in every little gap you can find, you have wasted a lot of opportunities, and it's not even lunchtime yet. But if the morning has been characterized by at least some spaciousness, some openness in your mind and heart, some gap in your usual way of getting caught up, sooner or later that is going to start to permeate the rest of your day.

If you haven't become accustomed to the experience of open-ness, if you haven't got any taste of it, then there is no way the after-noon is going to be influenced by it. On the other hand, if you've given openness a chance, it doesn't matter whether you are medita-ting, working at the computer, or fixing a meal, the magic will be there for you, permeating your life.

As I said, our habits are strong, so a certain discipline is required to step outside our cocoon and receive the magic of our surroundings. The pause practice—the practice of taking three conscious breaths at any moment when we notice that we are stuck—is a simple but power-ful practice that each of us can do at any given moment.

Pause practice can transform each day of your life. It creates an open doorway to the sacredness of the place in which you find your-self. The vastness, stillness, and magic of the place will dawn upon you, if you let your mind relax and drop for just a few breaths the story line you are working so hard to maintain. If you pause just long enough, you can reconnect with exactly where you are, with the immediacy of your experience.

When you are waking up in the morning and you aren't even out of bed yet, even if you are running late, you could just look out and drop the story line and take three conscious breaths. Just be where you are! When you are washing up, or making your coffee or tea, or brushing your teeth, just create a gap in your discursive mind. Take three conscious breaths. Just pause. Let it be a contrast to being all caught up. Let it be like popping a bubble. Let it be just a moment in time, and then go on.

You are on your way to whatever you need to do for the day. Maybe you are in your car, or on the bus, or standing in line. But you can still create that gap by taking three conscious breaths and being right there with the immediacy of your experience, right there with whatever you are seeing, with whatever you are doing, with whatever you are feeling.

Another powerful way to do pause practice is simply to listen for a moment. Instead of sight being the predominant sense perception, let sound, hearing, be the predominant sense perception. It's a very powerful way to cut through your conventional way of looking at the world. In any moment, you can just stop and listen intently. It doesn't matter what particular sound you hear; you simply create a gap by listening intently.

In any moment you could just listen. In any moment, you could put your full attention on the immediacy of your experience. You could look at your hand resting on your leg, or feel your bottom sitting on the cushion or on the chair. You could just be here. Instead of being not here, instead of being absorbed in thinking, planning, and worrying, instead of being caught up in the cocoon, cut off from your sense perceptions, cut off from the power and magic of the moment, you could be here. When you go out for a walk, pause frequently—stop and listen. Stop and take three conscious breaths. How precisely you create the gap doesn't really matter. Just find a way to punctuate your life with these thought-free moments. They don't have to be thought-free *minutes* even, they can be no more than one breath, one second. Punctuate, create gaps. As soon as you do, you realize how big the sky is, how big your mind is.

When you are working, it's so easy to become consumed, particularly by computers. They have a way of hypnotizing you, but you could have a timer on your computer that reminds you to create a gap. No matter how engrossing your work is, no matter how much it is sweeping you up, just keep pausing, keep allowing for a gap. When you get hooked by your habit patterns, don't see it as a big problem; allow for a gap.

When you are completely wound up about something and you pause, your natural intelligence clicks in and you have a sense of the right thing to do. This is part of the magic: our own natural intelligence is always there to inform us, as long as we allow a gap. As long as we are on automatic pilot, dictated to by our minds and our emotions, there is no intelligence. It is a rat race. Whether we are at a retreat center or on Wall Street, it becomes the busiest, most entangled place in the world.

Pause, connect with the immediacy of your experience, connect with the blessings; liberate yourself from the cocoon of self-involvement, talking to yourself all of the time, completely obsessing. Allow a gap, gap, gap. Just do it over and over and over; allow yourself the space to realize where you are. Realize how big your mind is; realize how big the space is, that it has never gone away but that you have been ignoring it.

Find a way to slow down. Find a way to relax. Find a way to relax your mind and do it often, very, very often, throughout the day continuously, not just when you are hooked but all the time. At its root, being caught up in discursive thought, continually self-involved with discursive plans, worries, and so forth, is attachment to ourselves. It is the surface manifestation of ego-clinging.

So, what is the most important thing to do with each day? With each morning, each afternoon, each evening? It is to leave a gap. It doesn't matter whether you are practicing meditation or working, there is an underlying continuity. These gaps, these punctuations, are like poking holes in the clouds, poking holes in the cocoon. And these gaps can extend so that they can permeate your entire life, so that the continuity is no longer the continuity of discursive thought but rather one continual gap.

But before we get carried away by the idea of continual gap, let's be realistic about where we actually are. We must first remind ourselves what the most important thing is. Then we have to learn how to balance that with the fact that we have jobs to do, which can cause us to become submerged in the details of our lives and caught in the cocoon of our patterns all day long. So find ways to create the gap frequently, often, continuously. In that way, you allow yourself the space to connect with the sky and the ocean and the birds and the land and with the blessing of the sacred world. Give yourself the chance to come out of your cocoon.

Healing Pain and Dressing Wounds

Thich Nhat Hanh

*The Vietnamese monk and activist Thich Nhat Hanh teaches how
mindfulness—the simple recognition of what's going on in the present
moment, without judgment or critique—can calm our emotional
upheavals. When we have an idea that makes us suffer, we can
learn to simply let it go.*

Here is a practice poem that you can use in everyday life, at any
time, no matter where you are:

> I breathe in, I breathe out.
> Deeper, gentler.
> I become calm, I let go.
> I smile, I am free.

You can recite this no matter what you are doing—while you
are driving your car, while you are watering your garden, while you
are cooking, or before falling asleep—as well as during walking or
sitting meditation.

"I breathe in; I breathe out." This phrase comes to us directly
from the Buddha. What it means is, "Breathing in, I know that I am

breathing in. Breathing out, I know that I am breathing out." That's the whole thing. It's simple recognition of what is happening: an in-breath happens, and then an out-breath happens.

Mindfulness is first of all the ability to recognize what is happening in the present moment. It is simple recognition—without judgment or critique, without suppression or attachment. I breathe in, and I am aware that the in-breath is here. I breathe out, and I am aware that the out-breath is here. There is no critique or struggle. There is no effort either to reject anything or fit in with it.

I breathe in, I breathe out.
I breathe in toward the inside.
I breathe out toward the outside.

You could also say, "In-breath, out-breath." Or even just, "In, out." It's very simple, yet you can regard this practice as recognition of everything that is happening in the present moment. "I breathe in; this is an in-breath. I breathe out; this is an out-breath."

During this time, all thoughts stop. The past, the future, your memories and plans—you drop everything. You are your in-breath, and becoming one with your in-breath, concentration occurs. This will give you a great deal of pleasure.

"Breathing in, I know that I am breathing in." Let me remind you again that this practice comes to us directly from the Buddha. You are free of any intention to judge, find fault, reject, or cling, and you maintain that freedom in relation to whatever is happening. When you get angry or depressed, it is the same. You simply recognize what is there—anger, depression, and so forth—without any sense of disapproval or rejection. If you recognize emotion as existing in the moment, you will not feel upset. There is no battle to win or lose—this is Buddhist meditation.

When you drink whiskey, learn to drink it with mindfulness. "Drinking whiskey, I know that it is whiskey I am drinking." This is the approach that I would recommend. I am not telling you to absolutely stop drinking. I propose that you drink your whiskey mindfully, and I am sure that if you drink this way for a few weeks, you will stop drinking alcohol. Drinking your whiskey mindfully, you will recognize what is taking place in you—in your body, in your liver, and so on. When your mindfulness becomes strong, you will just stop.

You do not have to struggle against a desire. There is no need for a battle within you. Mindfulness is something that embraces and includes things like desire, that recognizes them with great tenderness. Meditation is not some battlefield where one side fights the other, because the basis of Buddhist meditation is nonduality. The habits of drinking alcohol or getting angry are also you, and therefore you must treat them with great tenderness and nonviolence. The essential point is not to create a conflict, a fight, within yourself.

So we begin with simple recognition. Then, when the energy of mindfulness is strong and you have concentration, you can practice deeply looking into the nature of whatever is arising, and from that comes insight. When you have deep insight, it will liberate you from all negative tendencies.

"Breathing in, I know that I am breathing in. Breathing out, I know that I am breathing out." This is very, very simple, yet it can give you a lot of pleasure. You cultivate concentration, and with that concentration, you touch life deeply. You are free at that moment.

Let me say a few words about adding the words "deeper, gentler" to this practice of breath awareness. "Deeper" in this case does not mean trying to make our inhalation deeper. It simply means that after a few minutes of practicing "I am breathing in, I am breathing out," you will notice that your breathing has become deeper and gentler. As you breathe in, you notice that your in-breath has become longer. As you breathe out, you notice that your out-breath has become gentler. As a result, your practice becomes pleasurable, and this pleasure nourishes and transforms you.

You should make use of this pleasure. The practice should be enjoyable and pleasant. The elements called joy and pleasure, *priti* and *mudita* in Sanskrit, are a very important part of meditation. If you are suffering during meditation, your practice is not correct. Practice should be enjoyable and pleasant. It should be full of joy.

So whether your practice is walking or sitting meditation, do it in such a way that joy and pleasure are possible. It is not supposed to be hard labor. And in your everyday life, just as you do not do violence to your breathing, do not do violence to your body, nor to your anger or depression. We need to treat them with a great deal of tenderness, because the essential thing in Buddhist meditation is not to create tension, conflict, or disruption in yourself. The positive elements within you are you, and the negative elements within you are you also. It is necessary for the positive elements to acknowledge and cradle the negative elements, and if you do that, a transformation will take place. There is no need for the two to battle.

SURVIVING EMOTIONAL STORMS

I am becoming calm, I am letting go.

If you find there is not enough peace in your emotions, your perceptions, or your feelings, you should practice calming them.

Breathing in, I calm my feelings.
Breathing out, I smile at my feelings.

When you are the victim of strong emotions, you can practice like this. Assume a seated posture in which you can be solid, or you can lie down. As you breathe, bring your attention to your navel and to the movement of your abdomen. Your abdomen rises and falls— follow that movement. Do not think about anything. The object of your attention is solely the movement of your abdomen. "I breathe in, I breathe out. I breathe in, I breathe out."

A strong emotion is like a storm. If you look at a tree in a storm, the top of the tree seems fragile, like it might break at any moment. You are afraid the storm might uproot the tree. But if you turn your attention to the trunk of the tree, you realize that its roots are deeply anchored in the ground, and you see that the tree will be able to hold.

You too are a tree. During a storm of emotion, you should not stay at the level of the head or the heart, which are like the top of the tree. You have to leave the heart, the eye of the storm, and come back to the trunk of the tree. Your trunk is one centimeter below your navel. Focus there, paying attention only to the movement of your abdomen, and continue to breathe. Then you will survive the storm of strong emotion.

It is essential to understand that an emotion is merely something that arises, remains, and then goes away. A storm comes, it stays a while, and then it moves away. At the critical moment, remember that you are much more than your emotions. This is a simple thing that everybody knows, but you may need to be reminded of it: you are much more than your emotions. Many people have no idea how to face their emotions, and they suffer because of it. A lot of young people are like that, and they think the only way to put an end to their suffering is to kill themselves. So we must practice this ourselves, and we must help young people to practice it.

You should not wait for emotion to appear before you begin practicing. Otherwise you will be carried away by the storm. You should train now, while the emotion is not there. So sit or lie down and practice mindfulness of the breath, using the movement of your abdomen as the object of your attention. I am positive that if you do this exercise for twenty days, ten minutes per day, then you will know how to practice whenever a strong emotion comes up. After ten or twenty minutes, the emotion will go away, and you will be saved from the storm.

THE PRACTICE OF LETTING GO

If there are things that are causing you to suffer, you have to know how to let go of them. Happiness can be attained by letting go, including letting go of your ideas about happiness. You imagine that certain conditions are necessary to your happiness, but deep looking will reveal to you that those are the very things that are making you suffer.

One day the Buddha was sitting in the forest with some monks. They had just finished their lunch and were about to begin a dharma discussion when a farmer approached them. The farmer said, "Venerable monks, did you see my cows come by? I have a dozen cows, and they all ran away. On top of that, I have five acres of sesame plants, and this year the insects ate them all up. I think I'm going to kill myself. It isn't possible to live like this."

The Buddha felt strong compassion toward the farmer. He said, "My friend, I'm sorry, we didn't see your cows come this way." When the farmer had gone, the Buddha turned to his monks and said, "My friends, do you know why you are happy? Because you have no cows to lose."

I would like to say the same thing to you. My friends, if you have some cows, you have to identify them. You think they are essential to your happiness, but if you practice deep looking, you will understand that it is these very cows that have brought about your unhappiness. The secret of happiness is being able to let go of your cows. You should call your cows by their true names.

I assure you that when you have let your cows go, you will experience happiness, because the more freedom you have, the more happiness you have. This is strange but true. The Buddha taught us that joy and pleasure are based on surrender, on letting go. "I am letting go" is a powerful practice. Are you strong enough to let go of things? If not, your suffering will continue.

You must have the courage to practice letting go. You must develop a new habit—the habit of freedom. You must identify your cows. You must regard them as bonds of slavery. You must learn, as the Buddha and his monks did, to set your cows free. It is the energy of mindfulness that helps you to identify your cows and call them by their true names.

I am becoming calm, I am letting go.

When you have an idea that is making you suffer, you should let go of it, even if it is an idea about your own happiness. Every person and every nation has an idea of happiness. In some countries, people think that a given ideology must be followed to bring happiness to the country and its people. They want everybody to approve of their idea of happiness, and they believe that those who are not in favor of it should be imprisoned or put in concentration camps. It is possible to maintain such thinking for fifty or sixty years, and in that time to create enormous tragedy, just with this idea of happiness.

Perhaps you are the prisoner of your own notion of happiness. There are thousands of paths that lead to happiness, but you have taken only one. You have not considered other paths because you think that yours is the only one that leads to happiness. You have followed this path with all your might, and so the other paths, the thousands of others, have remained closed to you.

We should be free to experience the happiness that just comes to us without our having to seek it. If you are a free person, happiness can come over you just like that! Look at the moon. It travels in the sky completely free, and this freedom produces beauty and happiness. I am convinced that happiness is not possible unless it is based on freedom. If you are a free woman, if you are a free man, you will enjoy happiness. But if you are a slave, even if you are only the slave of an idea, happiness will be very difficult for you to achieve. That is why you should cultivate freedom, including freedom from your own concepts and ideas. Let go of your ideas, even if abandoning them is not easy.

Conflict and suffering are often caused by a person not wanting to surrender his concepts and ideas of things. In the relationship between a father and a son, for example, or between partners, this happens all the time. It is important to train yourself to let go of your ideas about things. Freedom is cultivated by this practice of letting go. If you look deeply, you may find that you are holding on to a concept that is causing you to suffer a great deal. Are you intelligent enough, are you free enough, to surrender this idea?

> I am becoming calm,
> I am letting go.
> Having let go, there is victory.
> I smile.
> I am free.

The dharma that the Buddha presented is radical. It contains radical measures for healing, for transforming the present situation. People become monks and nuns because they understand that freedom is very precious. The Buddha did not need a bank account or a house. In the time of the Buddha, the possessions of a monk or a nun were limited to their robes and a bowl in which to collect alms. Freedom is very important. You should not sacrifice it for anything, because without freedom, there is no happiness.

How to Experience the Miracle of Life

Joy and happiness are born of concentration. When you are having a cup of tea, the value of that experience depends on your concentration. You have to drink the tea with 100 percent of your being. The true pleasure is experienced in the concentration. When you walk and you are 100 percent concentrated, the joy you get from the steps you are taking is much greater than the joy you would get without concentration. You have to invest 100 percent of your body and mind in the act of walking. Then you will experience that being alive and taking steps on this planet are miraculous things.

The Rinzai Zen master Linji said, "The miracle is walking on the earth, not walking on water or fire. The real miracle is walking on this earth." Why should you not perform a miracle just by walking? A step taken with mindfulness can lead you to the Kingdom of God. This is possible. You can do it today. Life is too precious for us to lose ourselves in our ideas and concepts, in our anger and our despair. We must wake up to the marvelous reality of life. We must begin to live fully and truly, every moment of our daily lives.

When you are holding a cup of tea in your hand, do it while being 100 percent there. You know how to do this—one deep in-breath, one gentle out-breath, and the body and mind come together. You are truly there, absolutely alive, present! This only takes ten or fifteen seconds, and suddenly the tea reveals itself to you in all its splendor and wonder.

When I pick up a book or open a door, I want to invest myself in this act 100 percent. This is what I learned during my monastic training, when my teacher taught me how to offer a stick of incense. A stick of incense is very small and very light, yet the right way to hold it is with two hands. When offering the incense, you have to invest 100 percent of your being in your hands and in two of your fingers—the energy of mindfulness must be concentrated there. This may look like a ritual, but it is a really an act of concentrated awareness. I put my left hand on my right hand, and during this time, I concentrate 100 percent. The incense is an offering to the Buddha, but does the Buddha really need incense? This is actually an offering of peace, of joy, and of concentration.

During my first year of training at the temple, my teacher asked me to do something for him. I loved him so much that I became quite excited, and I rushed out to do it. I was in such a hurry that I did not leave the room as I should have. I did not close the door properly, with 100 percent of my being.

He called me back. "Novice," he said, "come here." I knew right away that something was wrong. He said only, "My son, you can do better." He did not have to teach me this a second time. The next time, I did walking meditation to the door, I opened the door mindfully, and I closed the door behind me perfectly.

Since that day, I have known how to close a door behind me. It must always be done with mindfulness—not for the sake of the Buddha, not for the teacher, but for myself. This is the way you create peace; this is the way you bring about freedom. You do it for your own happiness, and when you are happy, the people you relate with benefit from your presence and are happy too. A happy person is an important thing, because their happiness spreads all around them. You can be a happy person too and become a refuge for those around you.

Concentration is the practice of happiness. There is no happiness without concentration. When you eat an orange, try to practice concentration. Eat it in such a way that pleasure, joy, and happiness are possible the whole time. You could call this orange meditation. You take an orange in the palm of your hand. You look at it and breathe in such a way that it reveals itself as the miracle it is. An orange is nothing less than a miracle. It is just like you—you are also a miracle of life. You are a manifest miracle.

If I am 100 percent there, the orange reveals itself to me 100 percent. As I concentrate on the orange, I get deep insight from it. I can see the sun and the rain that are in it. I can see the flowers of the orange tree. I can see the little sapling sprouting, and then the fruit growing. Then I begin mindfully to peel the fruit. Its presence—its color, its texture, its smell and taste—is a real miracle, and the happiness that comes to me from entering into deep contact with it can become very, very great. A single orange is enough to give you a great deal of happiness when you are truly there, entirely alive, entirely present, entering into deep contact with one of the miracles of life that surround you.

Little by little you must train yourself for life, for happiness. You probably received a college degree that you spent years working for, and you thought that happiness would be possible after you got it. But that was not true, because after getting the degree and finding a job, you continued to suffer. You have to realize that happiness is not something you find at the end of the road. You have to understand that it is here, now. Mindfulness practice is not an evasion or an escape. It means entering into life strongly—with the strength generated by the energy of mindfulness. Without this freedom and concentration, there is no happiness.

Engaged Buddhism means engagement not only in social action, but in daily life. The object of this practice is joy in everyday life, which is freedom. We should use our time with a great deal of intelligence, because time is not only money, it is much more precious than that. It is life. A day is twenty-four hours long: do you know how to manage it? You are intelligent and have lots of different talents, but do you know how to manage your days? You must invest yourself 100 percent in organizing the days that are given to you to live. You can do it.

With mindfulness practice, transforming your pain will become much easier. Joy and happiness will be your counterbalance as you reestablish your equilibrium and heal your pain.

You know that good blood circulation is necessary for the well-being of your body. The same is true for your psyche, your consciousness—you must live and practice in such a way that your consciousness benefits from good circulation. Bad circulation of psychological elements creates problems. Accumulations of suffering, fear, jealousy, and distress are congealed in the depths of your consciousness. They cannot circulate, and they make you feel fear. That is why you have closed the door to your mental depths, because you do not want these things to come to the surface. You are afraid of the pain in you, and so whenever you have a gap, you fill your mental space with books or television so these accumulations of suffering do not come up to the surface.

That is what most of us do. It's a policy of embargo. You do your best to forget what is inside you and consume whatever is available to help you do that. In this way you create bad psychological circulation, and mental problems will soon appear. While you are sleeping, accumulations of suffering will reveal themselves to you in your dreams. They cry out for help, but you continue to practice suppression and repression. Depression, fear, and confusion may also manifest in the realm of the soma, in the body. You will have headaches and all kinds of other aches and pains, but your doctor will not be able to identify the source of the pain, because it is psychological in nature.

Buddhism teaches that the body and mind are two aspects of the same thing. There is no duality between the physical and the mental aspects. There is a Sanskrit expression, *namarupa. Nama* is our mental aspect, and *rupa* means form. We cannot make a distinction between the physical and the mental. Your hand is not just a physical formation; it is a mental formation at the same time. The cells of your body are not physical alone; they are also mental. They are both at the same time.

Buddhism has found that reality sometimes manifests as psyche and sometimes as soma. "Psychosomatic" is the Western term; *namarupa* is the equivalent in Sanskrit. Therefore, we should train ourselves to regard physical things as not solely physical realities. In fact, "physical" and "mental" are no more than expressions.

The Humanist Manifesto, which was written in 1933, says that the mind-body duality should be rejected, including the idea of a soul that survives after death, because that idea also represents a duality. What do Buddhists say about this? Buddhism agrees that the mind-body duality should be rejected, but it does not say that the disintegration of the body represents a total negation. Buddhism helps us to see that neither the concept of permanence nor the concept of annihilation are applicable to reality.

BEYOND BIRTH AND DEATH

If we look deeply into the nature of reality, we will see that nothing is created or lost. As the Buddhist text called the Prajnaparamita says, there is neither birth nor death. Birth is a concept, and death is too, and neither of these concepts is applicable to reality. We must make the effort to look into this truth deeply to confirm it for ourselves.

In our minds, we think that birth means we start from nothing and become something—that starting as nobody we become somebody. That is our definition of birth: from nothing comes existence, from nothing comes being. But that is absurd, because it is impossible for anything to come from nothing.

This piece of paper I am holding in my hand is something that exists right now. Can we establish a time and place of birth for this paper? That is very difficult to establish, impossible actually, because before it manifested as a piece of paper, it was already here in the form of a tree, of the sun, of a cloud. Without the sun, without the rain, the trees would not have lived, and there would have been no piece of paper. When I touch this piece of paper, I touch the sun. When I touch this piece of paper, I also touch the clouds. There is a cloud floating in this piece of paper. You do not have to be a poet to see it. If I were able to separate the cloud from the piece of paper, the paper would not exist anymore.

The true nature of this piece of paper is interbeing. Before taking the form of paper, it already existed in the form of sun, cloud, rain, and trees. In the same way, a human is not born from nothing. Birth is a moment of continuation. It is only a concept, not a reality. And if there is no birth, there is no death either.

The tradition of Zen Buddhism invites us to look deeply at reality with the help of koans. For example, what was your face before the birth of your grandmother? Where were you at that moment? You are invited to discover that. Following this invitation, you embark on a journey in which you look deeply and see back before your birth, even before the birth of your grandmother.

You did not come from nothing. That is impossible, just as it is impossible that the piece of paper came from nothing. It manifests in the present moment as a piece of paper, but in the past it manifested in other forms. You are asked to seek and discover your own face, your original face before the birth of your grandmother. This is a wonderful practice. If you embark on this journey of seeking, you will have the opportunity to touch the nature of non-birth and of non-death, and fear will disappear. This is the language of Zen.

When the French scientist Antoine Lavoisier said "Nothing is created and nothing is destroyed," he was saying exactly the same thing. The concept of death is that being turns into nonbeing. That is impossible. Can somebody go back to being nobody? No. If we burn the piece of paper, we cannot reduce it to nothing. The paper will turn into heat, which will go out into the cosmos. It will turn into smoke, which will join the clouds in the sky. Tomorrow a drop of rain will fall on your forehead, and you will make a new contact with the piece of paper. The ashes produced by the burning will rejoin the earth, and one day they will manifest as daisies. Do you have enough mindfulness to recognize the piece of paper in those daisies?

It is our idea of birth and death that takes away our peace and happiness in everyday life. And it is meditation that will rid us of the fear that is born from the idea of birth and death. This is the virtue of deep looking in meditation. It helps you to see the heart of reality very deeply. To touch the nature of interbeing is to touch the very nature of non-death and non-birth.

The notion of death, of nothing, is very dangerous. It makes people suffer a lot. In Buddhist teaching nothingness is only a concept, and it is never applicable to reality. The Buddha said, "When conditions are sufficient, the thing manifests, and when they are not sufficient, the thing remains hidden." There is neither birth nor death. There is only manifestation, appearance. Concepts like birth and death, being and nonbeing, are not applicable. The wave on the water is free from birth and death. It is free from being and nonbeing. The wave is the wave.

The word "suchness," meaning "it is such," describes reality as it is. Concepts and ideas are incapable of expressing reality as it is. Nirvana, the ultimate reality, cannot be described, because it is free of all concepts and ideas. Nirvana is the extinction of all concepts. It is total freedom. Most of our wretchedness and fear arise from our ideas and concepts. If you are able to free yourself from these concepts, anxiety and fear will disappear. Nirvana, the ultimate reality, or God, is of the nature of non-birth and non-death. It is total freedom. We need to touch this reality to leave behind the fear connected with the idea of birth and death.

We are afraid of nonbeing. "I am somebody, I am something," we feel. "Today I am, and I am afraid that one day I will no longer be." But it is impossible for being to become nonbeing. The Buddha said it in absolutely simple terms: "If this exists, that exists." This refers to the manifestation of phenomena on the basis of the law of interdependent origination. When conditions are sufficient, there is a manifestation. You could call that "being," but that would be false. In the same way, you could call the situation before manifestation arises "nonbeing," but that is equally false. The situation is simply one of manifestation or non-manifestation.

Just because something is not manifest, you cannot say that it is nonexistent, just so much nothing. In April at Plum Village, you do not see sunflowers. The hills are not covered with their blossoms, but you cannot say that there are no sunflowers. The sunflowers are hidden in the earth; they are just lacking one of the conditions for their manifestation, sunshine. It is false to say that the sunflowers do not exist.

So what is death? It is simply the cessation of manifestation, followed by other forms of manifestation. In wintertime, we do not see dragonflies or butterflies. So we think that everything is dead. But suddenly spring comes, and the dragonflies and butterflies manifest again. That which is currently not perceivable is not nonexistent. But we cannot say that it is existent either.

Existence and nonexistence are just concepts. There is only manifestation and non-manifestation, which depend on our perception. If you have perception that is deep enough, a deep insight into life, then you are free from all these concepts such as being and nonbeing, birth and death. This is the highest level of the Buddha's teaching. You come looking for relief for your pain, but the greatest relief that you can ever obtain comes from touching the nature of non-birth and non-death.

In Buddhism, we go beyond the concepts of creation and destruction, of birth and death. We also go beyond the concepts of self and no-self. We have seen, for example, that a flower cannot exist by itself. The flower cannot be. It can only inter-be. We must go back to what the Buddha said—"If this exists, that exists"—and train ourselves to look at things in the light of interdependence. We can see the entire universe in a flower. We can see not only the entire universe but also all our ancestors and our children in every cell of our own body.

Through Buddhist meditation you will experience the happiness of seeing and discovering wonderful things that will liberate you. We live in a time when everyone is too involved in the business of everyday life, and we do not have enough time to live in suchness, with mindfulness. We do not take the time to touch things in depth, to discover the true nature of life. You are invited to use your intelligence, your time, and your resources to taste this historic meditation that was handed down to us by our original teacher, the Buddha.

Mindfulness and Compassion

Tools for Transforming Suffering into Joy

Phillip Moffitt

The insight meditation teacher Phillip Moffitt offers easy-to-understand instructions for the Buddha's practice of mindfulness, and he tells us how it benefits our health and well-being.

The Buddha taught that suffering comes from ignorance. "Ignorance is the one thing with whose abandonment clear knowing arises," he said. By "ignorance" he meant the misperceptions and delusions that your mind has about its own nature. Thus, the way to free the mind from suffering is through gaining insight into what truly is. Insight is a profound level of understanding that transcends mere intellectual cognition and can only be known by experiencing it. One of the tools the Buddha taught for gaining insight is mindfulness, the ability to be fully aware in the moment.

Mindfulness enables you to go beneath the surface level, moment-to-moment life experience, which is clouded with emotions, to clearly see the truth of what is happening. The untrained mind is just the opposite of mindfulness. It is often described as "monkey mind," because it is continually distracted by one thought, emotion, or body sensation after another. The monkey mind repeatedly identifies with the surface experience and gets lost in it. The insights that arise through mindfulness release the mind from getting caught in such reactivity and can even stop the cycle from beginning.

An important aspect of practicing mindfulness is *sampajanna*, which translated means "clear comprehension"—the ability to see clearly what needs to be done, what you are capable of doing, and how it relates to the larger truth of life. Obviously it is not easy to be mindful in such a manner, let alone experience the deep insights that lead to full liberation, but you can develop mindfulness through the practice of meditation.

Mindfulness in Daily Life

First let's look at how the insight from mindfulness might manifest in daily life. Suppose someone at work says something that upsets you, and you become angry or defensive and react by saying something you later regret. The incident ruins your day because you can't stop thinking about it. Of course you are aware of your feelings; they have registered in your brain. But this kind of "ordinary awareness"— simply being conscious of your emotional reaction to an experience— is not what the Buddha meant by mindfulness.

Mindfulness enables you to fully know your experience in each moment. So when your colleague upsets you, if you are being mindful, you witness that her words generate thoughts and body sensations in you that lead to a strong emotion with still more body sensations. You have the insight that these feelings are being created by a chain reaction of thoughts in your mind. While this chain reaction is going on, you acknowledge how miserable it makes you feel. But instead of reacting with harsh words when you feel the impulse to speak unskillfully, you choose not to. Your mindfulness allows you not to identify with the impulses of your strong emotions or act from them. Moreover, because you witnessed the impersonal nature of the experience, you don't get stuck in a bad mood for the rest of the day. It is an unpleasant experience, but you are not imprisoned by it. When you are being mindful, you are aware of each experience in the body and mind and you stay with that experience, whether it is pleasant or unpleasant, such that you see what causes stress and harm to you or another and what does not.

Mindfulness as a Meditation Practice

It truly is possible to experience this wise awareness in your daily life, but you need to train yourself to do so, and mindfulness meditation is the most effective means to accomplish this. Through the practice of mindfulness meditation you develop your innate capacity to:

- Collect and unify the mind (at least temporarily)

- Direct your attention

- Sustain your attention

- Fully receive experience no matter how difficult

- Investigate the nature of experience in numerous ways

- Then let go of the experience, no matter how pleasant or unpleasant it may be

Formal meditation practice involves sitting in a chair or on a cushion in a quiet space with your eyes closed for a period of time and slowly training the mind. You can practice meditation by simply sitting, doing nothing special, and just watching what happens, but the more common approach is to direct the mind by cultivating your power of attention. By being mindful, you train or condition your mind to be more mindful. It is not unlike training the body and mind to play the piano, dance the tango, speak a foreign language, or play a sport. You learn forms in order to train the mind, in the same way that a pianist learns scales. You learn what to pay attention to in the same way a dancer learns to feel the music and to be aware of her body and her partner's.

Mindfulness meditation training begins with practicing techniques for concentrating your attention on an object, which enables you to notice how your mind is reacting to what it is experiencing. Concentration is the ability to direct your attention and to sustain it so that it becomes collected and unified. It is a skill everyone already has, but for most people it is limited to only certain specific tasks and is not within their control. When concentration and mindfulness are combined, the power of attention is transformed into a spotlight that illuminates a particular experience in the same way that a theater spotlight holds steady on a single actor until it's time to focus the audience's attention elsewhere. You learn how to direct and sustain your attention on a single experience, rather than letting the mind jump from one thought or feeling to another as it usually does. In Pali the ability to direct attention is called *vitakka* and the ability to sustain it is called *vicara*. The Buddha referred to these skills as "factors of absorption."

Traditionally, in *vipassana*, or mindfulness, meditation you use your breath initially as the object of concentration to collect and unify the mind. You typically stay with the experience of the breath as it touches the body in a single spot, such as the tip of the nose as it moves in and out, or the rise and fall of the chest, or the in-and-out movement of the belly, or the feeling of the breath in the whole body. There are many ways to follow the breath, including counting, noticing its speed, and making mental notes of what is happening, using labels such as "in" and "out" or "rising" and "falling." You can also learn to stay with the breath by coupling a word with each breath. Some teachers insist on a particular method of developing concentration, while others are more flexible.

At first you won't be able to stay with the breath, but soon you will at least be able to be with one or two breaths throughout the complete cycle of inhalation and exhalation. You will also develop the ability to notice when your mind has wandered and to firmly and gently bring it back to the breath.

When your mind starts wandering, the breath becomes your anchor to which you return in order to stabilize and focus your attention. This anchor object is important because meditation is so hard to do. You may get distracted by what's worrying you or by some longing, or you may get bored, sleepy, or restless, or you may start doubting the whole process. Staying with the breath calms the mind, collects your scattered attention, and unifies the mind so that you are able to continue. It is never a mistake or a bad meditation if all you do is work on staying with the breath. Even when you constantly struggle and don't actually spend much time with the breath, it's good practice. By repeatedly returning to the breath, you are learning to just start over. Starting over is a key step in meditation. It expresses your intention to be present, and *the power of your intention is what determines your ability to be mindful in daily life.*

The manner in which you stay with the breath in meditation is called "bare attention"—you simply feel the movement of the breath and body's response and notice whether the breath is warm or cool, long or short. You observe the arising of a breath, its duration, and its passing. You might stay with only one of these experiences or a combination of them. In practicing bare attention you don't judge the breath or think about how you might improve it. You simply register the experience of the breath without reacting to the experience with mental commentary or physical action.

Moving beyond the Breath in Meditation

Once you're somewhat able to stay present with the breath, you start to open your field of attention to ever-more-subtle objects of experience that arise in the mind. This process continues until you are able to respond to all of your experiences as opportunities for mindfulness. In order to meditate in this manner, the Buddha taught what are often called the Four Foundations of Mindfulness, in which you systematically learn how to pay attention to and investigate what arises in your mind, whether the experience comes from one of your five body senses or from the mind generating thought. The four modes of investigation he prescribed are:

- knowing how any experience feels in the body (First Foundation),

- noting the pleasant-, unpleasant-, or neutral-feeling tone that accompanies every moment's experience (Second Foundation),

- witnessing your mental state and your emotions in the moment (Third Foundation), and finally,

- opening to the impersonal truth of life that is revealed in this moment (Fourth Foundation)

These Four Foundations of Mindfulness and all the practices associated with them are described in depth in the Buddha's Satipatthana Sutta. By building your awareness utilizing these four foundations, you gradually develop clear seeing (*sampajanna*), the ability to be mindful in the present moment. In so doing you begin to have insight about what is true and how to respond skillfully in any situation.

When you are just beginning this practice, you serially investigate all Four Foundations of Mindfulness. For instance, if the mind is pulled away from the breath by a strong body sensation, then you temporarily abandon the breath as an object and let that body sensation become the object of your attention. When the mind gets tired of staying with the body and starts to move to other objects, return to the breath.

At this stage of practice you do not investigate your emotions or your mind states, only body sensations. The challenge is to sustain your attention on a particular body sensation in such a way that you can feel it. Is it a pulsation or a wave? Is it expanding or contracting? If it's painful, what kind of pain is it? Does it twist, stab, burn, pinch, and so forth? If it's pleasant, is it sweet, warm, tingly? In the First

Foundation of Mindfulness the attention is to be focused on the body from within the body, meaning that you are not training your mind to be a distant, indifferent observer of your body: rather you are being with your aching back. This same method of keeping attention within the experience is used for all Four Foundations of Mindfulness.

The Buddha started vipassana practice with mindfulness of the body because for most people it is far easier to stay present with the body than with the mind and because the body participates in all other experiences you have in ordinary consciousness. He said, "If the body is not mastered [by meditation], then the mind cannot be mastered; if the body is mastered, mind is mastered." He went on to say, "There is one thing, monks, that cultivated and regularly practiced, leads to a deep sense of urgency . . . to the Supreme Peace . . . to mindfulness and clear comprehension . . . to the attainment of right vision and knowledge . . . to happiness here and now . . . to realizing deliverance by wisdom and the fruition of Holiness: it is mindfulness of the body."

Many experienced students of meditation tend to skip over the body and focus on the emotions and the mind states, thinking they are getting to the really juicy part of practice, but as the Buddha's quote indicates, this is a significant misapprehension. I encourage you to develop an almost continual awareness of your ever-changing body experience. I have found that cultivating this body-awareness is the surest way for most students to start to impact their daily life with their mindfulness practice. Therefore, as you move from the First Foundation of Mindfulness of the Body to the Second Foundation, remember that through the practice you use the breath as an anchor to collect and unify the mind while expanding your mindfulness to an ever-greater range of experience.

After you develop mindfulness of the changing nature of body experience, you are ready to work with the Second Foundation— the feeling tone of your experience. You start to include the pleasant, unpleasant, or neutral flavor contained in each moment of body sensation in your field of attention. You don't try to control these sensations but simply to know them. For instance, you notice how pleasant the warm sun feels on your face on winter mornings, or how an aching leg feels unpleasant, from within the experience. When body sensations are neither pleasant nor unpleasant, they are neutral. Ordinarily you don't notice the neutral sensations, but with mindfulness they become part of your awareness and expand your experience of being alive. Developing awareness of pleasant, unpleasant, and neutral sensations and how they condition the mind is a critical factor in finding peace and well-being in your life.

After you have worked with body sensations, you are ready to work with the Third Foundation, mental events (your emotions, mental processes, and mind states), in your meditation. At first just take emotions as a field for investigation. Notice when your mind is pulled away from the breath by an emotion. What is the nature of the emotion? How do you feel it in the body? In my experience, all emotions are accompanied by body sensations. What is an emotion, really, when you deconstruct it? Is it not an internal image, or words, or a pleasant or unpleasant feeling accompanied by many coarse or subtle sensations? I'm not referring to what caused the emotion, which is a combination of perception, belief, intent, and response, but rather to what happens when the mind registers an emotion. Does the mind keep feeling the emotion, or does it arise and pass like a body sensation? Remember to continue to use your anchor object so that you don't get lost in your emotions.

Many times you will discover that you do not know what emotion you are feeling or that there is more than one emotion competing for attention. In these instances, just be aware of emotions; do not try to name them. Likewise, sometimes you can't name a body sensation, so it only feels like numbness; numbness then *is* the body sensation. Don't insist on specificity; just be aware that there is a body.

Now you are ready to examine your mental processes. You will quickly notice that the mind is almost always thinking and that much of this thinking is based on the past or future in the form of remembering, planning, fantasizing, and rehearsing. Observe each of these. Are they pleasant or unpleasant? What happens to them as you turn your attention on them? Do they stop or intensify? Or do you get lost in them and lose your mindfulness? What underlies your constant planning? Is it anxiety? When you bring up a fear or a worry over and over again, is it really unpleasant or does it induce a kind of reassurance? What happens if you stop? Is the constant worrying really a false reassurance? Does it actually induce a habit of anxiety? Remember to feel your mental processes from within them—the fuzziness and excitement of fantasy, the heaviness of worry and fretting, and the speed of planning. Notice what it is and how it then changes.

Finally, you are ready to experience the Buddha's insights as they manifest in your life—the life you have been examining until now, which includes your body sensations, emotions, mind states, and mental processes, and the pleasantness and unpleasantness that accompanies each of them. With the Fourth Foundation of Mindfulness, you see how each moment constantly changes and that most of what you take personally is actually impersonal and is not about you. For instance, in our earlier example, the person at the office who upset you was not really focused on you but was reacting to her own inner turmoil, and you just happened to receive the eruption. You also notice which mind states lead to suffering and which don't, and you begin to live more wisely.

IMMEDIATE AND LONG-TERM BENEFITS OF MINDFULNESS MEDITATION

Being present or awake empowers your life. It gives you a presence that you feel and others can feel, and it opens you to the experience of being fully alive. Many people complain that something is missing in their lives or they have some vague sense of incompleteness, dissatisfaction, or unease with life. As you wake up, such emotions start to diminish and lose their hold on you. You also begin to realize you have more choice in how you react to whatever arises and you discover that it is genuinely possible to dance with life.

Mindfulness meditation strengthens the mind so that you can more easily be with difficult emotions or uncomfortable physical sensations that cause your mind to abandon the present moment. Mindfulness also strengthens the nervous system such that physical and mental pains don't have the same degree of "hurt," because the mind isn't contracting in anticipation of more pain in the future. For the first few years of practice you are literally reprogramming your nervous system to free it from habitual reactivity. This alone will bring much ease and flexibility to your mind.

The most life-changing benefits of mindfulness meditation are the insights, which arise spontaneously the way a ripened apple falls from the tree of its own accord. Insight is what changes your life. Through insight you realize what brings well-being to yourself and others as well as what brings stress, discomfort, and dissatisfaction into your life. Such insights can be small or quite dramatic. Moreover, they have a cumulative effect such that previous insights become building blocks for still more insights.

Each insight is a direct knowing or "intuitive knowing" of the truth of your experience as contrasted with the conceptual perception, which comes from your usual way of thinking. This direct knowing is what enables mindfulness meditation to have such impact in your life—you feel the truth of your experience, instead of conceptualizing it, reacting to it, or being lost in the past or the future.

During meditation, you will most often have personal insights about your life and how it has been conditioned. Such insights help you grow and understand yourself better, leading to a fuller life. For this reason, many psychotherapists teach their clients a simple form of mindfulness practice.

Less frequent, but having far greater impact when they arise, are the insights about the nature of life itself. These are universal insights about the ever-changing and impersonal nature of your life experiences. These universal insights are what constitute the Buddha's teachings of *dhamma* (in Pali) or *dharma* (in Sanskrit), which is often translated as "truth." For example, mindfulness meditation helps you realize the impersonal nature of difficult experiences, that they are just part of life. This is known as *anatta,* or "not-self," the realization that much of what you previously identified as "you" is actually "neither me nor mine." Therefore you do not take defeat or loss as personal failures, and you are much less reactive to them. You also become aware of *anicca,* the rapid and endlessly changing nature of all things in life. Not-self and the constancy of change are basic characteristics of life, but the truth of them, in the sense of being life altering, can only be known through direct insight, which comes from mindfulness.

How Will I Use This Day?

Sakyong Mipham Rinpoche

We're meditating all throughout our day, Sakyong Mipham Rinpoche says, but we're often simply meditating on "me." If we cultivate a different outlook on our day and how we spend it, our meditation can turn toward more positive and creative qualities. And they will give us the inspiration and strength to make the decisions we need to encounter life's challenges.

Our modern culture does not encourage awakening, and without a sense of inner strength, we are easily invaded by the difficulties around us. If we don't orient our day toward spiritual growth, the speed of our life takes over, fueled by habitual patterns. While some habitual patterns are a source of inspiration, others just drain our energy. Meditation trains us to notice these patterns, which create the fabric of the entity known as "me."

When we wake up in the morning, our first meditation is often "What about me?" We can loosen this pattern by setting a different kind of view. Instead of "What do I have to do today?" or "Will I ever get enough sleep?" we can ask ourselves, "How can I use this day to let the dharma change my thoughts, words, and actions? What positive qualities shall I cultivate?"

Carrying this view to the cushion will enrich our morning meditation. Yet no matter how well our meditation goes, entering into everyday life presents a schism: "I finished my practice and now I have to go to work." It's an insidious dilemma that lowers our energy and hampers our growth. Thinking practices over when we leave the house weakens our ability to engage wholeheartedly with the world outside.

So how do we carry a dharmic view into the day? By seeing the day as our life, and our life as the path, we learn to regard everything we meet as an opportunity to practice. There are seven facets of awakened mind that we can consciously cultivate to enhance the path-like texture of our life.

The first is *egolessness*. In order to grow, we must be willing to give up territory. We may look fervently for the teacher, teachings, or situation that fits into our comfort zone, but the path is not going to happen on our own terms. Are we prepared to abandon our habitual patterns—to give up the support of concepts, opinions, and comforts? To make progress, we need to be willing to change.

The great Tibetan saint Milarepa said that to give up territory, we have to understand impermanence. If we don't understand impermanence, we don't have a sense of immediacy. Without a sense of immediacy, we remain under the influence of the protracted illusion that we are eternal. In other words, we become very comfortable in our habits. Our practice is lazy and our mind tends to be thick. So every day we need to cultivate the willingness to give up the habitual patterns that warp our experience.

The second element to awaken is *faith*. The word "faith" often has the sense that even though we're not really sure about something, we believe in it anyway. The faith we're talking about here, however, is based on knowing what we're doing, not in hoping for the best. It's as if we've checked our boat for holes and found none, so we set sail with a yearning to be completely engaged in practice because we're certain that the teachings will work. The active ingredient of our yearning manifests as strength and compassion.

There are three kinds of faith. First is the faith of inspiration. Seeing a teacher, hearing the dharma, or visiting a meditation center, we feel an immediate inspiration. Faith suddenly arises as a very powerful hit. It hooks our mind and we become excited about it. We just *know*.

But that kind of faith is not sustainable. We must supplement our inspiration with curiosity, from which the second kind of faith arises, understanding. We ask ourselves, "What made that person that way? Why is this place so powerful?" Unless we investigate our inspiration, we will lose our motivation to practice. So we get curious—reading, studying, and hearing dharma. That's how we increase our understanding, which leads to a deeper kind of faith because we know why we were inspired in the first place.

The third kind of faith is following through. Having been impressed, then curious, we now think, "I want to be like that, so I will follow this through." The three kinds of faith naturally sequence into a potent driving force, combining inner strength and compassion.

Being willing to give up, having trust, and yearning to go forward, we now need to be *daring,* which is a third facet of cultivating awakened mind. But daring to do what? We dare to jump out of our samsaric habitual tendencies into more dharmic ones. When we see ourselves falling into the "me" meditation, we emerge from our hallucination and courageously take a leap into a more open place. This can be as simple as giving up our place in line to someone in a hurry.

If we dare to jump out of laziness, we might become slightly aggressive, so a fourth quality to cultivate is *gentleness.* That means slowing down so that we synchronize our intention with our speech and action. Our intention is to use the day as a spiritual path. What is the path? It is a place to grow. With gentleness, we provide the space and warmth for growth, but we don't force progress—our own or others'. If we're not in a rush with our own mind, we have the patience to let things unfold naturally.

If we become too gentle, however, we might become feeble. So *fearlessness* is a fifth element of achieving awakened mind. In terms of how we engage in our life, we're no longer second-guessing ourselves, because we're not afraid of our mind. We can look at it head-on. Although we encounter obstacles, we steadfastly move forward; we're not afraid of giving up territory or taking a leap. Fearlessness has a decisive element, too: at some point we can respond to a situation with a simple "yes" or "no"—the "maybes" go out the door.

With fearlessness comes *awareness*. No longer cloaked in habitual pattern, no longer using hope and fear to manipulate the environment, we are aware of what's happening in our life. We have more energy because we're not burdened by trying to maintain the concept and polarity of "me." Our practice becomes more three-dimensional.

The last entry on this list is a *sense of humor*. I haven't met any great practitioner who didn't have a good sense of humor. It's a sign of pliability and intelligence. Who wants to be a brow-heavy practitioner, squinting hard as we try to push out realization? With a dharmic eye, we're able to see things with some levity because we're connected to our wholesomeness.

Each morning we can choose one of these elements as a daily contemplation and practice. Throughout the day, we can train ourselves to bring the mind to "egolessness," "faith," or "gentleness," for instance—as words, then actions. In the evening, we can take a moment before going to sleep and reflect on what happened: "How did I use this day to nurture my mind and heart?"

Training to increase our dharmic habitual tendencies is a perpetual source of inspiration and strength that provides a standard for decision-making at every level. It's how we become perpetually forward-thinking, visionary people who can use every situation as an opportunity to cross over from the transcendent to the practical—and back.

The Practice of Loving-Kindness for All

Joseph Goldstein

When we find ourselves in difficult circumstances, we find it easy to get caught up in a spiral of inward-focused thoughts. Insight Meditation Society cofounder Joseph Goldstein discusses how, paradoxically, focusing outward gives us the greatest inner strength.

When I first began the practice of *metta* (loving-kindness), I had an experience that revealed a lot about my mind and the way I was relating to others. At the time, I was developing loving-kindness toward a neutral person—although I wasn't really sure what a "neutral person" meant. My teacher, Anagarika Munindra, simply said to pick someone nearby for whom I didn't have much feeling, one way or another.

I was in India at the time, and there was an old gardener at the little monastery where I was staying. I saw him every day, but I had never really given him any thought at all. He was just somebody I noticed in passing. It was quite startling to realize how many such people there were around me, beings for whom I had completely neutral feelings. That in itself was an illuminating discovery.

So every day for weeks, I began visualizing this old gardener in my meditation, repeating phrases like "May you be happy, may you be peaceful, may you be free from suffering." After a while, I began to feel great warmth and caring for him, and every time we passed my heart just opened.

This was a great turning point in my practice. I understood that how I feel about someone is up to me and that my feelings do not ultimately depend on the person, his or her behavior, or the situation. The gardener remained the same. He did not change what he was doing or how he related to me. But because of a turn in my own understanding and practice, my heart began to fill with genuine feelings of kindness and care.

WHAT LEADS TO TRIUMPH OF HEART?

There is an important lesson here about the sustaining power of loving-kindness. Because it does not depend on any particular quality in the other person, this kind of love does not transform easily into ill will, anger, or irritation, as love with desire or attachment so often does. Such unconditional love—love literally without conditions—comes only from our own generosity of heart.

Although we may recognize the purity and power of this feeling, we may fear or imagine that this kind of love lies beyond our capacity. But metta is not a power that belongs only to the Dalai Lama or Mother Teresa or some extraordinary being categorically different from ourselves. We can all practice this power within ourselves and actually learn to love in this way. The question for us is *how* can we do it? What makes this inclusiveness possible?

A number of years ago, the *Harvard Medical Journal* included an article about a Tibetan doctor named Tenzin Chodak, who had been a personal physician to the Dalai Lama. In 1959, Dr. Chodak was imprisoned by the Chinese for twenty-one years. For seventeen of those twenty-one years, he was beaten and tortured daily—physically and psychologically—and his life was continually threatened.

Astonishingly, he emerged from this twenty-one-year-long horror virtually free from signs of any kind of posttraumatic stress.

In the article, Dr. Chodak distills the wisdom we need to understand into four points of understanding, which made possible not only his survival—people survive horrendous conditions in many ways—but also the great triumph of his heart. A short biographical sketch of him by Claude Levenson describes him in this way: "An appearance almost of timidity on first meeting, a voice so quiet it might be a whisper . . . Dr. Chodak could easily pass unnoticed, until you meet his gaze—a gaze filled with the perception of one who has seen so much that he has seen everything, seeing beyond the suffering he has experienced, beyond all the evil and the abuses he has witnessed, yet expressing boundless compassion for his fellow human beings."

Four Insights in Times of Distress

We must endeavor to see every situation in a larger context. Like the Dalai Lama—who often speaks of how one's enemy teaches one patience—Dr. Chodak saw his enemy as his spiritual teacher, who led him to the wisest and most compassionate place in himself. Accordingly, he felt that even in the most dreadful and deplorable circumstances some human greatness, some greatness of heart, could be accomplished. Of course, thinking this is easy; the challenge is to remember and apply this understanding in times of difficulty.

Second, we must see our enemies, or the difficult people in our lives, as human beings like ourselves. Dr. Chodak never forgot the commonality of the human condition. The Eastern "law of karma" means that all our actions have consequences: actions bear fruit based on the intentions behind them. People who act cruelly toward us are actually in adverse circumstances, just as we are, creating unwholesome karma that will bring about their own future suffering.

But we mustn't fall into thinking of karma as "They'll get theirs," as a kind of vehicle for cosmic revenge. Rather, seeing the universal human condition can become a wellspring of compassion. The Dalai Lama said, "Your enemies may disagree with you, may be harming you, but in another aspect, they are still human beings like you. They also have the right not to suffer and to find happiness. If your empathy can extend out like that, it is unbiased, genuine compassion." Understanding karma—that we all reap the fruit of our actions—as a vehicle for compassion is the wisdom we could now integrate into our lives. We're all in the same situation with regard to the great law of karmic cause and effect.

Third, we must let go of pride and feelings of self-importance. These attitudes, which can arise so easily in times of conflict, become the seeds of even more difficulty. It doesn't mean that we should adopt a stance of false humility or self-abnegation. Rather, we let go of the tendency toward self-aggrandizement, whether interpersonally or within the framework of our own inner psychology. A story from ancient China uses nature to illustrate the great protection of true humility:

> The sage Chuang-Tzu is was walking with a disciple on a hilltop. They see a crooked, ancient tree without a single straight branch. The disciple says the tree is useless, nothing from it can be used, and Chuang-Tzu replies, "That's the reason it's ancient. Everyone seems to know how useful it is to be useful. No one seems to know how useful it is to be useless."

Dr. Chodak actually attributed his survival to the ability to let go of self-importance and self-righteousness. This insight provides a tremendous lesson on the spiritual journey, a lesson that can come up for all of us again and again.

Finally, the insight that nourished Dr. Chodak's amazing triumph of the heart, and one we must truly understand ourselves, is that hatred *never* ceases through hatred; it ceases only in response to love. Many spiritual traditions acknowledge this truth. In situations of conflict, loving-kindness and compassion grow when we understand them to be the most beneficial motivation for responsive and effective action.

Hopefully, most of us will never be tortured by our enemies; but can we hold these perspectives, even in less trying circumstances? When someone is very angry with you or you're in some difficult situation, remember that this difficulty, itself, can strengthen patience and love. In these situations, we can investigate what greatness of heart we might accomplish, remind ourselves that everyone involved shares the common bond of humanity, let go of pride, and understand that, in the end, hatred and enmity will only cease by love.

Years ago I was practicing meditation in India and facing a circumstance that, at the time, felt quite challenging to my inner peace and well-being. The summer months had grown very hot on the Indian plains, and I decided to continue my meditation in a rented cottage in the mountains. Situated at seven thousand feet, the hill station of Dalhousie has spectacular views of the high Himalayan peaks. It was beautiful and quiet, and I settled into a routine of silent, intensive practice.

Just below my cottage was a big, open field, and a few weeks after I arrived, a group called the Delhi Girls pitched their tents. The Delhi Girls were a kind of paramilitary Girl Scout troop. Not only did they set up camp, they also set up loudspeakers, blaring loud Hindi film music from six o'clock in the morning until ten o'clock at night.

I watched my mind go through a tremendous range of emotions, from real frustration and anger to an outraged feeling of self-importance—"How can they do this to me? I came all the way to India to get enlightened!"

It took quite a while for my mind to work through all that, to let go of the feelings of self-importance and self-righteousness and *just let things be.* As Ajahn Chah, a great Thai meditation master of the last century, once said of a noisy celebration near his meditation hut: "If my mind doesn't go out to disturb the noise, the noise won't disturb me." There in the mountains of India, when my mind finally did settle down, the continual din of film music in the middle of a meditation retreat was no longer a problem.

OPENING TO COMPASSION

In Buddhist practice, we develop awareness of the different motivations that underlie our actions. We also open to the possibility of expanding our highest motivation and aspirations. This actually enlarges our sense of what we can accomplish in our lives.

Bodhichitta is a Sanskrit and Pali word that literally means "the awakened heart." This refers to that deep wish to awaken from the dream of ignorance in order to benefit all beings. Through cultivating this aspiration, we dedicate our spiritual practice and our very lives to the happiness and welfare of all.

But is this aspiration realistic? Is it really possible to cultivate such an altruistic motivation, given the great mix of qualities within our minds?

Even His Holiness the Dalai Lama has said, "I cannot pretend I always practice bodhichitta, but it does give me tremendous inspiration. Deep inside me I realize how valuable and beneficial it is. That is all." If we, too, can realize how valuable and beneficial it is, we can simply *plant the seed* of bodhichitta in our minds and trust that it will slowly take root and grow in our lives. Repeated short moments of bodhichitta are powerful imprints in our minds. Just as a small seed can become a giant redwood, these moments of bodhichitta are the seeds for many wholesome actions. As the great naturalist Henry David Thoreau wrote, "Convince me that you have a seed there and I am prepared to expect wonders." We might begin each day or each period of meditation with whatever resolve expresses our deepest wish, finding the words that most inspire us. For example, we might say, "May I quickly attain liberation for the welfare and happiness of all beings." Doing this regularly leads us from the understanding that our spiritual practice inevitably helps others, simply by becoming kinder and more peaceful ourselves, to making the benefit of others the very motivation for our practice.

This shift in understanding transforms the way we move through the day with a generous heart, a heart that wishes well to all beings rather than just a few, a heart full of peace. With such a heart, whenever we come close to suffering in the world, we are moved to help alleviate it. That *impulse to act* is compassion.

PART THREE

Transforming Difficulty into Awakening

Erring and Erring, We Walk the Unerring Path

The Dzogchen Ponlop Rinpoche

Adverse circumstances help us to see that we always face a "moment of opportunity," according to the Dzogchen Ponlop Rinpoche, one of the foremost Tibetan teachers living in America today. In that moment, we can choose to fall under the sway of another round of self-defeating emotions or we can choose to work with our mind. Choosing to face our mind directly is not a panacea. We will make many, many mistakes, but those very errors will bring ever more moments of opportunity.

Across much of the nation and the world, people have been losing their jobs and homes due to the global economic decline. Everyone is asking: how much worse will it get; how soon before it gets better? We wonder if we'll be able to take care of our families and what else could possibly go wrong. The ghost of the Great Depression hangs over us like a bad dream that scares and fascinates at the same time. Meanwhile, the bickering of politicians entertains and annoys us nightly.

We are clearly living through a time of great challenges, and yet Mother Earth has witnessed the rise and fall of humanity's fortunes many times over. I recall that during the cold war years someone once asked the Sixteenth Karmapa to comment on that time's worst-case scenario. His Holiness simply smiled and said, "The world has always been this way." We've endured through cycles of prosperity and poverty, peace and war, confidence and doubt. Life is a journey, and it is full of adventures. Some of these may be hard to appreciate in the beginning, but they all contribute to the richness and depth of our journey—they become the knowledge and vision that can transform our dreams and aspirations into reality.

It is our basic instinct to search for happiness. Everything we do is for that: we work, play, create art, join churches, wage wars, count our money, and occasionally make clowns of ourselves. The irony is that we often end up sacrificing our sense of joy in life in our pursuit of this happiness. Since that is the case, we should ask ourselves, "What is this happiness to which I am so devoted that I am willing to sacrifice so much?" A greater mystery is that we do not seem greatly concerned to know what it is. We think money, prestige, and relationships will bring us happiness, but time and again, we experience disappointment and boredom in the midst of having it all.

At some point, our life can become machinelike. We find ourselves running on automatic pilot, without any clear sense of purpose—our momentum fueled by a chronic sense of need, a vague feeling that something is missing in our life. Nothing we have is enough to relieve the pressure we feel. So we keep on with our superhuman efforts to design a life that looks like the happiness we imagine. We've read all the recipes and assembled the right ingredients, but the meals we prepare don't look like the pictures in the book. When it depends on material things or external valuations, happiness has a history of being short-lived.

When we are looking at failed hopes, expectations, and desires, it is a perfect time to see our underlying poverty mentality, because it is so vivid. Our mind of poverty and the actual condition of our pocketbook are usually not the same. Moreover, our capacity to experience happiness and contentment depends more on a sane mind and a kind and generous heart than on wealth. On the other hand, discontent is like a hunger that can never be satisfied. To relieve our sense of emptiness, we consume endlessly. We will buy, beg, or steal whatever makes us feel better, if only for a moment. When we are stuck in discontentment, we become collectors of stuff. At some point, our garage is full, but we go on collecting. We don't stop until our basement is full, our attic is full, and we are paying for public storage. Then we have a garage sale. But our precious collection, which we have hung onto for years, is worth only a few bucks.

We might also collect computer applications that sit on our hard drive. The problem is that, one day, they may cause our computer to crash, and then we will lose everything, including our sixteen-hundred-dollar hard drive. That destroys the whole point of collecting, doesn't it?

In the same way, when we approach the spiritual journey with the attitude of poverty and unchecked discontentment, we can crash our mind. We collect instructions and practices, but despite possessing such spiritual wealth, we still feel insufficient. When one practice doesn't pay off, we go to another. When that doesn't work, it's on to the next. Eventually, we end up back at the beginning for another try. We spin in a circle that has no end, which is the very definition of cyclic existence, which is known as "samsara." This is not a path to enlightenment but to deeper confusion.

That is no different from the confusion of our ordinary life, where our quest is for more and better material possessions. For years, the trend was to have bigger cars and houses. Station wagons morphed into SUVs and Hummers. Houses grew family rooms, media rooms, sun rooms, offices, and decks. We do such things simply to feel better, to be happy. We think if only we can get that new house, that cool car, the latest laptop, it's going to be different. We tell our friends, "I'm going to be much happier. I'll be more satisfied." Sure. But once you get the big, new house and the thrill wears off, you start thinking, "I need to change the paint. Maybe get a new carpet. This couch has got to go." When will it stop? Never. It goes on and on, in your spiritual journey and in your life, until you can transform your discontentment into contentment: the state of being happy and at ease with what you have and using it in the best way that you can. That is the practice of contentment, which, in itself, is a seed of enlightenment. As far as samsara is concerned, our dissatisfaction will continue forever if we let it.

When we've truly discovered the happiness we are searching for and found a genuine purpose to our life, temporary environmental changes do not have any disastrous impact. According to the wisdom of the historical Buddha, true happiness can only be found within. Outer conditions such as wealth and friendships can serve as supports for our happiness and as instruments to connect with an inner experience of joy, but if we see them as our only source of happiness, we are in deep trouble. In the vernacular, we are totally screwed.

Instead, with a calm and clear mind, and with an attitude of kindness, we can acknowledge the reality of impermanence, which is simply that change is inevitable, and move forward with confidence. As we say in the West, "Where there's a will, there's a way." To exercise our will is to engage the power of mind to accomplish our purpose. First, we think, and, second, we act, which coincides with the Buddhist teaching that mind is the primary agent, the instigator, of all actions. It's clear that when mind is calm and stable, we can think more clearly and precisely. So, when conditions are difficult and we must act, there are a few basic things we can do to support our decision-making.

Take some time to contemplate your situation. First, connect with your basic heart of sanity, calm your mind and relax; then, within that, contemplate what you truly desire and what your options are for accomplishing it. Finally, translate that into action, step by step, with an attitude of kindness toward yourself and others. In this way, you can start to bring a sense of clear seeing and equanimity into stressful situations.

FEARLESS JOURNEY

Sometimes our view of our spiritual path can be overly theoretical. From the Buddhist point of view, there is no reality outside the set of experiences we go through every day. While our theories may be quite impressive, they can also be somewhat vague when it comes to practical matters. We may be able to speak coherently about the enlightened nature of mind and all phenomena, but when it comes to our experiences of daily life, it can be hard to see the connection. In order to get to the reality of all that—to actually taste the pure nature of mind—we have to be open to all experiences of life, especially those we regard as negative.

There are positive flashes of awakening going on all the time, in the midst of the ups and downs of our daily grind. We may be wishing for something more, or better, or wanting desperately to escape what we feel is a dire predicament. Whatever our situation looks like, there is tremendous value in simply being present with it. Why? Because no experience ever repeats itself. Each is a once-in-a-lifetime, singular moment that is as precious as meeting the Buddha. This is our only chance to not miss the reality of being who we are and where we are, beyond all our speculations and theories. That is the whole process of the path and spirituality.

Being *who* we are begins with being *where* we are. Being where we are is easy when the experience is pleasant. When we are in the Bahamas, lying down on a nice beach or going for a swim, it is easy to say, "Oh yeah! I can be here. I don't want to be anywhere else." We can be present perfectly in that situation; however, it is more difficult to be where we are when we don't want to be there. That's when we have to try our best to experience reality and be where we are.

When we encounter adverse circumstances, we often feel that the situation is personal, and we lose confidence and faith in ourselves. Yet, when we can work with unfavorable circumstances, that is the time when the quality of our life being a path, rather than a fixed destination, can manifest. In such moments, we can take full advantage of the situation by turning it into an opportunity to reconnect with our basic heart and see the interdependent nature of our existence. At the same time, when we are in situations of joy, of pleasure, of appreciating the beauty of the natural world, we should be there as well. If we miss those moments, we are missing another big opportunity. The sunset you see will never reoccur. The sky you see will never happen again. The formation of clouds, the waves, the tide, whatever you are experiencing now will not come again. It only happens once. Appreciating and being fully present for each moment without either hanging onto it or rejecting it is a powerful practice.

It's not a question of whether we have opportunities to work with our mind or not. We have plenty of opportunities, which is why in Buddhism we talk about a "precious human birth." When the Buddha taught the practice of reflecting on our precious human birth, he didn't mean that we should just be grateful for having a human body instead of some other physical form. From the Buddhist perspective, not every human life possesses the same opportunities. Our birth becomes a precious birth only when we possess the skills and wisdom to understand and apply the instructions for taming and training our mind. In other words, when we have an opportunity to realize the true nature of our mind, which is in the state of primordial buddhahood. In this sense, we have in our hands a rich treasure. Once we realize the preciousness of our opportunity, we should definitely take advantage of it.

MOMENT OF OPPORTUNITY

We have two choices, always. We can just sit around and do nothing as our mind slips under the influence of one disturbing emotion after another, or, when an opportunity presents itself, we can relate to our experience and make the best use of it. That's what we call working with the thought of impermanence. When we realize how ephemeral each moment is, how quickly it comes and goes, never to repeat, then we're more inspired to make our time meaningful rather than wasting it. In this way, our emotions become useful; we are not wasting them. It's like putting our newspapers in the recycling bin; if we just throw them out, they are nothing but junk.

In the same way, when a confused thought or emotion arises

and we make use of it instead of throwing it away, we become a real practitioner. We are genuinely practicing, because we are working with our mind. We are making our best effort, taking our opportunity in the best way we can. Then our life is meaningful. We are not just caught in a vicious cycle of habitual patterns—we are working with our mind to break those patterns. At this point, our emotions are no longer ordinary emotions; they are sacred. Why? Because we are taking them onto the path, which is a sacred dharma journey. We are not talking about just intellectual dharma, here, and we are not talking about just the physical form of dharma practice— shrines, cushions, and sitting meditation. We are talking about dharma that is alive in the movement of our thoughts and emotions. This is how we make the dharma present in our ordinary life, and it is how we can actually see a real transformation taking place. Otherwise, dharma is limited to classroom theory, or it becomes more of a cultural convention than a genuine practice, like going to the church or synagogue on weekends and holidays. In that case, the dharma is not taking root in our heart. It is not affecting our life and journey. Therefore, we don't see any results from our practice. In order to really experience a result from dharma, we have to integrate it into our life, bring it into our experience.

If you grab every opportunity to work with your mind—at home, at school, at work—you'll end up with many more chances to work with strong emotions than in one hour of sitting on your cushion with some vague idea of "meditation." In fact, your practice of working directly with your mind moment to moment will be much more powerful and bring more success because it will really affect your mind; it will change your mindstream. From the Vajrayana point of view, when you recognize an emotion with mindfulness, and penetrate it with some degree of recognition of the nature of mind, that very process is self-transforming. There's nothing more that you need to do. When you can work with your mind in this way, you can see the power of the path. You can clearly see its effect, not just in you, but in the environment—in your family and in your community. That's what practice should produce, a clear result. And that result comes from persistence, from doing it, again and again, whenever you can.

If we sincerely want to engage in dharma practice, we shouldn't make the dharma something "out there" while we are "here." Then we are in a situation of trying to connect the dots, so to speak. One dot is "me and my life" and the other dot is "the dharma and my spiritual path." When we make such a separation, we have to try to bridge that gap, and it becomes a dualistic enterprise, which is harder on us, psychologically speaking. From the point of view of our own journey, the practice of dharma is nothing more than the practice of working with our mind.

In challenging times, we need to remember that the path is a mixed bag. On the one hand, there is a process of transformation taking place; in some areas, we are, indeed, overcoming obstacles and experiencing some level of psychological liberation. In other areas, however, we are still struggling, still engaged in negative, unproductive actions, and therefore experiencing the results of that. We are not always perfect and our life includes blunders and burdens of various kinds. One of the greatest yogis of our time, Khenpo Tsultrim Gyamtso Rinpoche, always says, "Erring and erring, we walk the unerring path." So, when we realize that we have made some mistakes in this life, or that we are caught up in a fit of emotion or fear, we should not take that to mean that we're not progressing on the path or being successful in life. We are likely to feel that we've failed, but so long as we are working with our mind, applying the dharma in whatever way we can, that is regarded as a success. As long as you make an effort to recognize and work with your emotions, thoughts, and any tendency to commit negative actions, you are doing your work. Whether you fail or succeed in a particular instance, in either case, you will actually have been successful. From this perspective, failure is part of what makes up our accomplishments. We usually don't see this.

Success on the path and in life does not come only with being perfect. If you expect that each time a turbulent state of mind arises, the "normal" thing is to look and see, "Oh, there is its non-arising nature," and then when it is fully present and vibrating in your mind, "Oh, there is its non-abiding nature," and finally, when it dissolves, "Oh, there is its non-ceasing nature," that will never happen! You cannot say it's not possible at some point, but it is not the "norm" on the path. In the same way, if you expect that each year your income will increase and your business will grow, that your next home will be larger than your last, and that you are building toward a more and more secure and comfortable future, as befits the American Dream, you are mistaking the ideal for what's normal. That is not only a mistake, it sounds somewhat boring, like a feel-good movie where you know from the beginning exactly what's going to happen. In actual life, anything can and does happen. That is the truth of impermanence and change, and it is what makes our life such an adventure. Remembering this and taking it to heart allows us to be more pragmatic and courageous at the same time. We need to move away from chasing after an impossible ideal and connect as closely as possible to our life as a personal journey—full of surprises and fresh opportunities to make it meaningful.

We need warrior-like courage to be able to face and accept defeat from time to time, and we need to be honest, true to ourselves and our original intention, to transform our suffering and confusion into liberation and awakening. Like champions in boxing or the martial arts, we have to accept some defeats and be willing to learn from them in order to be victorious in the end. We learn from setbacks. We learn from getting beaten up, from being punched again and again, whether it is by our own emotional turmoil or the phenomenal world outside. Sometimes, when you're down, it feels like the world sees you as just a punching bag, and you are taking hits from all sides. That is when we need to remember that loss, disappointment, sadness, and pain are part of our life and the lives of everyone. We are no exception; many others are in worse shape right now. When you have some sense of guidance, when you have some skill in working with your mind, you are better off than most. Let that thought touch your heart and bring you some resolve to "work out your own liberation," as the Buddha taught.

So, remembering that the path is a mixed bag, look at the instructions you have been fortunate to receive, and apply them to your life. Do not see your life and practice as having *any* separation. Your instructions are simply guidelines; they are like the skeleton or backbone of your path. It is you who puts the meat on those bones. You make your path yourself. It is your wisdom, your journey to take, and how it goes and what it looks like is up to you. Be patient about getting to the fruition, however, and let the result come in its own time. You cannot see a minute-by-minute change in your heart or mind; it takes a little time. On the other hand, don't think of success as being too far away. Then you might think, "I'll never reach it, so forget it." With a more balanced, realistic view, we can practice the dharma more pragmatically and arrive at an experience of realization that will benefit us and, in turn, also benefit others.

It is helpful to remember, too, that as much as acute intelligence, insight, or *prajna*, is critical to our journey to enlightenment, we need to bring our understanding into the world with genuine compassion. While it is through our intellect that we actually come to know the path and see clearly how to follow and accomplish it, only through compassion can we manifest in the world what we know and see in a way that will benefit others. No matter how sharp your intelligence is, don't forget to filter it through the heart of compassion before you manifest it in the suffering world. Don't push your wisdom onto others. It doesn't work. If you really want to help someone, simply let your compassion blaze.

If you want to get something across to another person, whether it is the wisdom of enlightenment or how to do a job more efficiently, compassion seems to be the gateway to communication. When your heart is lit with compassion and you are beyond self-interest or self-gratification, your message will get through. Your colleague will listen to you. The world will understand you. Your aspiration to benefit others can actually be realized. That's why compassion is often referred to as "a wish-fulfilling gem": it can fulfill all your desires. When wisdom and compassion are together, it brings heart to your path and the path to your heart. Therefore, when the road gets rocky and your way uncertain, make your journey personal, not theoretical. Make it genuine, not philosophical. Make it ordinary, not religious. Then, you can really embark on the path to enlightenment.

What Lies beyond Blame

Chögyam Trungpa Rinpoche

Many great teachers have commented on the profound—and profoundly practical—teachings of lojong, *mind training, which come from the Tibetan tradition known as Kadampa. These practical instructions—contained in a short text called* The Seven Points of Mind Training—*outline the attributes we need to develop in our mind in order to be supple and adaptable to all conditions. The instructions are encapsulated in groups of short sayings, or slogans. Here, Chögyam Trungpa Rinpoche discusses slogans focusing on the cultivation of patience. These slogans show how reversing our point of view in the face of bad circumstances transforms them: they become vehicles for making our life more workable and enjoyable.*

Whatever happens in your life should be included as part of your journey. That is the basic idea in this group of slogans, which is connected with the *paramita* of patience. (*Paramita* means perfection, or crossing over to the other side, and it refers to six virtuous practices that make up the Mahayana path of the bodhisattva, one who works for the benefit of all beings.) The definition of patience is forbearance. Whatever happens, you don't react to it. The obstacle to patience is aggression. Patience does not mean biding your time and trying to slow down. Impatience arises when you become too sensitive and you don't have any way to deal with your environment, your atmosphere. You feel very touchy, very sensitive. So the paramita of patience is often described as a suit of armor. Patience has a sense of dignity and forbearance. You are not so easily disturbed by the world's aggression.

The basic slogan of this section is:

WHEN THE WORLD IS FILLED WITH EVIL,
TRANSFORM ALL MISHAPS INTO THE PATH OF *BODHI.*

Whatever occurs in your life—environmental problems, political problems, or psychological problems—should be transformed into a part of your wakefulness, or bodhi. Such wakefulness is a result of the practice of mindfulness-awareness discipline as well as your basic understanding of soft spot, or *bodhichitta.*

This slogan says practically everything about how we can practice generosity as well. In our ordinary life, our immediate surroundings or our once-removed surroundings are not necessarily hospitable. There are always problems and difficulties. There are difficulties even for those who proclaim that their lives are very successful, for those who have become the president of their country, for the richest millionaires, for the most famous poets or movie stars or surfers or bullfighters. Even if our lives go right, according to our expectations, there are still difficulties. Obstacles always arise. That is something everybody experiences. And when obstacles happen, any mishaps connected with those obstacles—poverty mentality, fixating on loss and gain, or any kind of competitiveness—should be transformed into the path of bodhi.

That is a very powerful and direct message. It is connected with not feeling poverty-stricken all the time. You might feel inadequate because you have a sick father and a crazy mother and you have to take care of them, or because you have a distorted life and money problems. For that matter, even if you have a successful life and everything is going all right, you might feel inadequate because you have to work constantly to maintain your business. A lot of those situations could be regarded as expressions of your own timidity and cowardice. They could all be regarded as expressions of your poverty mentality.

You should also begin to build up confidence and joy in your own richness. That richness is the essence of generosity. It is the sense of resourcefulness, that you can deal with whatever is available around you and not feel poverty-stricken. Even if you are abandoned in the middle of a desert and you want a pillow, you can find a piece of rock with moss on it that is quite comfortable to put your head on. Then you can lie down and have a good sleep. Having such a sense of resourcefulness and richness seems to be the main point.

We have found that a lot of people complain that they are involved in intense domestic situations: they relate with everything in their lives purely on the level of pennies, tiny stitches, drops of water, grains of rice. But we do not have to do that—we can expand our vision by means of generosity. We can give something to others. We don't always have to receive something first in order to give something away. Having connected with the notion of generosity, we begin to realize a sense of wealth automatically. The nature of generosity is to be free from desire, free from attachment, able to let go of anything.

DRIVE ALL BLAMES INTO ONE.

This slogan is about dealing with conventional reality. No matter what appears in our ordinary experience, whatever trips we might be involved in, whatever interesting and powerful situations arise— we do not have any expectations in return for our kindness. When we are kind to somebody, there are no expectations that there will be any reward for that. Drive all blames into one means that all the problems and the complications that exist around our practice, realization, and understanding are not somebody else's fault. All the blame always starts with ourselves.

A lot of people seem to get through this world and actually make quite a comfortable life by being compassionate and open—even seemingly compassionate and open. They seem to get along in this world. Yet although we share the same kind of world, we ourselves get hit constantly. We get blamed and we get into trouble—emotional problems, financial problems, domestic, relationship, and sociological problems are happening all the time.

We might have entirely the same lifestyle as somebody else. For instance, we could be sharing a room with a college friend, eating the same problematic food, sharing the same shitty house, having the same schedule and the same teachers. Our roommate manages to handle everything okay and find his or her freedom. We, on the other hand, are stuck with that memory and filled with resentment all the time. We would like to be revolutionary, to blow up the world. But who did that to us? We could say that the schoolteacher did it, that everybody hates us and they did it. But *why* do they hate us? That is a very interesting point.

The blame for every mishap that happens to us is always directed naturally to us; it is our particular doing. Everything is based on our own uptightness. We could blame the organization; we could blame the government; we could blame the police force; we could blame the weather; we could blame the food; we could blame the highways; we could blame our own motorcars, our own clothes; we could blame an infinite variety of things. But it is we who are not letting go, not developing enough warmth and sympathy—which makes us problematic. So we cannot blame anybody.

Of course, we could build up all kinds of philosophies and think we are representing the voice of the rest of the world, saying that this is the world's opinion, that is what happens in the world. "Don't you see that you should not make me suffer this? The world is this way, the true world is that way." But we are *not* speaking on behalf of the world, we are simply speaking on behalf of ourselves.

This slogan applies whenever we complain about anything, even that our coffee is cold or the bathroom is dirty. It goes very far. Everything is due to our own uptightness, so to speak, which is known as ego holding, ego fixation. Since we are so uptight about ourselves, that makes us very vulnerable at the same time. We consequently provide the ideal target. We get hit, but nobody means to hit us—we are actually inviting the bullets. So there we are, in the good old world. Driving all blames into one is a very good idea.

The intention of driving all blames into one is that otherwise you will not enter the bodhisattva path. Therefore, you do not want to lay any emotional, aggressive blame on anybody at all. So driving all blames into one begins with that attitude. On that basis, you drive all blames into one again at the level of *vipashyana* (insight). This involves actually experiencing the real, visible, logical consequences of doing otherwise. For instance, you could drive all blames into Joe Schmidt, but instead you drive all blames into yourself. In this case, you actually begin to see the possibility that aggression and neurosis are expanded if you drive your neurosis into somebody else. So instead, you drive your blames onto yourself. That is the basic point.

All of this seems to come under the general categories of compassion for others and having a loving attitude to oneself, known in Sanskrit as *karuna* and *maitri*. In other words, the experience of karuna and maitri is to drive all blames into one. So this slogan is connected with the basic discipline of the bodhisattva path, which is to refrain from any kind of ill-doing.

This slogan is the essence of the bodhisattva path. Even though somebody else has made a terrible booboo and blamed it on you, you should take the blame yourself. In terms of power, it is a much simpler and more direct way of controlling the situation. In addition, it is the most direct way of simplifying complicated neuroses into one point. Also, if you look for volunteers around you to take the blame, there will be no volunteers other than yourself. By taking that particular blame on yourself, you reduce the neurosis that's happening around you. You also reduce any paranoia existing in other people, so that those people might have clearer vision.

You can actually say, "I take the blame. It's my fault that such and such a thing happened and that such and such things took place as a result." It is very simple and ordinary. You can actually communicate with somebody who is not in a defensive mood, since you already took all the blame. It is much better and easier to talk to somebody when you have accepted the blame already. Then you can clarify the situation, and quite possibly the person you are talking to, who might be the cause of the particular problem, would realize that he has done something terrible himself. He might recognize his own wrongdoing. But it helps that the blame, which is just a paper tiger at that point, has already been taken on by you. That helps.

This kind of approach becomes very powerfully important. I've actually done it thousands of times. I've taken a lot of blame personally. A person may actually do a terrible thing based on his or her understanding of my recommendation. But that's okay, I can take it on wholeheartedly as my problem. In that way there is some chance of working with such a person, and the person begins to go along and fulfill his actions properly, and everything is fine.

That's a tip for people working in organizations. If individuals can take the blame themselves and let their friends off to continue their work or duty, that will make the whole organization work better and allow it to be much more functional. When you say, "You're full of shit! I didn't do such a thing. It wasn't me, it's you who did it. There's no blame on me," the whole thing gets very complicated. You begin to find this little plop of a dirty thing bouncing around in the bureaucracy, something like a football bouncing back and forth. And if you fight over it too much, you have tremendous difficulty dissolving or resolving that particular block, plop, slug. So the earlier you take the blame, the better. And although it is not really, fundamentally, your fault at all, you should take it as if it's yours.

This seems to be the interesting point where the two aspects of the bodhisattva vow, *mönpa* and *jukpa* (desiring to enter and actually entering into bodhisattva discipline), come together. It is how you work with your fellow sentient beings. If you do not allow a little bit of blame and injustice to come to you, nothing is going to work. And if you do not really absorb all the blame, but say it is not yours since you are too good and are doing so well, then nothing is going to work. This is so because everybody is looking for someone to blame, and they would like to blame *you*—not because you have done anything, but because they probably think you have a soft spot in your heart. They think that if they put their jam or honey or glue on you, then you actually might buy it and say, "Okay, the blame is mine."

Once you begin to do that, it is the highest and most powerful logic, the most powerful incantation you can make. You can actually make the whole thing functional. You can absorb the poison—then the rest of the situation becomes medicine. If nobody is willing to absorb the blame, it becomes a big interrelational football. It is not even tight like a good football, but filled with a lot of glue and gooey all over the outside as well. Everybody tries to pass it on to each other and nothing happens. Finally that football begins to grow bigger and bigger and bigger and bigger. Then it causes revolutions and all the rest.

As far as international politics are concerned, somebody is always trying to put the blame on somebody else, to pass that huge, overbuilt, gooey, dirty, smelly, gigantic football with all sorts of worms coming out of it. People say, "It's not mine, it's yours." The communists say it belongs to the capitalists and the capitalists say it belongs to the communists. Throwing it back and forth doesn't help anyone at all. So even from the point of view of political theory—if there is such a thing as politics in the Mahayana or in Buddhism—it is important for individuals to absorb unjustified blame and to work with that. It is very important and necessary.

Usually, with any problems at all that might occur in your life—political, environmental, psychological, or, for that matter, domestic or spiritual—you always decide to blame it on somebody else. You may not have a particular individual to blame, but you still come up with the basic logic that something is wrong. You might go to the authorities or your political leaders or your friends and demand that the environment be changed. That is your usual way of complaining to people. You might organize a group of people who, like yourself, blame the environment, and you might collect signatures for a petition and give it to some leader who might be able to change the environment. Or, for that matter, your complaint might be purely individual: if your husband or wife is in love with somebody else, you might ask him or her to give up his or her lover. But as far as you yourself are concerned, you feel so pure and good, you never touch yourself at all. You want to maintain yourself one hundred percent. You are always asking somebody else to do something for you, on a larger scale or on a smaller scale. But if you look very closely at what you are doing, it becomes unreasonable.

Sometimes, if he is brave enough, your husband might say to you: "Isn't there some blame on your side as well? Mightn't you also have to join in and do something about it?" Or if your wife is brave enough, she will tell you that the situation might have something to do with both of you. If your spouse is somewhat timid and intelligent, he might say, "Both of us are to blame." But nobody says, "It is *you* who has to change." Whenever anybody does say, "It's your problem, not anybody else's," you don't like it at all.

The text says: "Drive all blames into one." The reason you have to do that is because you have been cherishing yourself so much, even at the cost of sacrificing somebody else's life. You have been cherishing yourself, holding yourself so dearly. Although sometimes you might say that you don't like yourself, even then in your heart of hearts you know that you like yourself so much that you're willing to throw everybody else down the drain, down the gutter. You are really willing to do that. You are willing to let somebody sacrifice his life, give himself away for you. And who are you, anyway? So the point is that all blames should be driven into oneself.

This slogan does not mean you should not speak up. If you see something that is obviously destructive to everybody, you should speak out. But you can speak out in the form of driving all blames into yourself. The question is how to present it to the authorities. Usually you come at them in an aggressive, traditionally American way. You have been trained to speak for yourself and for others in the democratic style of the "lord of speech." You come out with placards and complaints: "We don't like this." But that only solidifies the authorities even more. There could be a much better way of approaching the whole thing, a more intelligent way. You could say, "Maybe it's my problem, but personally I find that this water doesn't taste good." You and your friends could say, "We don't feel good about drinking this water." It could be very simple and straightforward. You don't have to go through the whole legal trip. You don't have to use the "lord of speech" approach of making public declarations of all kinds, "Freedom for all mankind!" or anything like that. Maybe you could even bring along your dog or your cat. I think the whole thing could be done very gently.

Obviously, there are social problems, but the way to approach that is not as "I—a rightful political entity," or as "me—one of the important people in society." Democracy is built on the attitude that I speak out for myself, the invincible me. I speak for democracy. I would like to get my own rights, and I also speak for others' rights as well. Therefore, we don't want to have this water. But that approach doesn't work. The point is that people's experience of themselves could be gathered together, rather than just having a rally. That is what you do in sitting practice.

In an extreme case, if I happened to find myself in the central headquarters where they push the button that could blow up the planet, I would kill the person who was going to push the button for the bomb right away and without any hesitation. I would take delight in it! But that is slightly different from what we are talking about. In that case, you are dealing with the threshold of the power of society altogether. In this case, we are simply talking about how we can collectively smooth out this world, so that it could become an enlightened society. Creating an enlightened society requires general cultivation of that nature.

BE GRATEFUL TO EVERYONE.

This slogan also is dealing with conventional reality. That is to say, without this world we cannot attain enlightenment, there would be no journey. By rejecting the world, we would be rejecting the ground and rejecting the path. All our past history and all our neurosis is related with others in some sense. All of our experiences are based on others, basically. As long as we have a sense of practice, some realization that we are treading on the path, every one of those little details that are seemingly obstacles to us becomes an essential part of the path. Without them we cannot attain anything at all—we have no feedback, we have nothing to work with, absolutely nothing to work with.

So in a sense all the things taking place around our world, all the irritations and all the problems, are crucial. Without others we cannot attain enlightenment—in fact, we cannot even tread on the path. In other words, we could say that if there is no noise outside during our sitting meditation, we cannot develop mindfulness. If we do not have aches and pains in our body, we cannot attain mindfulness, we cannot actually meditate. If everything were lovey-dovey and jellyfish-like, there would be nothing to work with. Everything would be completely blank. Because of all these textures around us, we are enriched. Therefore, we can sit and practice and meditate. We have a reference point—encouragement, discouragement, or whatever. Everything is related to the path.

The idea of this particular teaching is actually to give our blood and flesh to others. "If you want me, take me, possess me, kidnap me, control me—go ahead, do it. Take me. I'm at your service. You could bounce on me, shit on me, cut me into pieces, or anything you want. Without your help I would not have any way to work with my journey at all." That is a very, very powerful thing. In fact, one of the interesting sayings of Langri Thangpa, one of the Kadampa teachers, was: "I realize that all mistakes belong to me and all virtues belong to others, so I cannot really blame anybody except myself."

There is a little phrase that might be good to memorize. In Tibet we used to stick it on our door handles and things like that. The saying goes: "Profit and victory to others; loss and defeat to myself." That sounds terribly self-flagellating if you look at it the wrong way. In particular, the popular idea of Catholicism is to blame everything on oneself as an ultimate guilt concept. But in this case, we are not talking about guilt or that we did something terribly wrong. It is seeing things as they are. By "profit and victory," we mean anything that encourages us to walk on the path of dharma—that is created by the world. Yet at the same time we are filled with loss and defeat all the time—that is ours. We are not supposed to sulk on that particular point, but we are supposed to take pride in that. It is a fantastic idea that we are actually, finally fearless persons—that profit is others' and loss is ours. That is great, fantastic! We may not find that to be so when it is early morning and we have just woken up and feel rather feeble; although at the end of the day, when we have had a few drinks and our belly is filled and we are relatively comfortable, we might feel that way. But fundamentally it is true.

These statements are not based on guilt or punishment, like the Jewish idea of *oy vey*. But it is actually true that a lot of things that we tend to blame others for are our own doing—otherwise we wouldn't get in trouble. How come somebody else doesn't get in trouble and we do get in trouble? What causes that? It must be something happening to us, obviously. We can write our case history and employ our own lawyer to prove that we are right and somebody else is wrong—but that is also trouble we have to go through. It is all trouble, problems. And trying to prove our case history somehow doesn't work. In any case, hiring a lawyer to attain enlightenment is not done. It is not possible. Buddha did not have a lawyer himself.

The slogan "Be grateful to everyone" follows automatically once we drive all blames into one. We have a feeling that if others didn't exist to hassle us, we couldn't drive all blames into ourselves at all. All sentient beings, all the people in the world, or most of them, have a problem in dealing with "myself." Without others, we would have no chance at all to develop beyond ego. So the idea here is to feel grateful that others are presenting us with tremendous obstacles—even threats or challenges. The point is to appreciate that. Without them, we could not follow the path at all.

When Things Fall Apart

The Eight Worldly Dharmas

Pema Chödrön

Bouncing between opposing conditions like gain and loss, we are trapped in the unending cycle of dissatisfaction known as "samsara." By exploring how these "things we seek and things we avoid" shape our lives, says Pema Chödrön, we can learn to "use our life" instead of being trapped in it. When we look at the work of these opposites with the curiosity of a young child, what seemed like a problem becomes a source of wisdom.

One of the classic Buddhist teachings on hope and fear concerns what are known as the eight worldly dharmas. These are four pairs of opposites—four things that we like and become attached to and four things that we don't like and try to avoid. The basic message is that when we are caught up in the eight worldly dharmas, we suffer.

First, we like pleasure; we are attached to it. Conversely, we don't like pain. Second, we like and are attached to praise. We try to avoid criticism and blame. Third, we like and are attached to fame. We dislike and try to avoid disgrace. Finally, we are attached to gain, to getting what we want. We don't like losing what we have.

According to this very simple teaching, becoming immersed in these four pairs of opposites—pleasure and pain, loss and gain, fame and disgrace, and praise and blame—is what keeps us stuck in the pain of samsara.

Whenever we're feeling good, our thoughts are usually about things we like—praise, gain, pleasure, and fame. When we're feeling uncomfortable and irritable and fed up, our thoughts and emotions are probably revolving around something like pain, loss, disgrace, or blame.

Let's take praise and blame. Someone walks up to us and says, "You are old." If it just so happens that we want to be old, we feel really good. We feel as if we've just been praised. That gives us enormous pleasure and a sense of gain and fame. But suppose we have been obsessing all year about getting rid of wrinkles and firming up our jawline. When someone says "You are old," we feel insulted. We've just been blamed, and we feel a corresponding sense of pain.

Even if we don't talk about this particular teaching any further, we can already see that many of our mood swings are related to how we interpret what happens. If we look closely at our mood swings, we'll notice that something always sets them off. We carry around a subjective reality that is continually triggering our emotional reactions. Someone says, "You are old," and we enter into a particular state of mind—either happy or sad, delighted or angry. For someone else, the same experience might be completely neutral.

Words are spoken, letters are received, phone calls are made, food is eaten, things appear or don't appear. We wake up in the morning, we open our eyes, and events happen all day long, until we go to sleep. A lot is happening in our sleep, too. All night long we encounter the people and events of our dreams. How do we react to what occurs? Are we attached to certain kinds of experiences? Do we reject or avoid others? How hooked do we get by these eight worldly dharmas?

The irony is that we make up the eight worldly dharmas. We make them up in reaction to what happens to us in this world. They are nothing concrete in themselves. Even more strange is that we are not all that solid either. We have a concept of ourselves that we reconstruct moment by moment and reflexively try to protect. But this concept that we are protecting is questionable. It's all "much ado about nothing"—like pushing and pulling a vanishing illusion.

We might feel that somehow we should try to eradicate these feelings of pleasure and pain, loss and gain, praise and blame, fame and disgrace. A more practical approach would be to get to know them, see how they hook us, see how they color our perception of reality, see how they aren't all that solid. Then the eight worldly dharmas become the means for growing wiser as well as kinder and more content.

To begin with, in meditation we can notice how emotions and moods are connected with having lost or gained something, having been praised or blamed, and so forth. We can notice how what begins as a simple thought, a simple quality of energy, quickly blossoms into full-blown pleasure and pain. We have to have a certain amount of fearlessness, of course, because we like it all to come out on the pleasure/praise/fame/gain side. We like to ensure that everything will come out in our favor. But when we really look, we're going to see that we have no control over what occurs at all. We have all kinds of mood swings and emotional reactions. They just come and go endlessly.

Sometimes we're going to find ourselves completely caught up in a drama. We're going to be just as angry as if someone had just walked into the room and slapped us in the face. Then it might occur to us: "Wait a minute, what's going on here?" We look into it and are able to see that, out of nowhere, we feel that we have lost something or been insulted. Where this thought came from we don't know, but here we are, hooked again by the eight worldly dharmas.

Right then, we can feel that energy, do our best to let the thoughts dissolve, and give ourselves a break. Beyond all that fuss and bother is a big sky. Right there in the middle of the tempest, we can drop it and relax.

Or we might be completely caught up in a delightful, pleasurable fantasy. We look into it and see that, out of nowhere, we feel we have gained something, won something, been praised for something. What pops up is out of our control, totally unpredictable, like the images in a dream. But up it comes, and we're hooked again by the eight worldly dharmas. The human race is so predictable. A tiny thought arises, then escalates, and before we know what hit us, we're caught up in hope and fear.

In the eighth century a remarkable man introduced Buddhism into Tibet. His name was Padmasambhava, the Lotus-Born. He is also called Guru Rinpoche. The legend is that he simply appeared one morning sitting on a lotus in the middle of a lake. It is said that this unusual child was born completely awake, knowing from the very first moment that phenomena—both outer and inner—have no reality at all. What he didn't know was how everyday things functioned in his world.

He was a very inquisitive boy. He found out on the first day that because of his radiance and beauty, everyone was attracted to him. He saw too that when he was joyful and playful, people were happy and showered him with praise. The king of this country was so taken with the child that he took Guru Rinpoche to live in the palace and treated him like a son.

Then one day the boy went up to play on the flat roof of the palace, taking with him the king's ritual instruments, a bell and a metal scepter called a *vajra*. Completely delighted, he danced around on the rooftop, ringing the bell and spinning the vajra. Then with great curiosity, he tossed them into space. They fell to the street below, landing on the heads of two passersby and killing them instantly.

The people of the country were so outraged that they demanded that the king exile Guru Rinpoche. That very day, without any baggage or food, he was sent off into the wilderness alone.

This inquisitive child had learned a powerful lesson about the workings of the world. The story goes that this brief but vivid encounter with praise and blame was all he needed to figure out the everyday operations of samsara. From then on he abandoned hope and fear and worked joyfully to awaken others.

We can also use our lives this way. We can explore these familiar pairs of opposites in everything we do. Instead of automatically falling into habitual patterns, we can begin to notice how we react when someone praises us. When someone blames us, how do we react? When we've lost something, how do we react? When we feel we've gained something, how do we react? When we feel pleasure or pain, is it as simple as that? Do we just feel pleasure or pain? Or is there a whole libretto that goes along with it?

When we become inquisitive about these things, look into them, see who we are and what we do, with the curiosity of a young child, what might seem like a problem becomes a source of wisdom. Oddly enough, this curiosity begins to undercut what we call ego pain or self-centeredness, and we see more clearly. Usually we're just swept along by the pleasant or painful feelings. We're swept away by them in both directions; we spin off in our habitual style, and we don't even notice what's happening. Before we know it, we've composed a novel on why someone is so wrong, or why we are so right, or why we must get such-and-such. When we begin to understand the whole process, it begins to lighten up considerably.

We are like children building a sand castle. We embellish it with beautiful shells, bits of driftwood, and pieces of colored glass. The castle is ours, off limits to others. We're willing to attack if others threaten to hurt it. Yet despite all our attachment, we know that the tide will inevitably come in and sweep the sand castle away. The trick is to enjoy it fully but without clinging, and when the time comes, let it dissolve back into the sea.

This letting things go is sometimes called nonattachment, but not with the cool, remote quality often associated with that word. This nonattachment has more kindness and more intimacy than that. It's actually a desire to know, like the questions of a three-year-old. We want to know our pain so we can stop endlessly running. We want to know our pleasure so we can stop endlessly grasping. Then somehow our questions get bigger and our inquisitiveness more vast. We want to know about loss so we might understand other people when their lives are falling apart. We want to know about gain so we might understand other people when they are delighted or when they get arrogant and puffed up and carried away.

When we become more insightful and compassionate about how we ourselves get hooked, we spontaneously feel more tenderness for the human race. Knowing our own confusion, we're more willing and able to get our hands dirty and try to alleviate the confusion of others. If we don't look into hope and fear, seeing a thought arise, seeing the chain reaction that follows—if we don't train in sitting with that energy without getting snared by the drama, then we're always going to be afraid. The world we live in, the people we meet, the animals emerging from doorways—everything will become increasingly threatening.

So we start by simply looking into our own hearts and minds. Probably we start looking because we feel inadequate, or in pain, and want to clean up our act. But gradually our practice evolves. We start understanding that, just like us, other people also keep getting hooked by hope and fear. Everywhere we go, we see the misery that comes from buying into the eight worldly dharmas. It's also pretty obvious that people need help and that there's no way to benefit anybody unless we start with ourselves.

Our motivation for practicing begins to change, and we desire to become tamed and reasonable for the sake of other people. We still want to see how mind works and how we get seduced by samsara, but it's not just for ourselves. It's for our companions, our children, our bosses—it's for the whole human dilemma.

What Suffering Teaches

Polly Young-Eisendrath

The respected psychoanalyst and longtime Zen and Vipassana practitioner Polly Young-Eisendrath celebrates the path of resilience. When we decide, as individuals and a society, to accept suffering, we become self-aware. Out of that grows compassion, recognition of our humanity, and a sense of purpose in life. We learn, she says, to thrive in adversity.

> Zen Master Dogen has pointed out that anxiety, when accepted, is the driving force to enlightenment in that it lays bare the human dilemma at the same time that it ignites our desire to break out of it.
> —Philip Kapleau

The elite ranks of medicine, psychiatry, biology, and sometimes even psychology show an almost uniform lack of interest in the value of suffering. They focus instead on avoiding or eliminating it. This contemporary strategy tends to increase our worst fears—that pain and suffering are intolerable and wasteful of our energy. As a practicing Buddhist and psychoanalyst, I see it differently. Hardships are the major catalysts for change and development in our lives; they wake us to how we create suffering through our own attitudes and intentions, our actions and relationships.

I'm writing, though, against a strong current that includes a widespread assortment of psychiatric and New Age formulas for how to stay happy and in control, as well as the hard-core scientific ideologies of genetics and brain chemistry that promise us cures for all major diseases and problematic moods—even the possibility of conquering death. Trying to find a gene for criminality, a physical basis for happiness, and ever better drugs for our negative moods, we have directed our gaze to Nature to locate the origin of our suffering. This is a grave error, from the perspectives of Buddhism and psychoanalysis.

Seeing Yourself or Blaming Nature

Much of our suffering originates with our own discontent, emanating from the evaluations and attitudes that arise in protecting ourselves and separating ourselves out from the context of our own engagement. As a Jungian psychoanalyst, I look upon much of this discontent as arising from the psychological complexes that derive from our emotional adaptations of childhood. These complexes, archetypal at root, drive us to create images of grandiosity and devaluation and dominance and submission both within ourselves and between ourselves and others. The ego complex, with its core of an archetypal self (the universal predisposition to create an identity of coherent individual subjectivity), forms as the central aspect of personal identity. Defenses of the ego can lead to suffering through shame, envy, fear, pride, or guilt as we feel ourselves separated off or alienated from others. Tendencies to identify with and/or project complexes of Terrible Parent and Victim Child are universal emotional difficulties of adulthood that are sometimes rigidified as aspects of personality and sometimes felt as neurotic inner conflicts. If we can map the psychic terrain of our subjective lives, we can begin to find a path to freedom—that middle path between dissociation or repression and enactment.

As we attempt to explain more and more of our personal difficulties through biology and genes, society and culture encourage us to avoid such a middle path. We are invited to put down the mirror of self-recognition and to stop our search for a self-awareness that could set us free.

From the perspective of Buddhist teachings, dropping the mirror of self-recognition can result in falling into the lowest realms of hell where we are continuously driven by greed, ignorance, fears, and cravings into terrible states of misery and restlessness. I fear that I see these hellish states in every shopping mall, every subway, every parking garage and supermarket that I enter. People have lost their ability to know how to be human. They often appear to be drifting around in the confusions of greed, ignorance, and fear—perhaps searching for something to relieve their misery.

NEUROSIS AND AUTHENTIC PAIN

Without the capacity to see how we create a lot of our own difficulties, we are morally and spiritually adrift on all levels of existence. In our society, we are deeply perplexed about the increase in violence and suicide and destruction among young people, especially in our cities. But it is obvious that there is no widespread understanding or teaching of the "ethic of suffering": that one is the creator of oneself and that whatever one does, one becomes heir to those intentions and actions.

Through the ethic of suffering we come to recognize a boundary between our own subjectivity and what lies beyond our control. Our thoughts, feelings, intentions, and actions become ours, and we recognize the power of being conscious, of making meaning. Knowing our own subjective freedom, we are able to surrender more fully to the effects of loss, aging, illness, and death, which are the inevitable natural processes of life.

Jung talks about the difference between neurosis and authentic pain. Neurosis arises from the ways in which, conscious or unconscious, we are dissatisfied, thrown off-center, full of childish wishes and complaints. This neurotic suffering distracts us from the authentic and inevitable miseries of life. Without a true understanding of the constraints and limitations of human existence, we have no knowledge about what it means to be *human* (not animal, not divine). We have no answers to life's major questions: Who are they? (the mystery of our parents in childhood), Who am I? (the perennial question of adolescence), and Who are we? (the exquisite question of adulthood). When we get caught in the unending repetitions of our neuroses, we lack the inner freedom even to ask these human questions, much less seek their answers.

Within the contemporary ideology of biological psychiatry, genetic engineering, and psychopharmaceutical remakes, there is no felt personal connection between our actions and their consequences, no belief that anxiety may be the springboard for development, that illness and loss are the impetus to wake up to discoveries of self-knowledge. Our cultural messages have themselves become neurotic: stay young forever, try to escape the boredom that arises from sealing off your inner life, and protect yourself from too much insight.

THE MEANING OF LIMITATION

Keeping our attention on the limits and constraints of human life arouses spiritual yearning. In both psychoanalysis and Buddhism, practitioners discover the meaning of limits—of time, wishes, desires, control, responsibility, omnipotence, ideals, power, and even love. These limits teach us. From the facts of our discontent, dependence, vulnerability, and lack of omnipotence and omniscience, we learn what it means to be truly human. These "negative" experiences open our hearts and allow us to connect to others through gratitude and compassion. Moreover, they insist that we ask those fundamental questions: Who are they? Who am I? Who are we?

The only real freedom from suffering and death is to accept limitations, to be interested, and to begin to see how they connect us to ourselves through meaning and to others through compassion. Although we may discover many cures for illnesses and some relief for pain, we cannot transform our own discontent without recognizing how we create it. This is at the heart of the Four Noble Truths of Buddhism, the first teachings of the Buddha Shakyamuni after his supreme enlightenment. Although the core teachings of the Noble Truths are often translated into English as teachings about "suffering," it would probably be more accurate to call them teachings about stress. The Sanskrit word translated as "suffering" is *dukkha*, which literally refers to off-centeredness, like a wheel riding off its axle or a bone out of its socket. So I refer to the Noble Truths as teachings about stress and its relief.

Taken as a whole, the Noble Truths state that stress has an identifiable cause, and if this cause can be eliminated, then so can its effect. In other words, the goal of Buddhist practice and theory is to achieve lasting flexibility. This is understood as possible only when the actual causes of stress have been eliminated. Most forms of Buddhism teach that the ultimate root of our stress is the concept of a permanent, lasting individual self. Many practices and theories of Buddhism demonstrate that nothing in reality corresponds to the notion of our having a permanent self or soul.

In fact, nothing is permanent and lasting in human life—not our most up-to-date knowledge, not ourselves, not any of the world as we know it. It is all subject to change. When we can experience this impermanence as the fact of our existence and live within its reality—that is, within the ongoing death and rebirth from moment to moment of existence—then we are attuned to the nature of being human. What grounds us and keeps us centered in this existence is the recognition of our actual interbeing—our embeddedness in a context. When we have a proper sense of ourselves supported by a fluid context, with the freedom to alleviate stress, our hearts are opened by compassion to everything that lives and suffers from limitation. There is an almost natural sense of purpose that arises from such compassion, an inspiration about how one might help others with the knowledge that has come from one's own suffering.

SOCIAL ETHIC OF SUFFERING

As a society we need far more opportunities to hear stories of adversity and resilience, to explore our own experiences of stress, and to be mentored or guided through fundamental transitions from pain to compassion and self-knowledge. This would allow us to engage with the ethic of suffering—the knowledge that we create the conditions of our own lives through intentions, attitudes, actions. Such knowledge might enable us to cope more effectively with our cultural symptoms of idealization.

In Western societies we have a long history of idealizing ourselves through visions of heroic control and dominance—over ourselves, our environment, others. Our contemporary platform of a "free-market economy" is one in which environmental resources are used without knowledge of future effects, often without any thought of the consequences of our actions. We separate ourselves out as individuals, from other species, even from other humans, and attempt to bring Nature under our dominion.

This kind of idealized control has often led to a tendency to feel exempt from the natural limitations of life, limitations that may now have put our own species at greater risk of extinction. Many aspects of Western culture—from our stories of heroes and geniuses to our theories of bringing Nature under our control—arise from the belief in the right of an individual self to promote itself in isolation. From the perspective of Buddhism, this way of thinking causes ultimate harm to all.

The human ability to think abstractly, manipulate symbolic concepts apart from concrete situations, and theorize about ourselves is perhaps the greatest resource of our species. Our capacities to "decenter" and act at a distance from ourselves lead to some of our greatest discoveries, but they can quickly run amok if we do not curb our need for control and dominance.

Moreover, some theorists argue that humans are characterized, as a species, by a sort of "instinct" of competence. This instinct emerges in our predisposition to separate ourselves out from our experience and then to evaluate our experience negatively. As the psychologist and researcher Mihaly Csikszentmihalyi says:

The . . . reason that the freely roaming mind usually attends to negative thoughts is that such a pessimistic bias might be adaptive—if by "adaptation" we mean an increased likelihood of survival. The mind turns to negative possibilities as a compass needle turns to the magnetic pole, because this is the best way, on the average, to anticipate dangerous situations.

This instinct of competence seems to me to be unchecked in our society. We don't question the limits of its usefulness. Both Buddhism and psychoanalysis, as I said above, insist that we face the limits of our control and, in facing those limits, allow ourselves to awaken to the knowledge of our dependence, a mature dependence when it is grounded in both giving and taking. The knowledge of mature dependence—of our interconnection with and responsibility to other living beings—is not readily available at this time in America.

Our economic system has achieved world dominance, but it is grounded in competition, individualism, and greed. Although we have the potential, through our valuable methods of democracy, for complex responsiveness to a range of needs and points of view, we seem more and more to be immersed only in competence and control—*my* pocketbook and *my* safety—with the results of greater and greater self-protection and isolation. Rather than fostering shared goals and responsible interdependence, many Western societies end up protecting only those forms of life that are essential to their own economic stability. In large part, this is the result of a fundamental belief in individual rights to happiness, even when these put other beings at risk for greater and greater adversity.

THE LESSON

Unless we can begin to see the problems of our inherent discontent and grandiosity, we may put our species at risk of suffering catastrophes that result from unchecked competence. Although knee-jerk negative thinking might have benefited us earlier in the evolutionary process, compelling us to greater and greater manipulation of the environment to fulfill our needs, it may now put us out of business if we cannot respond wisely to the demands for cooperation, collaboration, and sharing that characterize our future on this planet.

What suffering teaches us today is the necessity of developing personal responsibility for our own subjective lives, in order to awaken thoughtful compassion about the critical limitations that face our own and other species here on earth. This is what I have learned from practicing Buddhism and doing psychoanalysis for thousands and thousands of hours. My patients in therapy have taught me the path of resilience—from suffering to personal self-awareness, then on to compassion, self-knowledge (of what it means to be human), and a sense of purpose in life. What is striking about the capacity to thrive in adversity, known now as resilience, is how resilient people have a meaningful story that places them in a context of helping others for some larger purpose. This might seem like a sleight-of-mind trick if it did not come from the authentic struggles to develop personal responsibility in the face of misery. Instead, it seems to me to be a fundamental witnessing of exactly why human life is so interesting. From psychoanalysis and Buddhism, I have learned how a mature spirituality can develop from a confrontation with one's own neurosis, one's individual stress and suffering.

Our meanings and intentions are vitally important in shaping our lives. When we shift the paradigm for our own perceptions—the grounds of meaning and expectation—then the perceived also changes. Subject and object are joined in the ground of our perceptions. The account of a world resting on consciousness may still seem far-fetched in terms of most Western psychology and philosophy, but it is not unfamiliar in some theories of contemporary physics, and it seems immediately apparent when we dissolve our belief in a strongly bounded, separate, individual self. When we conceive of the self as wholly embedded and impermanent, as a function rather than a thing, then we appreciate more deeply our true freedom in this world. It is the freedom of making new meanings, of opening ourselves especially to the conditions of our own limitations and exploring these into the roots of our suffering.

When we cross the bridge from self-protection and isolation to gratitude and compassion, then we have changed the world. Without the ordinary occasion of human suffering—our own stress and discontent—there would be no bridge.

PART FOUR

Facing Fear and Other Strong Emotions

Have Courage and a Sense of Humor

Dzigar Kongtrül Rinpoche

Fighting and rejecting the natural ebb and flow of life, which brings with it inevitable loss and decay, is a futile pursuit that robs us of our ability to truly enjoy life. When we face it directly, our anxiety about loss can turn into the courage to live without trying to make things always stay the same. In that way, our self-obsessed drama can become amusing, like watching children at play.

Practitioners who train in courage become true warriors. The war we wage is not with enemies outside of ourselves but with the powerful forces of our own habitual tendencies and negative emotions. The greatest of these is fear. In order to become fearless, we need to experience fear. Facing fear changes our perspective and gives rise to the courage to face our neuroses as well as our enlightened qualities.

Fear and worry are understandable at times. It would be stupid not to be concerned for our personal well-being and selfish not to be concerned for others. Feeling concern is a natural part of human goodness. But when it prevents us from accepting our life, fear is crippling. We find ourselves saying no to the world; no to our karma; no, no, no to everything—which is a very painful way to live. When we spend our life wishing it were different, it's like living someone else's life. Or, we could say, it's like living our life despite ourselves. Meanwhile, the full spectrum of our life experience goes by unnoticed.

Someone asked me recently if I am afraid to die. Truthfully, I am more afraid of not living my life fully—of living a life dedicated to cherishing and protecting myself. This fear-driven approach to life is like covering your couch in plastic so it won't get worn. It robs you of the ability to enjoy and appreciate your life.

It takes courage to accept life fully, to say yes to our life, yes to our karma, yes to our mind, emotions, and whatever else unfolds. This is the beginning of courage. Courage is the fundamental openness to face even the hardest truths. It makes room for all the pain, joy, irony, and mystery that life provides.

We especially need courage to face the four streams of human life: birth, old age, sickness, and death. A mother can't say after nine months, "I don't want to deliver my baby because I am afraid." Afraid or not, she has to go to the hospital and give birth. Mothers do this very beautifully. It's hard nowadays to find a truer sense of courage.

We cannot say, "I don't want to get old." We're getting older day by day. The way to grow old beautifully is to accept our aging and do it well. Everything is impermanent and comes to an end. Every moment that comes into being is a moment of destruction. If we accept aging as the natural process of impermanence, we will still have a sparkle in our eyes when we're old. We cannot say, "I don't want to get sick." Sickness is an integral part of having a body. Our body is like a complex machine with many moving parts; it is subject to the suffering and impermanence of all compounded things. Think of how often you have to repair your car, which is a much simpler machine; you'll be amazed that your body functions as well as it does. If we accept this compounded body, surprisingly, we might experience illness in a very different way!

Finally, we cannot say, "I don't want to die." Everything that is born is subject to decay. We will all need tremendous courage and acceptance on our deathbed. No matter how much our loved ones care for us, we must leave them behind. Clinging to them only makes our parting more painful. We must make this journey alone. No one can experience our pain or prevent it from happening. Our death is part of our life. If we accept it with courage and joy, we will make the transition from this world to the next beautifully.

Going against the four streams of existence is like building a castle of sand by the ocean. The waves will inevitably knock it down. If we don't accept the ebb and flow of the tide, we will persist in building our castle—all the while fearing its destruction. Then we will never enjoy our life, let alone fully experience what it's like to age, fall ill, or die. But if we accept and reflect on the natural flow of aging, illness, and death, we will have nothing to fight or reject. We will not be disappointed when confronted with the inevitable—and we will have nothing to fear.

With an open mind, fear can become your greatest ally—because facing fear means facing your life, and facing your life means *living* your life. You become courageous and victorious over the world of good and bad, right and wrong, comfort and pain. This notion means a great deal to me, as my birth name, Jigmé Namgyel, means "fearless victory." But I think it is good advice for everyone.

SENSE OF HUMOR

We could all use more humor in our lives. Having a sense of humor doesn't mean laughing and being cheerful all the time. It means seeing the illusory nature of things—and seeing how, in this illusory life, we are always bumping into the very things we meticulously try to avoid.

Humor allows us to see that ultimately things don't make sense. The only thing that truly makes sense is letting go of anything we continue to hold on to. Our ego-mind and our emotions are dramatic illusions. Of course, we all feel that they're real: my drama, your drama, our confrontations. We create these elaborate scenarios and then react to them. But there is nothing really happening outside of our mind! This is karma's cosmic joke. You can laugh about the irony of this, or you can stick with your scenario. It's your choice.

We need to bring a sense of humor to all aspects of our lives—even to positive aspects such as well-being, harmony, and peace. When we take these things too seriously, joy becomes pain, peace becomes annoying, and harmony becomes contrived. To have genuine harmony, peace, and joy, we need to cut through seriousness with a sense of humor.

Humor can't be described in words. It arises in our heart and a smile appears or laughter comes out of our mouth. It brings a new vision and perspective to everything. And it can also be a great friend—at times our only friend. In especially difficult times, when we're deserted by everyone else, we still have our sense of humor. We don't have to take this short life—with its fathers, mothers, husbands, wives, lovers, children, jobs, and money—so seriously. In fact, it's funny to be so serious. Especially knowing that ultimately we will have to drop all of it and leave this life, as in the Tibetan saying, "like a hair pulled from butter." The brief time that we have in this world would be well spent trying to wake up from seriousness.

There is a lot we could accomplish in this brief human life. We could actually realize the nature of reality and the truth of phenomena—including ourselves. How ridiculous is it then to be so serious about carrying a briefcase, driving a BMW, or talking on the cell phone to our friends? At some point, we have to say, "OK, that's enough." This doesn't mean ignoring our mind and emotions, or not addressing or discussing things. It means simply asking ourselves whether seriousness is all that useful.

Seriousness can be a curse. Before we even get out of bed in the morning, we start planning our day—because if we don't plan ahead, we might just lie there and get nothing done. Then our boss would fire us, our spouse would think we're a terrible person, everyone would think we're a terrible practitioner—and we might agree! Obviously, we must do some planning. But when we take it too seriously, we just torment our mind and body and waste one whole precious day in stress, pain, and confusion.

When we wake up in the morning, thoughts and feelings naturally arise. It's up to us how seriously we take them. Some people don't take things very seriously at all; they may even seem a bit spaced out. But these people get through the day with less stress on the mind and body than people who take things so seriously. This is not to say we should never be serious or responsible. It just means that we may need some perspective and a more positive attitude.

A positive attitude doesn't mean just thinking good thoughts. It means not getting caught up in the seriousness of everything we do, hear, see, feel, and relate with. I myself am very tired of being so serious—exhausted, actually. But it doesn't help to just give up on the things we're so serious about. That doesn't really serve the purpose. What helps is having more lightness and humor.

When you find yourself stuck in seriousness—even if it's your karma to be a very serious person—you can just pop out of it. This is quite a profound practice. Like an old man watching children at play, we need to see through our own seriousness. No matter how seriously the children go about their games, the old man is amused and never for a moment takes them to be real. We can watch our thoughts and emotions in the same way. Without taking them so seriously, we can see them as children at play and give them lots of space. This is how the mind of a practitioner should be.

It is never too early—or too late—to start a "sense of humor practice." In the *Treasury of Dharmadhatu*, Kunkhyen Longchenpa describes the experience of all his ordinary reference points falling by the wayside. In essence, he says:

> Since I have come to this realization, all my reference points have fallen away. The ground for clinging to an "I" and "you" has now collapsed. Where is "you" and where am "I" myself? Who is friend and who is foe? In this wild, chaotic state, everything spontaneously arises in its own good time and in its own good way. When I look at others, they seem like children taking things to be real that are not real, taking things to be true that are not true, trying to possess the

unpossessable. Ha, ha! I burst out laughing at this amazing spectacle. (Paraphrased and translated from Longchenpa's Tibetan text.)

At this stage of realization, we can see the magical nature of appearances as they arise. Trying to nail them down as right or wrong, good or bad, accurate or inaccurate would seem to be a humorous and curious thing to do indeed.

The key to a better sense of humor and more positive attitude is self-reflection. This brings an appreciation of impermanence. Seeing that nothing is solid or permanent, you begin to make yourself at home in the unknown. Then you can experience the lightness and freshness of things as they truly are. It is possible to actually live your life this way.

The bottom line is this: don't take yourself and your emotions too seriously. Find another "self" to identify with. This doesn't mean creating a split personality; it means identifying with your true nature. Then you won't take ego's emotions so seriously. Even as you go about doing habitual things, if you have a sense of humor about it, ego won't rule your life. The most important heart connection you can have with yourself—just you and yourself—is a heartfelt sense of humor.

Imagine treating ego as a clown. Clowns are intriguing. They can make us laugh, but they can also become mean or even vicious. You need to be careful around clowns, because they could get you in trouble by making fun of you or making a scene at your expense. You might even want to sit at the back of the room and get ready to defend yourself if they get too aggressive. The point is, you have to be awake around clowns. In just the same way, you have to be on alert when it comes to ego. Otherwise ego's antics may throw you for a loop!

Once when I was talking about seeing ego as a clown, a man in the audience got very upset. Later I learned he was a professional clown, and he was very unhappy to hear clowns used as an example for ego. Since ego is generally vilified in Buddhist teachings, he felt I was putting down clowns—which shows that even clowns are tormented by taking ego so seriously. Later he took part in a bodhisattva vow ceremony. When he came up for his name, taken from a stack of names I'd written earlier that day, coincidentally it turned out to be "King of Laughter." After that, he was quite OK.

Sometimes when we're upset, depressed, or having physical difficulties, it's hard to have a sense of humor about anything, let alone ego. But not taking things too seriously is a good start. When the seriousness becomes too much, just say, "OK, that's enough!" And do something to shake it off: jump up and down, roll in the sand, dive into cold water to wake yourself up—just don't dive in with your eyeglasses on. But whatever you do, don't stay stuck. The more effort you put into letting go, the sooner you will see it really works.

As Shantideva said, "There is nothing that doesn't get easier with practice." When you can really laugh from your heart and your gut, everything opens up. Then you won't be like a professional clown: funny for others, but very serious about yourself.

Young girls are very fortunate because they giggle a lot. True giggles, not nervous or self-conscious giggles, are a kind of massage for the heart. They help us touch the joy in our lives. Giggles, laughter, and the kind of "ha, ha, ha" that old men make when they laugh with their bellies shaking—they all help us to not take this short life too seriously.

No matter how bad things seem, how could we expect them to be any better? Everything is part of the wheel of samsara. We can't escape from birth, old age, sickness, and death. And we can't just stare in the mirror squeezing our pimples or feeling awful about getting old. We *can* have a sense of humor about these stages of life.

When the time comes to be sick, we don't have to be grumpy or angry with ourselves and others. With a sense of humor, we can be pleasantly sick. And when the time comes to die, we can die with a real sense of humor and joy about our life because we have met the Three Jewels, become a practitioner, and glimpsed the nature of mind. We have seen the illusory quality of thoughts and emotions—and we know that taking them too seriously would defeat the purpose of everything we're trying to do.

Liberation is found wherever discursive thoughts truly dissolve. Whether they spin to the left or the right or around in circles, thoughts are just thoughts. They are dissolved through practice and a sense of humor. To get beyond them would be wonderful, but if you can't, it's wonderful just to have that inspiration. Discursive thoughts and emotions *themselves* are wonderful if we have a sense of humor. We can enjoy them the way an old man enjoys watching children at play. Then thoughts become what they truly are instead of something they're not.

This is what we want from practice. At every stage of the Buddhist path, we are in search of the truth. We can get to the truth of what is by letting things be. As is said, meditation is much better when it is not fabricated; lake water is much clearer when you don't stir it up—which means *let it be.*

Faith

Trusting Your Own Deepest Experience

Sharon Salzberg

When things go bad, says Sharon Salzberg, a leading teacher of insight and loving-kindness meditation, we feel as if we are falling endlessly. We are gripped by the fear that we will never gain control. When we recognize that we are not in control, we discover a faith in something greater—far beyond our impulse to control—that holds us no matter what happens.

A few winters ago there was a major exhibit of Vincent van Gogh's artwork at the Los Angeles County Museum of Art. The paintings included both exuberant outpourings and canvases tinged with foreboding. As I walked through the museum, my feelings kept shifting. What I found most heartrending in van Gogh's work were the contrasts, the intensity of the swings from one mood to another. The paintings of "light"—sun-drenched landscapes, still lifes of flowering branches, the bedroom at Arles—were tender, renewing, beckoning. Other, darker canvases—of twilight, ominous skies— drew me into his vortex of sorrow.

I imagined how van Gogh must have so poignantly grieved a mood's passing, as the light went and the darkness descended once more. I envisioned him engulfed by his changing states, with no refuge, no place to go to get perspective or feel safe. A close friend of mine was in the midst of a major bout of depression. Another had been hospitalized for the past several months with recurrent pneumonia, as well as a puzzling disease physician after physician was unable to diagnose. I stood in front of van Gogh's painting *Wheatfield with Crows,* thinking of the artist, of my friends, of myself— how all of us face the ungovernable nature of life and the suffering that comes from our powerlessness, our inability to stop the changes. Every day we might think that we have it all under control, only to once again suffer defeat.

I turned from the painting and set off for the museum gift shop to meet a friend. The shop was packed with people and souvenirs of the exhibit. At one point I found myself wedged between a pile of Vincent van Gogh pool towels and a display of Vincent van Gogh mouse pads. The contrast between my experience in the exhibit and what surrounded me in the gift shop was bizarre. As if the vast, untamable flow of life I'd seen evidenced in van Gogh's paintings could be captured and neatly packaged into manageable and marketable items—pool towels and mouse pads and umbrellas—to be bought, wrapped up, and tucked away. Nevertheless, for a moment I, too, was tempted to buy a souvenir that might serve as a totem against an out-of-control world.

The fact is that nothing we acquire—not even a Vincent van Gogh mouse pad today and a pool towel tomorrow—will put conditions under our command. Life is like an ever-shifting kaleidoscope—a slight change, and all patterns and configurations alter. A fight with a friend causes fifteen other relationships to stir and turn, our lives interconnected like a game of dominoes. One moment everything feels full and perfect—the next an accident happens or we fall sick. Settled comfortably into being single, we meet someone and fall deeply in love. We are going along in one direction when an unforeseen obstacle appears, and we have to swerve out of the way. Suddenly, stunningly, we are in a different life.

No matter how much we want it to be otherwise, the truth is that we are not in control of the unfolding of our experiences. Despite our search for stability and prediction, for the center of our lives to hold firm, it never does. Life is wilder than that—a flow we can't command or stave off. We can affect and influence and impact what happens, but we can't wake up in the morning and decide what we will encounter and feel and be confronted by during the day.

Invariably, when I think I have finally gotten some aspect of myself under control, life intrudes forcefully to show me otherwise. During the winter of the Vincent van Gogh mouse pads, I came down with a bad case of the flu. Nevertheless I continued to travel and teach until the flu turned to bronchitis so severe that I broke a rib coughing. One evening, when I was on the verge of another relapse, some friends took me to an outdoor mineral bath—supposedly healing waters.

We sat together in the warm water for some time, looking at the stars, enjoying easy, rambling talk. After a while the topic turned to fear, and how often it arises when we realize we aren't in control of events. We each told stories of when we had faced fear and how we had handled it, gracefully or poorly. Almost nonchalantly I commented, "It feels like it has been a long time since I had an experience of acute, intense fear—fear right down to my bones." Because of the greater serenity I had developed through meditation, I actually thought I had fear under control, that it was something I used to deal with, long ago, in my distant past. In terms of debilitating, crushing fear, I believed, "Never again."

Just two hours later my bronchitis turned to asthma, the first asthma attack of my life. Lying down, trembling, unable to breathe, I wondered if I was in fact dying. The air around me seemed to have changed to a viscous substance too thick to inhale. An astonishing primal, physical anxiety coursed through me. As I gasped for air, an image of my friend in the hospital with pneumonia came to mind, and I had a sudden, terrible conviction that he would die. Overwhelmed by the vision of someone struggling futilely to breathe, struggling until death, I realized that could also be me. Sure enough, the fear went right down to my bones.

The psychiatrist D. W. Winnicott once alluded to these moments in which we are utterly helpless as the feeling of falling endlessly. Winnicott used this image to describe the experience of growing up under the care of a depressed mother, but it is also one that describes what any of us might feel when no one seems to be in charge, when a situation we've relied on is coming apart, when everything around us is spinning out of control.

For most of us, when life feels out of control our most ready response is fear. When fear dominates, our sense of possibility collapses. Many years ago I attended a stress-reduction program led by Jon Kabat-Zinn. In one exercise, he stepped up to the blackboard and in the center drew a square made up of nine dots, arranged in three parallel lines with three dots in each line. Then he challenged everyone in the class to take the piece of chalk and see if we could connect all the dots using only four straight lines, without removing the chalk from the blackboard, and without retracing a line. One by one, all thirty of us went up to the blackboard. We tried beginning from the left, from the right, from the top, from the bottom, and returned to our seats frustrated, unable to do what he'd asked. The room was vibrating with stress.

Then Jon picked up the chalk and with great sweeping strokes that extended well beyond the perimeter of the small square, did exactly what he had challenged us to do. Every one of us had presumed that to succeed we had to stay within the circumscribed area formed by the nine dots. Jon had never said that we were limited to that little space, but all of us had concluded that was the only area in which we had to move, in which to find options. Not one of us could see beyond our assumptions.

Fear makes that same kind of assumption. It limits our options, strangles creativity, restricts our vision of what is possible. When the danger is physical, fear leads us in one of two directions: fight or flight. The body mobilizes to help us battle the menace or flee to safety. But even when we aren't in mortal danger, if we're lost in fear we respond the same way. We either resist what is happening by angrily insisting that it be different, or we tighten up and pull away, denying our experience. When we are deeply afraid, we view any change as a threat and the unfamiliar as a mortal enemy.

Being alive necessarily means uncertainty and risk, times of going into the unknown. If we withdraw from the flow of life, our hearts contract. We hold back so much that we feel separate from our own bodies and minds: separate from other people, even people we really care about. In the grip of other intense emotions, like grief and jealousy, we might feel anguish, but fear shuts us down, arrests the life force—to be driven by fear is like dying inside.

When the suffering is overwhelming, we may try to recoil from how bad it feels by numbing our reactions. Many of us survived childhood in just this way. But, ultimately, cutting ourselves off from what is happening locks us into fear and makes us unable to see that we might find another way to respond outside the small section delineated by the dots, defined by our assumptions.

Faith, in contrast, reminds us of the ever-changing flow of life, with all its movement and possibility. Faith is the capacity of the heart that allows us to draw close to the present and find there the underlying thread connecting the moment's experience to the fabric of all of life. It opens us to a bigger sense of who we are and what we are capable of doing.

To act with faith, however, means not getting seduced by any of its ready replacements. One of the most subtle ways fear can bind us, so quietly that we hardly know to call it fear, is what is known in Buddhist teachings as "fixated hope." Fixated hope, like hope itself, resembles faith in that both sparkle with a sense of possibility. But fixated hope is conditional, circumscribing happiness to getting what we want. We may, for example, have faith in our children's ability to have a meaningful life, but if to us that means they will grow up to be doctors or lawyers rather than custodians or waiters, what we are really doing is trying to manage life. Any insistence that people or circumstances meet our exact expectations is not faith but another effort at control, bound to end in disappointment.

I am not at all suggesting hopelessness. It's natural to want things to work out in ways that we believe will be for the good. When we are in pain, hoping for things to be another way can be essential to our health and even our survival. When we're unhappy, it is natural to picture how things might be better. True hope can open our hearts and remind us of light when we are in darkness. But when our hope for relief from suffering is based only on getting what we want, in the precise way we want it, we bind hope to fear rather than to faith.

Buddhism regards fixated hope and fear as two sides of the same coin. When we hope for a particular outcome to arise or a desire to be met, we invariably fear that it won't happen. Thus we move from hope to fear to hope to fear to hope to fear in an endless loop. Fixated hope promises to break us free of the circumscribed area in the middle of the blackboard, only to lead us right back to the narrow confines of that little square.

I saw myself caught in this cycle of hope and fear when Ram Dass, the Western spiritual teacher and author, suffered a massive stroke in 1997. He is an old and close friend of mine. Starting with our first Buddhist meditation retreat in Bodh Gaya, India, he and I often pursued spiritual practice together in many places around the world. We loved and respected many of the same teachers. A close confidant, Ram Dass once helped me through a long and difficult relationship breakup. We had a rich and ongoing dialogue on issues such as the role of spiritual awareness in social change. We also celebrated many of our significant life passages together, such as his sixtieth birthday. We had been fond of each other for decades.

During the hours immediately following news of his stroke, a few of our mutual friends gathered at my house. I wanted Ram Dass to recover from the stroke looking and acting just the way he had looked and acted before. I wanted him walking, funny, brilliant. I might have called my response true hope, but it was actually fixated hope. Fear kept me from letting in the reality: Ram Dass was immobile, unable to communicate, facing an uncertain outcome. Throughout the course of that night, I sat side by side with fear. As I acknowledged it, befriending myself despite the fear, my heart began to open. I met the unknown without a strategic plan for control.

With fear no longer dominating my mind, my love for Ram Dass could arise freely. Loving him didn't depend on a fixated hope for his recovery. The power of love wouldn't shatter in the face of change or disintegrate in the wash of my own terror.

We had all fallen silent, each of us with our own thoughts of Ram Dass, when, late into the night, one of his closest friends, Mirabai Bush, quietly spoke. "Here and now we have entered the mystery," she said. "This is a time for faith." As each of us accepted the fact of Ram Dass's stroke and surrendered to our inability to control the situation, tenderness and a tangible peace filled the room. None of us knew what would happen, but faith allowed us to relax into this vast space of *not knowing*. Even as I felt the ache of sorrow, I remembered that life is bigger than its constantly—sometimes drastically—changing circumstances. Looking around the room at all of us gathered there, I cherished the refuge of sangha, community, which has continually helped me open to a greater truth.

My eyes wandered to the mantelpiece in my living room, where there are two photos of my Tibetan Buddhist teacher, Nyoshul Khen Rinpoche, known as Khenpo. They were taken one afternoon in the Catskills when we visited a veterinarian's home together. As we sat and drank tea, a pet dove flew over and landed on Khenpo's hand. One photograph shows him smiling softly as he cradles the dove. In the other picture, the dove has just taken flight and Khenpo is laughing, as if rejoicing in its release. I had gazed at those pictures every day, and as I thought of Ram Dass they felt especially significant; Ram Dass and I had studied together with Khenpo and delighted in the playful nature of this extraordinary teacher. One of the great lessons I learned from Khenpo was the power of letting go in the face of the unexpected changes of life.

In Tibet, Khenpo was a highly regarded teacher. After his escape from persecution under the Communist Chinese regime, he lived for a time as a beggar on the streets of Calcutta. Through it all,

Khenpo's faith in the dharma, the truth of how things are, was unwavering. "Sometimes I was exalted and quite comfortable," he said. "More often I was bereft and poverty-stricken. Yet the inexhaustible wealth of inner truth and peace that is the dharma always sustained me well."

Looking at the photos, I was again inspired by Khenpo's faith. I could take refuge in the dharma, as if I were the dove cradled in Khenpo's hand, trusting that I was held by the quality of love he exhibited. I could also, like Khenpo, let go—and allow the moment to take flight.

Rather than searching for something that would keep me safe from change, I could reach for a home in the shifting shadows and light surrounding me. I couldn't demand Ram Dass's recovery: I couldn't deny that I was afraid for him. But I had a choice between acting out of fear masquerading as hope, or acting with faith.

Faith enables us, despite our fear, to get as close as possible to the truth of the present moment, so that we can offer our hearts fully to it, with integrity. We might (and often must) hope and plan and arrange and try, but faith enables us to be fully engaged while also realizing that we are not in control, and that no strategy can ever put us in control, of the unfolding of events. Faith gives us a willingness to engage life, which means the unknown, and not to shrink back from it.

The English word "courage" has the same etymological root as the French *coeur*, which means "heart." To have courage, just as to have faith, is to be full of heart. With courage we openly acknowledge what we can't control, make wise choices about what we can affect, and move forward into the uncultivated terrain of the next moment.

So it is with faith. That long night, I realized that for me to meet Ram Dass's stroke with faith instead of fear would mean experiencing him fully as he was and as he continued to change. It would mean that if I realized there was little I could do to help him, I wouldn't abandon my friend so as to avoid getting hurt if things didn't go well. With faith I could stay connected to him and not let dismay at my own powerlessness get in the way of my love for him. To act with faith would mean learning to care about Ram Dass in a way not based on language skills, mobility, or even on his staying alive. The closeness, the understanding, the devotion of love wouldn't diminish in letting go, as when Khenpo had let go of the dove.

About a year after his stroke, Ram Dass and I were sitting together on his front porch. He had regained considerable facility in speaking by then, but it was often difficult for him to freely express himself. This was particularly poignant because before his stroke Ram Dass's eloquence was his own special magic. His lectures had often been spellbinding.

Haltingly now, a few labored words at a time, he asked me how work on my book on faith was going. "It's really hard," I told him. "I've never had to go so deep inside myself before." Then I realized that what I'd just said wasn't exactly true. "Actually," I amended, "I've never had to go so deep inside myself before and bring out the words." He looked softly at me and slowly said, "That's how . . . I am . . . every day . . . now."

Having faith doesn't mean that we don't make an effort. When we are trying to create change, we can pour ourselves into the endeavor and do our best to accomplish our goal, doing our absolute best to speak, to heal, to create, to alleviate suffering—our own or others'. The particular gift of faith is that it allows us to make that intensity of effort guided by a more holistic vision of life, with all its mutability, evanescence, dislocations, and unruliness.

My porch visit with Ram Dass went on through the afternoon. There were long periods of silently being together, listening to the birds, feeling the breeze, being grateful to be alive. Periodically, one or the other of us tried to pull up some words from a deep place inside. At one point, Ram Dass mentioned someone's name, a person known to me as well, who had also had a stroke. "She has lost her faith," he declared. "For thirty years, she believed only . . . in the . . . beneficence of God, and then she had her stroke . . . and then she saw . . ." He looked right at me, and in his eyes I glimpsed the immensity of what he had seen since the stroke. It was like looking at a whole cosmos—of shock and pain and frustration and shame. But unlike that woman, whose picture of life excluded suffering, Ram Dass had opened his worldview wide enough to include it. And so he knew that in that cosmos, alongside pain was gratitude, love, care, and learning to receive. The look in his eyes was so intense, I almost fell over.

I told Ram Dass about what had happened to me the night of his stroke, how I'd had to open beyond my desires, beyond my fears, beyond my longing for neat and recognizable benevolence that would make him all better. Smiling, he said, "It seems . . . I've taught more about love through this stroke . . . than I have through all my thirty years . . . of lecturing about it." He also has taught us about a power of faith that doesn't depend on clinging to the known, but instead on opening to the vastness and mystery of what life provides in each moment.

Whatever takes us to our edge, to our outer limits, leads us to the heart of life's mystery, and there we find faith. In the process, however, we may have to confront many old habits. When my asthma attack began, my first impulse was to fight against it, to get through it with steely resolve. Flailing against my inability to breathe, I was swept up in the relentless momentum of panic. I was not only afraid, but worse, I was afraid of being afraid. I fought the fear and tangled with it, hating myself for my powerlessness in the face of it. The whirlwind of terror grew, and I pushed against it and pushed against it. The more I tried to resist the fear the stronger it became until, exhausted, I gave up the struggle.

Without the support of my tension and resistance, the fear immediately lessened, and I began to remember insights I'd gained through years of practice: "I don't really know what's happening here." "Beware of that determined slide to the worst possible, barely imaginable scenario." "You don't have to go there. Let's just see what happens now."

I was still afraid, but I wasn't cascading down the slippery slope of trying to claim control and feeling powerless when I couldn't.

I was afraid but I wasn't cut off from remembering the power of being in the moment, and the possibilities held latent there.

The panic, the grief, the gasping for breath didn't vanish, but now they seemed to float like buoys on an underlying calm. The thick atmosphere that had seemed so oppressive began to thin out. My mind, which had drawn back into a tight corner of dread, found there was room to move. I could feel my heart rise up in my chest. Though I still had fear, I also had faith.

In my mind I could hear the words a friend of mine had said when he received a terminal diagnosis: "I'm not going to make an enemy of my own death." If I was going to die, I didn't want to end my life scalded by my own acrimony at having failed to wrest control of the situation. If I was going to live, then I wanted to step out of the trap of an imagined, assuredly terrible future and reunite with my actual experience in the present. Whatever was happening to me, I wanted to be fully there for it. In faith, I surrendered to the moment.

Almost the next instant, it seemed I was transported, as if from the tumultuous edge of a hurricane to the still center. A peaceful courage filled me. Soon my breathing began to ease, and I knew I would be all right.

As long as we are alive, we will experience fear. No matter how deep our faith, when our life is threatened, or we think it is, we will feel afraid. But our reaction to fear can change. One time in India I went to see a well-known Advaita Vedanta teacher, Poonja. While in his presence one day, I had a powerful sense of connection to everyone else in the room and, by inference, to everybody in the city, in the country, and on the planet. When I told him about it, he said, "Now you'll never feel fear again." I thought, *Yeah, right. Unlikely!*

Not even fifteen minutes later I was back out on the streets of India as cars, trucks, bicycles, carriages, wagons, people, and animals swirled about the roads in no discernible pattern. Right next to me a pack of dogs went at one another, fighting for scraps of food. Life pressed in too far, too fast—I was afraid all right.

On the one hand, I could have been very disappointed—a scant fifteen minutes of freedom! On the other hand, something was different. I was afraid, but it wasn't the same experience of fear as I usually had. I had a deeper knowledge of the vastness of connection to life, within which fear was arising. I realized that Poonja hadn't meant fear wouldn't come up again in my mind but rather that my relationship to it could transform.

As our faith deepens, the "container" in which fear arises gets bigger. Like a teaspoonful of salt placed in a pond full of fresh water rather than in a narrow glass, if our measure of fear is arising in an open, vast space of heart, we will not shut down around it. We may still recognize it as fear, we may still quake inside, but it will not break our spirit.

More and more I've come to know that life will never be served up with guarantees of safety and security. We are not going to stop falling, but we can find faith in the midst of the fall. In his poem "Autumn," rendered here by the writer Jonathan Cott, Rainer Maria Rilke describes the bittersweet truth of inevitable change and offers his own statement of faith.

> As from the distance, leaves are falling.
> Fall as if the far-off gardens fade into the sky;
> They fall with gesture of relinquishing.
> And through the night there falls the pressing earth
> Down past the stars in lonesomeness.
> We are all falling. There, this hand falls too,
> Occurring to us all: just look around you.
> Still there is one who holds us tenderly
> As in his hands we fall, fall endlessly.

Through my asthma attack, I came to know that I was being held. I wouldn't use the phrase "in his hands" to describe my own sense of the connection Rilke is talking about, but I see the experience as the same. I feel I was indeed being held by the dharma, a deeper truth, that night. I could never have applied those insights through sheer will or determination. They came to me unbidden, like an act of nature, like a blessing. The understanding had risen up to support me, as though in response to the gift of my heart through all my years of meditation practice.

Experiencing the power of faith doesn't mean we've annihilated fear, or denied it, or overcome it through strenuous effort. It means that when we think we've conquered fear only to be once again overcome by it, we can still go on. It means feeling our fear and still remaining in touch with our heart, so that fear does not define our entire world, all we can see or do or imagine.

As we open to what is actually happening in any given moment, whatever it is or might be, rather than running away from it, we become increasingly aware of our lives as one small part of a vast fabric made of an evanescent, fleeting, shimmering pattern of turnings. Letting go of the futile battle to control, we can find ourselves rewoven into the pattern of wholeness, into the immensity of life, always happening, always here, whether we're aware of it or not.

Being held doesn't halt the falling, doesn't abruptly, according to our desires, change how things actually are. We're not able to stop the unknown from crashing into our expectations or get the whirlwind of circumstances under our command. What we can do is let go of the encrustations of the past and the fearful projections of the future to connect with the present moment, to find there the natural flow of life and the myriad possibilities within it.

We can recognize the mystery spreading out before us and within us all the time. We can step out of the hope-fear gyration and give our capacity to love a chance to flower. These possibilities are what hold us. This is where we can place our faith. Even as we fall, fall endlessly, with faith we are held as we open to each moment.

The Transformation of Desire into Abundance

Jack Kornfield

Desire is not a bad thing. It's a source of life and creativity. But unhealthy desire, says the renowned Buddhist teacher and psychologist Jack Kornfield, causes pain and suffering. If we pay intimate attention to the workings of desire, we can discover how to transform it into an experience of health, wealth, and well-being.

> Most people fail to see reality because of wanting. They are attached; they cling to material objects, to pleasures, to the things of this world. This very clinging is the source of suffering.
> —MAJJHIMA NIKAYA

> You, the richest person in the world, have been laboring and struggling endlessly, not understanding that you already possess all that you seek.
> —THE LOTUS SUTRA

Our world runs on desire. We would not have been born without sexual desire. Without continuing desire we would die. There is desire for love, connection, understanding, growth. When people lose their desire to live, they jump off a bridge or swallow pills. We need desire. And yet, desire is also a great challenge for us. Mistakenly, many people think that Buddhism condemns all desire. But there is no getting rid of desire. Instead, Buddhist psychology differentiates between healthy and unhealthy desire. Then it leads us to a freedom that is larger than the desire realm, where we can transform desire into true abundance.

How do we practice this principle? Buddhists connect the root of desire with the neutral mental factor called the will to do. It is part of the energy of life. When the will to do is directed in healthy ways, it brings about healthy desires. When the will to do is directed in unhealthy ways, it brings about unhealthy desires. The traditional description of unhealthy desires includes greed, addiction, overwhelming ambition, gambling, womanizing, and avarice. Unhealthy desire gives rise to possessiveness, self-centeredness, dissatisfaction, compulsion, unworthiness, insatiability, and similar forms of suffering.

Healthy desires allow us to feed and clothe and care for ourselves, to tend our body and our children, to develop our work and our community. Healthy desires are associated with caring, appreciation, and loving-kindness. This is evident in the healthy, caring bond between parents and children in Buddhist countries. Thai, Tibetan, and Sri Lankan children are held in every lap, with beaming faces, uninhibited playfulness, full of love of life. For all of us, these same healthy desires give rise to dedication, steadiness, stewardship, graciousness, generosity, and flexibility. They are the source of happiness.

Beyond healthy desire, Buddhist psychology describes a freedom that is outside our culture's understanding, yet we all know it. This is the place of inner freedom where the stickiness and clinging of desire is gone, where we can act, and yet not be caught up in desire. It's as if we were desperately hoping to buy a house and we lost it because someone else put in a higher bid. We let it go and then, two weeks later, the Realtor calls and tells us the other bid fell through and we can have the house. Now, without the compulsion, we get to reconsider. Do we really want the house? Will it serve the needs of our family? Finally, we may choose to buy the house and furnish it. But we do so more freely, without worry and grasping. It feels so much better. This is the ability to enter the world of desire without clinging, playfully and freely.

The Cost of Grasping Our Desires

> Although gold dust is precious, when it gets in your eyes, it obstructs your vision.
> —Hsi Tang

Buddhist psychology wants us to release unhealthy desires and to hold healthy desires lightly. To transform desire, we first have to feel how it works in the intimate experience of body and mind. Desire can lead us from sublime pleasure to raging addiction, from bodily survival to spiritual longings. Desire drives mushroom hunting and investment banking, Sufi dancing and rock and roll.

But these are the contents of desire. What does desire itself actually feel like when it is present? What is its effect? What happens when we grasp our desires most strongly? There is a tension in the body, an emotional contraction, a stickiness of mind, a focus on the future. There is a driven quality. Anxiety, jealousy, rigidity, insecurity, all become stronger.

Desire casts a spell, and we pay a price. When we are lost in desire, the heart closes. In India they describe it this way, "When a pickpocket meets a saint, all he sees is the saint's pockets." When we meet someone and are full of our own desire, we become calculating, measuring what we say by what it will get us. It's the same when we are hungry. If we walk down the street with an empty stomach, we only see the restaurants; we miss the trees lining the sidewalk, the glow of the late-afternoon sunlight and faces of the passersby. A well-traveled friend confided, "I've seen entire European cities through the lens of 'Where's the restroom?'" In Zen it is said, "The secret waits for eyes unclouded by longing."

In modern life, compulsive desire is visible on a global scale: in the greed for oil, the clearing of rain forests, the privatization of rivers and lakes, and the patenting of such human staples as beans and corn. "The world," said Ajahn Chah, "is in a feverish state." The Buddhist activist Helena Norberg-Hodge describes how modern desire has affected the Tibetan communities in Ladakh, India. For a thousand years, they believed they were blessed. They lived simply, with rainfall enough to grow their crops and time to tend their temples and follow the sacred rhythm of their year. When Ladakh first opened to the West in the 1970s, the Ladakhis told their visitors how abundant and rich they felt their lives were. Now, thirty years later, after exposure to television and wristwatches and music and fashion from India and America, the same Ladakhis and their children complain to visitors about how poor they are. It is all in comparison. Now feeling poor, many Ladakhis have left their villages to live in crowded, impoverished quarters in the city, seeking the happiness promised by the modern world. There are blessings in modernization, and we can understand the villagers' desire for running water and electric lights. But we can also recognize the costs of materialism when desire becomes out of balance.

To recover our innate freedom and balance, we have to study desire and be willing to work with it. How? It depends on our conditioning—on whether we are prone to indulgence or to suppression of desire. For those of us who easily indulge their desire, seeking to fulfill one desire after another, the wisest approach will require a powerful discipline of letting go. But for those of us who are afraid of desires, who have been conditioned to ignore, suppress, and fear them, another remedy is needed.

In my years as a monk at Ajahn Chah's forest monastery, our life was extremely simple. I would have thought that this simplicity would have eliminated desires. We did not have to decide what clothes to wear; there was no menu to sort through, no cable TV, no wine list. We had almost no possessions, just a robe and a bowl and a few books. But desire has a force of its own. As a new monk I had an old iron alms bowl, clunky and slightly discolored from rust. The senior monks had shapely stainless-steel bowls. I was shocked by my strong desire for a new bowl. I was like a middle school boy wanting cool clothes to wear. When I was finally given a stainless-steel bowl,

I set it up in my hut and spent days admiring it. So much for the humble mendicant.

From Grasping to Abundance

Through the practice of mindfulness and compassion, desire can be transformed. First we can release grasping, greed, our deficient sense of self. Then, naturally, through the psychological principle of reciprocity, there arise their opposites: states of generosity, abundance, dedication, and love of beauty. We discover that our natural state is one of wholeness and fulfillment beyond desire.

Abundance beyond desire is not well understood in the West. The Western psychoanalytic approach has been to liberate us from the repression of desire. Western behaviorists have focused on rewards and reinforcements. Even in motivational psychology, little has been studied about the absence of desire, except to acknowledge anhedonia, the painful lack of desire in depression. To study liberation from desire is a radical act. Imagine if the *Diagnostic and Statistical Manual of Mental Disorders* listed greed and driving ambition as human disorders. But we do not even recognize there is a problem here. We have come to the point where commerce has co-opted most of what we do. As the novelist Rita Mae Brown declares, "In America, the word revolution is used to sell pantyhose!"

It is revolutionary to step out of the thrall of desire. We lose touch with the joy and simplicity that letting go of desires can bring. A majority of the people I know say they would like to simplify their life. And it does indeed seem that happiness and simplicity go hand in hand. My good friend and colleague Joseph Goldstein tells the story of the winter Evie, his mother, came to visit him in India. Joseph had been practicing in Asia for seven years. He found his time there so inspiring that he persuaded his mother to join him. He wanted her to learn about the meditation practices guided by his wise and kindly teacher Anagarika Munindra.

After a long, hard journey—twenty-four hours of airports and airplanes, followed by a slow, crowded Indian train, a ramshackle taxi, and finally a horse cart—Evie arrived at the Burmese temple in Bodh Gaya, India. Used to comfortable American furnishings and modern conveniences, Evie was shocked when she entered her room, which was the best in the temple. It was a small hut in the back with a concrete floor, a metal bed and a mattress, and a wooden chair. The primitive latrine was a short walk away. With a make-do spirit, Evie set about joining Joseph for the teachings, and after some initial sightseeing, she undertook a disciplined training of mindfulness for a month. She lived a meditative life. Then she returned to the United States, to her well-stocked kitchen and study, her comfortable bed and bathroom, to piles of mail and visits with friends, to working and shopping. Afterward she said, quite simply, "Living in that concrete hut in India was the happiest month of my life."

Outer simplicity had allowed Evie to return to her inner abundance. But we do not have to go to a temple in India. We can live in the world without being lost in grasping and desire. A good example of how to do so is offered by Ajahn Jumnian, a teacher from southern Thailand who visits Spirit Rock Meditation Center every year. Ajahn Jumnian is a joyful monk who embodies desirelessness and aliveness. He doesn't want anything. Instead, he is appreciative of whatever comes. "If someone puts food in my bowl I am grateful. It gives me strength to teach. But if no one offers me food, this is good too—I get to go on a diet, which I could use! If students ask me to lead classes, I am happy to go anywhere. And if they take me sightseeing, I love to learn new things to help my teachings. But if no one invites me out, then I get to sit quietly and meditate. This makes me happy too. Whatever happens, I enjoy it."

How can this be done without grasping and desire? When asked, Ajahn Jumnian explained, "I relax and let my motivation be one of compassion and loving-kindness." The absence of greed and wanting does not bring about a withdrawal from the world. Instead, we awaken to the abundance of the world.

ABUNDANCE AND FULFILLMENT

The Indian sage Nisagardatta, another of my teachers, challenged his students, saying, "The problem with you is not that you have desires, but that you desire so little. Why not desire it all? Why not want complete fulfillment, joy, and freedom?" Nisagardatta did not mean boundless greed. He spoke from the state of consciousness that knows it is not separate from the world. Kabir, the Indian mystic poet, put it this way, "I laugh when I hear the fish in the sea are thirsty."

We all contain all that we desire. With this realization, we can undertake all things with a sense of abundance. Our inner abundance radiates a sense of worth, value, and ease, of having something to give to the world and enjoying doing so. Without abundance, we can be in the midst of riches and feel like a hungry ghost. Wise parents and teachers bring out abundance in their children by helping them feel that they each have so much to give, and providing them the opportunity to do so. For each of us, whether raising a child, building a business, planting a garden, or serving our community, a heartfelt dedication is required. Wise dedication springs from our own sense of inner abundance.

For me, letting go of wanting and opening to the rhythms of the rain showers and the cries of the wild fowl during my time in the forest monastery helped me learn to experience abundance. Students of mindfulness experience the same openness when they leave a meditation retreat. They enter the supermarkets we usually take for granted, and stand there smiling at the wildest abundance of food ever presented to an ancient emperor. When we open to abundance, we can enjoy the fog lifting from this morning's melting snow, and the steam rising from the hot bowl of tomato rice soup on our lunch table. We can appreciate the half smile of the tired waitress and celebrate the fact that we are here, breathing and alive on this marvelous earth.

In abundance the heart has a gracious and unshakable spirit. This fulfillment is far beyond the "prosperity consciousness" promulgated in books and workshops that urge us to visualize fancy cars, sprawling mansions, and burgeoning bank accounts. This prosperity seeking, however spiritual the trappings, is a reflection of limitation, a sense of insufficiency. The truly abundant heart is already whole. It knows our world includes joy and fear, gain and loss, nobility and selfishness. It embraces even death. When Zen Master Suzuki Roshi was dying of cancer he told his students, "If when I die, if I suffer, that is all right you know. No confusion in it . . . this is just suffering Buddha." He showed them how to include everything right up to the end. In the last stages of grave pain he hauled himself out of bed, put on his finest robe, and completed the long transmission ceremony for the next abbot of the temple. Then, with the same gracious presence, he lay down and a few days later he died.

The state of abundance is connected with a deep sense of gratitude. In Japan there is a form of Buddhist therapy called *naikan* that emphasizes gratitude as a way to heal depression, anxiety, and neurosis. In this approach we are asked to slowly and systematically review our whole life and offer gratitude for each thing that was given to us. A similar approach worked for Bob, a practitioner who had been homeless for a year and was now living at a nearby mountain Zen center. Because of his memory of sleeping in the park, lying half awake every night in fear that someone would try to rob him or stab him, Bob was afraid to sleep. He had a history of family trauma: he had left his addicted father and stepmother for the streets at age fifteen and had used drugs himself. In his life, he had been a carpenter and a mechanic.

When Bob went to the Buddhist center, he was trying to put his life together. The Zen teacher could feel his anxiety and mistrust. To help soften this state, the teacher instructed him in a simple practice of gratitude. Bob began offering thanks for whatever food, clothing, and shelter he had for the moment, living, as they say in AA, one day at a time. He was taught to stop and surreptitiously bow in gratitude ten times a day, wherever he found himself. Bob took to bowing. He bowed to his kitchen mates and to their shared breakfast. He bowed to his morning depression and to his feelings of unworthiness. He bowed to the carpentry tools he used in the shop, to his anxiety, to the afternoon sun, and to a fellow student driving the noisy tractor in the lower field.

A second instruction was given to Bob as well: to look beyond his suffering. Bob slowly began to notice moments of well-being, surprising breaks in his inner struggles, small periods of blessing. He loved being in the temple garden. He walked among the live oaks and mulch piles by the garden path, framed by sturdy redwood posts and delicate forget-me-nots and orange daisies. Bob described how his mind became quiet for the first time in years. The suffering he carried was still like a weight, but the vast silence was bigger. One day the temple bell rang for dinner, and his heart was pierced. His pain and longing was swept over by a sublime wave of gratitude for just being alive. Bob was returning to life.

NATURAL GENEROSITY

As desire abates, generosity is born. When we are present and con-nected, what else is there to do but give? An African proverb puts it this way, "It is the heart that gives; the fingers just let go." When someone in our family is hungry or in difficulty, we naturally want to help. When the heart is freed from grasping, our family grows. The people we meet are all our uncles and aunts, our grandparents and our cousins. The animal brothers and sisters are our siblings. We sense our interdependence with all beings.

In the abundant heart, our sense of welfare expands. It becomes common to all. The Iowa corn farmer whose corn always took first prize at the state fair had the habit of sharing the best seed corn with all the farmers in the neighborhood. When asked why, he said, "It's really a matter of self-interest. The wind picks up the pollen and car-ries it from field to field. So if my neighbors grow inferior corn, the cross-pollination brings down the quality of my own corn. That is why I am concerned that they plant only the very best."

To reawaken our sense of abundance, Buddhist psychology of-fers deliberate trainings and practices to cultivate generosity as a joyful way of being. There are daily practices of giving, vows of dedication to service, visualizations of our devotion to the welfare of all. These are repeatedly developed, until in the end there is no notion of separation, neither giver nor receiver. We are all the Buddha feeding ourselves.

Paul was a retired banker at loose ends whose Buddhist teachers suggested that he develop the path of service. Paul began to help at the temple, on committees, and at the community hospice. His life had been dedicated to success and self-importance, but as he began to serve others his self-interest faded, his unconscious fears passed. His work at the hospice taught him that what mattered was love. People who at first had been put off by his brusqueness and arrogance began to enjoy his presence. As he devoted himself to service, his heart mellowed like a good wine.

These generosity practices are not a way to become "good" but a way to become happy. We do not have to work at a hospice or an emergency room to serve. Sometimes our generosity is the giving of a smile, silence, listening, warm touch. Sometimes it involves action, time, money, our commitment to justice, our vision for a better world. Every form of giving is a blessing. Helping to run several large Buddhist centers, I have had to learn to become comfortable with money. There is so often shame and fear, judgments and expectations around money, whether it is having too much or too little. We have gotten the erroneous belief that money is not compatible with a genuine spiritual life. But money is a neutral energy that can be used in either unskillful or skillful ways. Gained skillfully and used generously, material abundance is honored by the Buddha. When money is wisely used, says the Buddha, it benefits our welfare and that of our family, and its generosity extends to our community, our spiritual life, and the common good.

As countless travelers from the West have observed, in Buddhist cultures generosity is especially visible. This was certainly true in Thailand. At Ajahn Chah's, every morning at dawn I walked on the small dikes between the rice paddies to nearby villages to collect alms food. At the remote branch monasteries, the villages were poor and the food was scarce. Yet every morning villagers would kneel in the dirt, lovingly offering food to the monks. I, a relatively rich Westerner, wondered if I should feel guilty about taking their food. But the villagers offered it with such generosity. It was as if they were saying, "We so value the teachings of the Buddha and the blessings of the monastery, that we joyfully give of the very little we have to support you." Because alms rounds are done in silence, I couldn't say thank you for the fish curry and dried mango. All I could do was accept their food as a blessing and an obligation, and to practice with as much integrity and compassion as I could.

DESIRE BECOMES ADORNMENT

Several years ago I read about a study done in an impoverished neighborhood of London. Two parallel streets were selected, a mile apart, each with similar poverty and concomitant problems, including a high level of crime. Unbeknownst to the residents, one of these streets was secretly selected to be cleaned every day for a year. All the trash was picked up, graffiti removed, curbside flowers replanted and watered, and broken lamps and signs repaired, repainted, and cared for. Nothing was said publicly about this extra cleaning and beautification. After a year, however, the streets were compared. The statistics showed a nearly 50 percent reduction in crime on the cleaned and beautified street.

As we release grasping and desire, the play of the world becomes like adornment for our wise heart. We appreciate and embody a natural love of beauty. The Buddha said, "When we find the way, we find the beautiful here and now; we know what beauty truly is."

In one Buddhist monastery, we were trained to notice what was beautiful and to abandon the unbeautiful. We went through the day deliberately observing whether our thoughts, words, and deeds were beautiful or unbeautiful. We could sense the pleasure in beautiful thoughts and words and deeds. We could sense the suffering in the unbeautiful ones. We began to incline toward appreciating the beauty. We consciously enjoyed our good moods. We found ourselves savoring a cup of tea as if in a tea ceremony. Our walks became more flowing and harmonious. Even when conflict arose between community members we entered the difficulties with more graciousness and dignity. All that arose became used as adornments for the way.

The Benedictine brother David Steindl-Rast explains it this way: "What is truly a part of our spiritual path is that which brings us alive. If gardening brings us alive, that is part of our path; if it is music, if it is conversation . . . we must follow what brings us alive." When we see its beauty, our world responds. When our heart is released from grasping, generosity and beauty flower.

A PRACTICE OF GENEROSITY

Life is giving to life every moment of the day. Take several days to pay attention to life's process of endless generosity.

As you go about your daily rounds, first notice the gifts of the natural world. Notice the way the gift of sunlight streams behind everything. It feeds the plants we eat and gives us the oil from ancient forests that fuel our cars and light our lamps at night. Notice too the rainfall and the rivers, the water that gives itself to the blood in your veins, to the neighborhood insects and trees, to the interdependent collaborative in which we swim. Now notice how generously you are held and supported by the earth under your home and your feet, and by the air you breathe, by the warmth of the day and the coolness of the evening.

Now look at the unending care and generosity in humans around you: parents with children, teachers with students, healers and businesspeople, all serving one another. People stop at red lights so you are safe to go. They line up in the market, they share the parks, they cooperate in a thousand ways at the office. The shopkeeper and the mechanic, the bank teller and the cook, the healer and the engineer give themselves to their work, supporting others with countless hours of unspoken generosity and love. Of course there are also times of resentment and being overwhelmed, when people are disgruntled and disaffected. But most of the time, the people around you are giving: in conversation, in action, adding the generosity of their life energy to the flow of the whole. Spend a day or a week just noticing, naming, bowing to this stream of generosity everywhere.

Now you can deliberately choose to add to this stream of generosity. Not as an obligation but as a way to be happy. Like all human beings, you already give in a myriad ways. Delight in whatever you do. And discover you can let it grow. Try this practice: whenever a thought of giving enters your mind, do it. Whether it is a gift of money, time, helping care, or offering a possession, if you even think of a generous act, follow it. Sometimes we worry that we will regret our generous acts, and we second-guess ourselves, a bit of doubt comes in. Don't believe the doubts. Instead, look for any spontaneous thoughts of generosity and follow them. You will find that they inevitably make you happy. Try it.

Smile at Fear

Carolyn Rose Gimian

When things get tough, fear can overwhelm us. Carolyn Rose Gimian shows us how we can discover the fearlessness of the great meditators— by welcoming fear as a precious opportunity to open up and let go. And that can make us smile.

Spiritually speaking, I come from an eccentric family. The patriarch of my family was the Indian *mahasiddha* Tilopa, who, while spiritually accomplished, was not motivated by worldly success. He held humble jobs: grinding sesame seeds into oil during the day, and at night, procuring clients for a prostitute. Later in life, having attained the supreme realization of the Vajrayana, he became a wandering yogi, known to feast on fish entrails left by fisherman down by the lake. At least, that's the story passed down to me, told with a great deal of family pride.

His spiritual son, Naropa, was a renowned scholar at the greatest Indian university of his era, Nalanda. After realizing that he didn't understand the inner meaning of the texts he was studying, he left the university to study with Tilopa. Naropa was subjected to a series of difficult trials by his teacher, such as jumping off buildings or lying in leech-infested water. Eventually, he attained complete, stainless enlightenment when Tilopa whapped him across the cheek with his sandal.

The next forefather, Marpa, owned a farm in Tibet and was married with children. From time to time, he traveled to India to study the dharma. There he found Naropa. Marpa had brought a bag of gold dust to make offerings to the teachers he encountered. When Naropa demanded the whole bag, Marpa didn't want to part with it, but he gave in. At that point, Naropa scattered the gold dust into the air, singing: "Gold, gold, what is gold to me? The whole world is gold to me." This was the beginning of Marpa's training with Naropa, which led to his ultimate liberation.

The next spiritual son, Milarepa, studied black magic and sent a hailstorm to destroy the farm of his aunt and uncle, who had made him and his mother into servants, but the vengeance did not fundamentally satisfy him. Eventually he found Marpa, who asked him to construct a series of buildings in exchange for receiving the teachings. Milarepa had to carry large boulders and shove them into place by himself, but Marpa would show up, often drunk, and ask Milarepa just what in the name of heaven he was doing. Ordered to dismantle the edifice, he would have to put up another somewhere else. Finally, when Mila was completely broken down and close to suicide, Marpa give him formal initiation. Mila eventually left to pursue meditation in solitude, spending the remainder of his life in caves, surviving mainly on nettles (to the point of developing a green glow). Milarepa sang to anyone who came by his cave, leaving thousands of songs of realization for us to contemplate.

These are some of the early forefathers of the Kagyu school of Vajrayana Buddhism, a lineage that has continued in this manner down to the present day. It is currently led by His Holiness the Seventeenth Karmapa, who had to make a dangerous escape from Tibet in order to receive thorough training and education. These life stories of the great figures of the Kagyu lineage show us what extreme human beings they were. The wisdom that comes from this family tree is *extreme* wisdom, and it may be just what is needed for the current situation.

This article is not intended to make you long for the "fish-entrails diet." Nor does it prescribe the "sandal-whap facial," the "throw your money in the air" freeing-therapy, or the "if you build it, you will tear it down" theory of insight. Rather, it asks: What helpful insights can we glean from the teachings of people like these? Why would we turn to such people now?

Because they were all *fearless*. They were not intimidated by external difficulties. In fact, they approached their lives with spontaneity, humor, and a sparkling sense of dignity and decorum that were completely independent of outside circumstances. They were not preoccupied with themselves or their problems. They were concerned about others; in fact, they embodied compassion, either ruthless or gentle depending on what was called for. And they were very, very wise, in the ways of the world, the ways of the heart, and the ways of the spirit.

In tough times, we need wisdom that is not dependent on conditions. When things are falling apart, we need wisdom that is not propped up. The basis for this wisdom is freedom—freedom from confusion, freedom from fear, and, interestingly enough, freedom from extreme views. "Extreme views" in this context means eternalism and nihilism, the belief in either existence or nonexistence as ultimate reality or saving grace. The origin of this wisdom is simplicity, or nonattachment, which is a bit less threatening than calling it "riding on the razor's edge," which might also apply.

Tilopa, Naropa, Marpa, Mila, and all their descendants exemplified the freedom of profound simplicity or naturalness of mind, which can adapt to and transform any external circumstance. Their lifestyles might look extremely unconventional to us, perhaps even unspiritual, but in fact these were people completely at ease in their world, having nothing more to attain and nothing more to give up.

How can we, as beginners on the path, relate to this way of being? To follow their example does not mean mimicking their behavior. Rather than trying to imitate or adopt something external, which will never be a thoroughly satisfying solution, we need to emulate their inner practice and, ultimately, their state of mind.

This may seem like a tall order, but to begin, at least, it is not that complicated. In the beginning, we need simply to examine what's taking place; we need to familiarize ourselves with ourselves. As long as we are in a state of panic, it is very difficult to actually see what is happening to us, to others, or to the world altogether. So in the beginning, developing simplicity means making friends with our fear. When the situation in the world around us inspires panic, we may regard that panic as something unusual or extraordinary. But actually, we are panicked all the time. Fear is already an old friend.

However, fear is so ingrained in us, as anxiety and denial, that we generally don't recognize it. We try to suppress our awareness of it. But in extreme times, this becomes harder to do. To keep ourselves from feeling panicked, we have to build a much denser wall of denial and self-deception, which we construct from the building blocks that the Buddhist teachings call the three poisons: passion, aggression, and ignorance.

On the other hand, we could take the approach that an extreme time is an opportunity as well as an obstacle. We could even celebrate and encourage the chance to bring fear to the surface, into the open. We could welcome our fear for the opportunity it brings us to develop fearlessness. Fear is not the enemy, unless we allow it to become that. Instead, fear can be conquered. But that requires that when we see fear, we smile—an image imparted to me by my teacher Chögyam Trungpa Rinpoche.

What does it mean to smile at fear? To begin with, it means to relax with our fear, by allowing ourselves to be fully with ourselves. One way to cultivate this relaxation is through the practice of meditation. In the Buddhist tradition, the practice of sitting meditation has two elements: simplicity, or peacefulness, and insight, or clarity. The application of mindfulness allows us to stop the world from spinning, by stopping the spinning of our own minds. This is the essence of the simplicity or peacefulness of *shamatha*. Then we can see the confusion. We can shine the light of *vipashyana*, or clear seeing, on confusion, and that brings the clarity of seeing things as they are. When we begin to see the situation as it is, and when we begin to see our own minds clearly, we defuse the panic.

From the experience we have in meditation, we also may begin to see how we can relax on the spot in the midst of the most difficult experiences in our lives. We begin to see that it is possible to be there in a simple and open way. What are we afraid of all the time? Often, it is the unknown. If we are willing to simply witness what is there, although it might in fact be devastating, it also turns out to be more benign, more manageable, and more ordinary and transparent than we expected. In the emptiness of our freak-out—which allows us to remain vulnerable—we begin to discover the quality of freedom.

The Buddha himself set the example for us. Here was an extreme human being if ever there was one. Having left the comfort of his father's palace and his own regal life, he tried every method he encountered to achieve liberation. Having practiced intense asceticism and arduous disciplines for a number of years, he realized that struggle was not the path to enlightenment. And this, I think, is when he began to smile at fear.

Make no mistake. The closer the Buddha got to enlightenment, the more forceful and insistent were the obstacles he encountered. We sometimes seem to approach the experience of enlightenment as though it were like a long drowsy soak in a warm perfumed bath. After our nap, we will arise as the Awakened One. The stories of the Buddha's enlightenment instead describe how the greatest obstacles, or *maras*, appeared to the Buddha the night before he attained enlightenment. Meeting their challenge required vigilance, or openness, rather than somnolence. As the Buddha sat in meditation beneath the bodhi tree, Mara sent his daughters in the guise of beautiful women to seduce the Buddha; he sent his troops of warriors to attack the Buddha. The Buddha manifested as the victorious one, *vijaya*, or the fearless one, the warrior of nonaggression. He remained unmoved by passion and aggression. He chose instead to be awake. Mara's arrows then became a rain of flowers.

In our own lives, it is difficult to be open yet unmoved by extreme situations, but we too, like the Buddha, have the choice to be wakeful. Whether it is the crash of the financial markets, the death of a loved one, the experience of chemotherapy, the failure of a relationship, or the violence of an angry mob—whatever the difficulties, they can be the bearers of good news, or at the very least, real news. That's quite an outrageous thing to say, but it is truly the message of people like the Kagyu lineage forefathers, who lived in the ground of reality beyond pain and pleasure, good and bad. This is not suggesting that the worse things get, the better it is; nor that we shouldn't have sympathy and feel compassion for our own and others' difficulties. However, unless we can make friends with what occurs in our life, we are simply subject to circumstances and controlled by them. Often, the worst—whatever it is—has already happened by the time we realize the need to apply these teachings. In that sense, we have no choice. We can't take our life back. It is not a rehearsal.

When circumstances bring our emotions to a sharp point, at that point both confusion and wakefulness emerge from the same ground. If we are willing to practice in that groundless ground, that too is smiling at our fear. In the Kagyu tradition, this is also called practicing in the place where rock meets bone. I always thought this phrase referred to the meditator's bony behind sitting on the bare rock of a meditation cave, but I learned recently that it refers to crushing bones for soup with a heavy rock mallet. That sense of crushing or breaking through our confusion and hesitation is also an expression of opening everything up, letting everything go, exposing the innermost marrow of the situation. It is about our ultimate vulnerability.

I can't offer you a finite list of things for you to do, nor can I tell you exactly how *you* can smile at fear. I'm working with turning up the edges of my mouth when I feel anxious. The advice I give myself is: don't avoid the opportunity to grin back at fear. And if you can dive into that empty feeling in the pit of your stomach, well, that would be excellent! We each have to find our own inner grin.

The time where rock meets bone turns out to be the time we are always living in, although we don't always acknowledge that raw mark of our existence. To do so is to meet the moment where neither past nor future exist and where we cannot hold on to the present for security. In that moment, the closing bell of the stock market is no different from the bell that calls us to the shrine room. In that moment, our dharmic ancestors will all applaud our fearless smile.

Getting to the Bottom of Stress

John Daido Loori

The conventional therapies and antidotes to deal with stress, says the American Zen master John Daido Loori, do not go deep enough. We need stress to live, but it becomes a problem because we cling to the sense of a solid separate self that needs to be de-stressed. In zazen— the simple mindfulness practice of just sitting—we can find that stress is relieved when we let down the needless protective boundary we erect around ourselves.

Quite a number of years ago in a psychology course, I came across what was called the "general adaptation syndrome," a description of the dramatic physiological changes that take place when a person is under stress. For instance, when you feel threatened, the body prepares itself for combat. The blood vessels are pulled back from the surface of the skin, so that if you are cut you do not bleed as much. Vision becomes very acute; strength is increased manifold; reaction time is shortened; reflexes become very sharp—all because of adrenaline pouring into the bloodstream. This is a survival mechanism that has been with the human race since its beginnings. If you are face to face with a saber-tooth tiger, that reaction takes place, and either you fight for your life or you run. Either way you need that heightened power. Whether the stimulus is some clear-cut physical danger or a more complex psychological situation that gets us tangled up in anxiety, anger, or frustration, the response to threat occurs to some degree, depending on the intensity of our feelings. If that power—that energy—is not used, there it is, racing around inside the body. You have no way to dissipate it.

That undissipated energy causes problems, particularly when there is no resolution and the stress situation is prolonged. As the stress continues day after day, the body-mind begins to respond in its own individual way—with chronic tension, pain, or disturbances in breathing, heart function, or digestion, with chronic anxiety, depression, panic attacks, and so on. As the situation continues, the trouble will get more serious. It is becoming very clear that stress can play a major role in triggering cancer, heart disease, arthritis, and all sorts of other diseases, as well as mental breakdown.

So what do we do about it? We may withdraw, psychologically or physically—if we have the chance. We try to avoid stress by putting up a barrier of time or space or creating some kind of mental barrier. Or we can take one of the hundreds of drugs prescribed for stress, or take illegal drugs, get stoned, or get drunk. We can make ourselves numb. Then there are therapeutic activities like running, aerobics, and massage, and the psychological therapies and the meditation therapies. It is true that these activities and therapies reduce stress. The big question is: do they ever really get to the root of it?

When you look at these therapies and the other ways of dealing with stress, you see that usually they have one thing in common. They are based on the assumption that the cause of stress and the effect of stress are two separate things. Either we are putting a barrier between ourselves and the apparent cause of the stress—drugging ourselves numb or running away in some other fashion—or we are trying to remove something or change something we believe to be the "cause" of the stress. But in actual fact, the cause of stress is not something "out there," and the cause and effect of stress are not different things.

We need to go deeper to really look at stress, to appreciate how it functions and how we can work with it as a fact of our lives. Life would be pretty dull without it. A lot of our vigor and alertness, and certainly the development of the species, has to do with dealing with stress, being stimulated by it. But when it reaches the point where it becomes unmanageable and debilitating, then there is something wrong with the way we are dealing with it. And the basic thing that is wrong is the illusion of separateness, of a separate self.

When you ask someone, "What is the self?" the answer will usually be a list of parts or items—the self is the body-mind, my history, my memory, my thoughts. Our most basic assumption is that everything inside this bag of skin is me and everything outside of it is the rest of the universe. That does not deal with the question "What is the self?" What is selfness itself? Obviously, the self that you are now is not the self that you were when you were three months old. You are not the same psychologically, chemically, physically. You do not look, act, think, or feel the same. And you are not the self at eighty that you are at forty. So the self is, first of all, something that is in a constant state of transition, a constant state of becoming.

That much is easy to understand. We can see, if we look at all this evidence, that, like everything else in the universe, the self is not fixed, not permanent. But the other side of it, the fact that there is no self separate from everything else in the universe, is not something that we can arrive at logically through an intellectual process. The nature of this no-separate-self has to be experienced.

Zen training provides us with the means to do that. Through *zazen*, sitting meditation, we learn little by little to drop the intellectual processes, to let go of the thoughts, the fantasies, that block the direct, intuitive experience of who and what we really are. Our constant mental activity is what holds up the illusion of a separate self and makes us vulnerable to stress.

In zazen, the first thing we learn is to just be still. Most of us are constantly engaged in activity, either inner or outer. If we are not directly focused on some activity, there is a constant mental dialogue. We are talking to ourselves and scattering our energy. We are preoccupied with the past, which no longer exists—it has already happened. Or we are preoccupied with the future, which does not exist—it has not happened yet. We generate a tremendous amount of stress in this type of preoccupation. We worry about what has happened, about what will or will not happen in the future; we think about the various things that make us feel anxious, frustrated, angry, resentful, depressed, afraid. And while we are so preoccupied, we are missing the moment-to-moment awareness of our life. It slips by and we hardly notice its passing; we eat without tasting, look without seeing, listen without hearing, live without ever knowing—perceiving—what is real.

What we do in zazen is take the scattered energy and focus it. Zazen has to do with being in the moment, without evaluating, analyzing, judging—just simply and directly experiencing, moment to moment. In Zen, the way this is done is through the breath. The breath is directly related to mental activity. When your mind is agitated, your breath is agitated. When the mind is at rest, the breath is at rest. Zen practice begins with counting the breath—inhalation is one, exhalation is two, inhalation is three, and so on up to ten. When you get to ten, you go back to one and start again. The only agreement you make with yourself is that when your mind begins to wander—when you begin to chase thoughts—you look at that, acknowledge it, and let go of the thoughts. And start again at one. With practice—and it takes time to get from one to ten even once—the internal dialogue begins to quiet down. It is like learning anything else. If you want to learn to walk a tightrope, you string a wire across the room, you take one step and fall off, come back and take another step and fall off, and keep doing that patiently until at one point you suddenly take two steps and then three steps, and as the days go by you are finally able to walk across the tightrope. It is the same with calming the mind.

When it is time to think, we should think. When it is time for the mind to shut up, we should learn to shut up. Being able just to be still and shut up is a facility that just about every creature on the face of the earth has. Humans seem to have lost that ability—even in our sleep we are constantly agitated. Meditation is one opportunity to really come to rest.

In Zen training, when we get the surface mind quiet, a lot of the deeper stuff that we do not want to think about begins popping up. We have been talking to ourselves to avoid these painful thoughts and feelings, and when the mind becomes calm, we begin to be aware of them. But through zazen we develop a way of dealing with what we have been avoiding: we look at it—without analyzing or judging, we acknowledge it, let go of it, and go back to the breath.

One of the things that is realized when you see the nature of the self is that what you do and what happens to you are the same thing. Realizing that you do not exist separately from everything else, you realize responsibility: you are responsible for everything you experience. You can no longer say, "He made me angry." How could he make you angry? Only you can make you angry. That understanding changes your way of relating to the world and your way of looking at stress. You see that stress is created in your mental processing of your experiences. It usually has to do with separation. Whenever a threat, barrier, or obstacle pops up, our immediate reaction is to pull back, to prepare mentally or physically to fight or run. If you become the barrier—become the fear, the pain, the anger—by experiencing it fully without judging or avoiding or running away, and then let it go, there is no barrier. Actually, there is no way to pull away from it; you cannot run away. There is nowhere to run to, nothing to run from: it is *you*.

None of the antidotes to stress—numbing ourselves, running away, the various therapies—will ever really get to the root of it. When we can acknowledge that we create our own stress and begin to look at how we create it, then we can begin to do something about it. Until then, we are just blaming, not taking responsibility. We say the trouble is my job, it is my boss, my wife, my husband, it is the kids, it is this, it is that . . . and we turn it into some kind of inner tension. We actually hold on to our stress. It is a way of holding on to our positions, our beliefs, our sense of being right—our self. In that tightness and rigidity, the body cannot deal with it and the mind cannot deal with it. We suffer because we will not let go. In zazen we learn how to let go, to let go of thoughts as they come up. When we begin doing that, we find that we can begin to let go of tension, anger, fear, pain. We begin to build confidence, trust ourselves, and not be dependent on something outside. There is nothing out there—there is only you. And how you deal with what is happening in your head makes all the difference in the world in how you live your life.

When we can let go of the idea of a separate self that we carry around in our heads, we have begun to make ourselves really free. What keeps us from being free is the boundary we create around ourselves. Just as we create pain and confusion, we can change them. Just as we make our body and mind sick, so we can heal ourselves. And we begin at the beginning, with that simple process of quieting the mind, focusing it, letting go of our thoughts.

Fearless Simplicity

Tsoknyi Rinpoche

One of the traditional Buddhist approaches to learning how to handle our emotions is to examine carefully their source. The investigation leads us back to ego and its primitive devices: pushing, pulling, and ignoring. And then we investigate that. Tsoknyi Rinpoche teaches that our investigation will reveal that in any given situation we have an innate quality of knowing, and along with that knowing comes a certain confidence or fearlessness, but suddenly ego pops up and wants to own everything. Do we really need to do this?

Most people I meet are to some extent afraid of themselves. Often they say something like, "Well, maybe I can handle it, maybe I cannot. Maybe I should listen to him, maybe I shouldn't. Maybe I can't take it."

All this doubt, all this reluctance, is based on fear, *fear of not being able to take it.* "If I do this, if I end up in that situation, maybe I couldn't stand it. Maybe I don't know how to deal with it, maybe it will be too much. I'd better not." There is a certain timidity, a feeling of dread, a way of imprisoning oneself inside a lack of confidence. Once we confine ourselves to that prison of timidity, ego will take the key, lock the door, and put the key in its pocket. We become prisoners of ego.

To illustrate the difference between simply knowing things as they are and ego's version, let's say you are looking at a flower. It's a beautiful flower, and it smells so sweet. The moment you see it, it delights you. If you're feeling a little bored, it invigorates you; if you're feeling a little chill, it makes you warm. The moment you look at it, the first thought is: "There is a flower." Next, you know it to be a nice flower. The third moment: "I want that flower. I must possess it. It should belong to me." In other words, ego enters.

Someone might say that it's not possible for there to be any knowing without ego. That is a big mistake, a serious false assumption. Knowing is not a function of ego but rather is a natural quality of mind, in the same way that a flame is hot or water is naturally wet. Mind's natural ability is to know. For the most part, ego steps in and takes over the knowing. It takes charge and then claims ownership, trying to make the knowing belong to itself.

Rather than simply allowing the first moment of perceiving to be as it is, ego wants to claim this knowing, to be in charge. In the moment of seeing the flower, to want to possess it is attachment. Or one could react with aversion: "I don't like having a flower here; it will smell up the room. Let's get rid of it. Don't even put it on the table; throw it outside." This way of being is not quite anger; it's more dislike, a source out of which anger can grow. Or, if one does not really care to know whether it's a flower or not a flower, but just shuts off from it, that is closed-mindedness or stupidity. These three poisons—attachment, aversion, stupidity—are ego's constant companions.

Ego knows no moderation. And it doesn't just stop with claiming ownership of experience—it wants to go all the way. For ego, this going all the way is endless. There is no stopping anywhere. If we could just remain with simply knowing whatever takes place, that would be fine. But ego is not happy with just that. It goes on and on: one thought, the next thought, and the next thought: "I want it. How can I get it?" Then it wants to get involved in more and more activity. It becomes a habit, and that habit can be endless. When a habit is reinforced by being used again and again, it's like we lose our freedom; every moment of perceiving seems an involuntary involvement. We get caught up all the time until we feel totally lost.

Ego always needs the support of the knowing quality; otherwise ego is nothing. Without the tool of the knowing quality, there is nothing it can do. When you dread doing a certain job, you are actually not afraid of the job; you are afraid of your emotions. There is never anything wrong with a job. It's more the fear of not being able to deal with the emotions that come up during the job, the emotions that are provoked by being involved in a certain sort of job. What happens is we blame the job at hand, because we feel incapable of handling our own emotions that might arise while doing the job. But honestly, without knowing how to handle our own emotions, it doesn't matter what job it is; we'll always have that feeling of being inadequate, which creates fear. And this fear makes us not want to do anything. We become closed in; we refuse to be involved in anything.

Maintaining the notion of "me" is separating oneself from others. It's as if one is holding on for dear life, being utterly concerned about "me" and pushing aside that which is other. This is ego-clinging. It is not the same as simply taking care of your business, making sure that the body is fed and able to experience and perceive. This basic process of taking care of oneself is not called ego, not at all.

"If I'm free of ego," some people ask me, "how can I eat, how can I walk, how can I do anything?" But simply eating or simply walking doesn't necessarily mean that there is ego-clinging. There could be, but it doesn't have to be that way. According to Buddhism, it is possible to function while being free of ego-clinging. It's possible to live in fearless simplicity.

In other words, when the body has to be fed, feed it; when it needs to be washed, give it a shower. But when something unfamiliar happens, it doesn't mean you have to claim ownership of it and make it your problem. If you always do that—collect problematic issues as if they were your own—then it's very hard to feel free in life. You're always collecting baggage, carrying a burden.

The Tibetan word for ego literally means "owner," as in claiming ownership or clinging to being the owner. This indicates that ego is something extra added into the situation. This is how to understand ego or self in the Buddhist context. It doesn't mean that being free of ego is like being switched off, like all the doors and windows are shut and there is no experience of anything ever again.

In order to understand the actuality of "no owner," no self, we need to understand two levels of reality: the seeming and the real— also called the relative and the ultimate. Really and ultimately, we don't own anything, because really and ultimately there are no things to own. Everything is impermanent and everything is devoid of any independent, true existence. There really are no entities to claim as one's own.

Nevertheless, the seeming level of reality also comes about because of not realizing how things actually are, ultimately. We need to respect that level as well, so that we can work with how things seemingly are experienced.

Here's an example. Let's say someone has given enough money to a hotel so that your bills are covered for your entire life, no matter how long you stay or what you eat or how much you spend. You move in and stay for a month or two. It is very nice, and you enjoy yourself a lot. You don't own the hotel, but you are allowed to stay there. Still, you respect the hotel. Something in your suite may break or get a little crack, but this doesn't really depress you; you don't fall into despair about it, because after all it's not really yours. Still you notice when something breaks, and you take care that it gets repaired. It doesn't mean that you have to think, "This is not mine, I don't care, let it break. In fact I'll even help a little to break it!" and so you kick the toilet and tear the curtains into pieces. That's not necessary at all. Just because you don't own it doesn't mean that it has to be destroyed. You don't have to disturb anything.

Because of respecting the relative level, you are careful about things breaking. Also, when you move to another room, it doesn't mean you pocket whatever you can carry. You don't have to be that way. But because you don't have the feeling of being the owner, because you don't have the ego feeling in your relationship to the room, you don't worry too much if something breaks, although you still take care of it and make sure it gets fixed. My main point here is that it's possible to live like one is staying in this hotel—in a way that is respectful but doesn't assume an extra degree of ownership. Your life is something like a hotel room. You don't own it forever. You might own it for sixty or seventy years, but it's not a permanent situation. You are staying as an honest, respectful guest in a hotel.

Ego-clinging in the Buddhist context refers mainly to the way we add something extra on top, beyond what is necessary to function. The word "ego" here is not the same as the modern psychological use of the term; that's not the way "ego" is used in the Buddhist sense. Go back to the original sense of the word, which just means "me." We need to clean up that word a little bit, wash off the modern connotation. If you really look into it for what it is, every single time you say "me," what is the "me" you refer to? It is only the sense of knowing—there is nothing else behind it. What can you really pinpoint?

When you look for this "me," for this "I" or ego, you find that it is mind. It is the knowing quality that you call "me." In fact, there is no "me" to find anywhere other than the knowing quality. When that knowing quality is misconstrued, it is given the name "me."

"Me" is not a "me" in the past or the future but rather the moment-to-moment, right-now feeling that "I am." Everything is measured from that. Above me, below me, to my right, to my left, and so forth. It's in the present. But if we look into that present, what is it? We don't find anything.

The present is actually egoless. We should think well about this to understand it correctly, otherwise we can have the feeling that all this is meaningless: "This is very weird, what's the point?" It seems like falling apart. It feels awkward, uncomfortable. We need to continue training in order to deepen this and make it an experience, so that our clinging to things as being real and our clinging to ego as something that truly exists is about to fall totally apart, but just as it's about to fall apart, ego starts spewing out more pollution. It rallies its forces again. In that moment, one feels scared: "Hey, this is too much." People get afraid of the feeling that everything is falling apart.

• • •

The United States is a prosperous country: there's lots of work, food is abundant, there is good housing, and people from countries with less wealth like India or Indonesia long to go there. Once they do, they feel they've arrived in a buddhafield. Their job may be lousy and low-paying, but they are so happy that they finally made it. Now look at the Americans themselves. One out of five takes antidepressant medication. Many people suffer in the United States who are not going hungry.

It is *mental* suffering, which can often come from not taking charge of oneself, one's own experience. So much pain is created by letting ourselves get lost in whatever happens. You project a thought, then the second thought believes the first one. The third, fourth, fifth thoughts are projected. The first thought is by this point already a reality, and then the tenth thought believes that the fifth thought has always been an actuality. And on and on, with more thoughts and more validating. That's how delusion is perpetuated. First an illusion is created in our mind, then a second thought takes the illusion to be true, and it goes on like that. It's possible to sit for fifteen or twenty minutes and believe that what we are thinking about is real.

As long as one is caught up in ego's world, there is no steadiness, since dualistic mind is impermanent. One is like a feather blown in a hurricane. There's no peace, only suffering. Dualistic mind's inherent instability is the basis for all suffering. Why is this? Because dualistic mind is unreal and insubstantial. Like foam or a bubble on water. It immediately gets overtaken by whatever happens, whatever the circumstance is. Dualistic mind is like a hungry Nepali street dog. It always feels, "I must eat, I must drink, I must take charge, be in control." A hungry dog may sometimes bite its owner; worse than that, when starving it may even try to eat itself. If we give free rein to the habit of conceptual mind, all sorts of terrible things can happen.

These are the negative traits of dualistic mind. Its function is to constantly grasp at and chase after objects. It pays attention to something, then another thing, then a third, and so on—always reaching out toward something other, thereby getting farther and farther away from its own nature. Dualistic mind's way of grasping is a hopeful, longing attitude, a wanting to take hold of something, of an object, and trying to get at it somehow by grasping again and again. But since all objects are impermanent and by nature insubstantial, there is ultimately nothing to grasp at. Therefore dualistic mind always ends up at a loss, disappointed in some way and not knowing how to come back to itself. One ends up completely homeless.

By pursuing and pursuing and pursuing in this way, chasing after one object after another, sooner or later one discovers that objects are futile to pursue; that there is nothing there to get. We learn that the attitude of chasing something meaningless is futile as well. At this point one is at a loss, like a lost child without a mother.

Mind is fickle and objects are seductive, it is said. The Buddha told us not to be that way. Don't chase after one object, then another, then a third. That pursuit is not your real home, your real mother. This futile pursuit is steered by, influenced by, and affected by circumstances. Whenever something feels unpleasant, one gets disturbed by it; if it's pleasant, one gets caught up in it. Throughout this course of events, we are so unstable, so unsteady. Sometimes the obsession becomes so intense that one can lose one's own life. This way of being creates incredible anxiety. One experiences fear, worry, feeling lost, feeling uncared for: "Nobody loves me, nobody takes care of me, nobody worries about me." This lonely frame of mind is because of being unstable, being steered by objects, being oversensitive in the wrong way.

Instead of this relentless chasing about, we ought to take a break.

PART FIVE

Skillful Means

Money, Work, and Family

At Times of Risk and Stress, Cultivate Stillness

Michael Carroll

Most of us spend a substantial part of our lives at work, and our workplaces can often be great sources of stress and tension. Michael Carroll, the author of Awake at Work, *discusses how we can walk a path between avoiding and overresponding to the challenges we face— and employ techniques for gaining composure in the midst of our most stressful moments.*

Uncertainty is woven into everything we do at work: launching a new product, starting a new job, prescribing a drug, even answering the phone. Each day, moment after moment, we deal with work's unknowns by taking risks. Sometimes these are small risks, like accepting a check for a hundred dollars: "Are the funds available or will the check bounce?" Sometimes they are large risks, like performing emergency surgery on an injured child: "Have we diagnosed the injuries correctly? Have we removed all the obstructions or did we miss something? Will the sutures hold?" Uncertainty requires choices, and taking risks is one of work's great demands.

In the face of crisis or risk on the job, we tend to hide out in the extremes of either hesitation or arrogance. Sometimes we underestimate the risks we are taking, failing to appreciate what's at stake. Maybe we are responsible for investing other people's life savings in stocks and bonds. Or maybe we are a CEO and responsible for guiding and growing the assets of a large corporation. The decisions we make in such roles impact thousands of people's lives. It would be the height of arrogance to treat such responsibilities frivolously. Overinvesting others' money in highly speculative funds or, as a CEO, applying "brinksmanship" accounting rules to shore up short-term profits would be blatantly foolhardy. Such overconfidence seriously misjudges the situation, underestimating the unknowns and risks.

On the other hand, we may overestimate the risks we are taking, exaggerating their importance. Maybe the very same financial investor invests his client's money too conservatively, getting a poor return on the investment. There are opportunities to consider—market segments that have strong track records, funds that are diversified sufficiently to prudently manage the risks—but he hesitates: "Maybe the market will go south tomorrow. Let me look at the companies' balance sheets once again. Maybe next week I'll run my risk-reward performance-predictor software on these investment ideas to see whether they are likely to perform or not." Or our CEO may not be willing to compete aggressively when confronted with marketplace pressures. Maybe she hesitates to invest in new product development or new technology to keep pace with change. Instead she hires a consulting firm to study the issue and make recommendations. She schedules a meeting in three weeks to hear new ideas and proposals. When we overestimate our risks, blowing them out of proportion, fearful of possible outcomes, we freeze and become indecisive. Such hesitation or lack of confidence is ponderous and halting, overestimating the unknowns and risks.

In order to avoid these extremes of arrogance and hesitation, we first have to be clear about what we are dealing with. When we take risks, we find ourselves feeling a range of powerful emotions. We can feel intrigued, bedeviled, excited, or afraid. The greater the risk we feel we are taking, the more complex and challenging our feelings. We should not regard these powerful emotions as problems or distractions, however. Rather, they are our natural instincts, our inborn intelligence, which can help us manage uncertainty, *if we know how to listen.* If we try to ignore them, treating them like distractions or unneeded worries, we are probably being overconfident and may be underestimating the risks. If we pay too much attention to our feelings, constantly agonizing over possibilities, chances are we are hesitating, lacking confidence, and possibly overestimating the risks. Properly listening to our emotions at times of crisis or risk in order to learn why they want our attention requires balance and poise.

To gain such composure at stressful moments, we can apply the mindfulness effort of letting go—abruptly shifting our attention from our thoughts to the immediacy of our physical environment. By suddenly being mindful in this way, we discover a visceral stillness, an "emotional space" of *not knowing*, like opening a door to an unfamiliar room or leaping from a diving board. When we are mindful in the immediate moment, the chaotic flood of emotions no longer vies for our attention like a crowd of loud, unruly voices. Instead, they focus and settle into a physical feeling, unclear and murky, but no less powerful—a tickle in the stomach, a vague softness around the heart, or an openness in the throat. Our senses, on the other hand, become extraordinarily vivid. The sound of the phone ringing is precise and distinct. The humidity or coolness of the air is no longer the background but is fully experienced. Our worn briefcase in all its familiarity is rich in detail. We discover that our emotions are actually bodily instincts—visceral, available, and informative. And our alertness gives us the precision and confidence needed to act.

By shifting our attention to our physical setting during times of crisis or risk, we acknowledge that our familiar feelings of control are gone and, ironically, we are at the same time alert and instinctively open to our circumstances, surprisingly calm and even. Such a space can be uncomfortable, since there are no familiar emotional signposts or reliable answers, and our impulse to seek assurances and closure can become quite strong. Our mindfulness practice, however, trains us to pause and rest in the "stillness of the unfamiliar." For a moment we have nothing to hold on to—we are just instinctively alert, resourceful, and open to the situation.

By stepping past our desire to resolve our emotions and making friends with this stillness, we finally discover the basis for making tough and risky decisions. From this open space, we can acknowledge our anxieties and powerful emotions in a balanced way, letting them play their role of alerting us to possibilities. The tickle in the stomach may remind us to call our most important client before making a critical investment. Seemingly out of nowhere we understand how best to finance a competitive bid. We experience a wave of relief, a physical calm, and we make the call and close the deal. A lingering doubt makes us check one last time before we close the accident victim's leg wound, and sure enough, we discover a small shard of glass. Over time we discover that our emotions and bodily sensations are actually guiding, not distracting, our decisions, prompting us to consider our gut feeling more deliberately and respectfully. We learn to listen through the stillness to our feelings, our work setting, our competitors, our colleagues. By learning to remain still in unfamiliar territory, we discover that we are expressing the very confidence that we have been seeking all along: a confidence guided by instinct and insight that is free from the anxiety of hesitation or the blindness of arrogance.

Developing our ability to listen to our emotions and body during times of stress and risk requires that we train thoroughly in mindfulness disciplines. Besides sitting meditation, the most effective technique I have used for listening deeply to the physical wisdom of the body is a practice called Focusing, developed by Dr. Eugene Gendlin from the University of Chicago. Gene and his colleague, Dr. Flavia Cymbalista, an economist from the Berlin Free University, spent many hours training and coaching me in listening to the language of the body as it seeks to guide and inspire decisions. I highly recommend learning this method of focusing as a powerful tool for making sound financial decisions, unblocking pent-up creativity, resolving conflicts, or just listening deeply to what your body is trying to tell you. (See my Web site www.awakeatwork.net for more information on this technique.)

"At times of risk and stress, cultivate stillness" proposes no magic for making difficult decisions and taking risks. We will need to be thorough and realistic. We will need to work through difficulties and make mistakes. At times we will need to have the courage of our convictions and possibly take risks that complicate our lives and those of others. But most of all, we will need to trust our inherent confidence to remain still in unfamiliar territory, listening deeply and precisely.

How to Help Your Family

Judy Lief

It hurts to see others, particularly our loved ones, struggling with intractable challenges and upheavals. We want so very much to do something. Yet knowing what we can and cannot do goes a long way toward being truly helpful to others we are close to.

As we go through life, we face many joys and discoveries and many problems and difficulties. We have continual ups and downs. Over time, most of us go through economic upturns and downturns, health ups and downs, relationship ups and downs—all sorts of ups and downs. As we are tossed about, we are gradually toughened and refined, like rocks tumbled in a stream. The more obstacles we encounter and manage to survive and overcome, the stronger we become. On the path of dharma, we are encouraged to view difficulties as opportunities for awakening, not simply as roadblocks. The combination of study and meditative training gives us tools to work with what arises as it arises, whether good or bad, happy or sad. But the more we increase our ability to deal with our own obstacles, the more we become painfully aware that we may not be able to help others—our family, our friends, people in our communities—who are struggling in similar ways.

In this world of duality, every experience has its shadow. The wish that others may be happy and not suffer is marked by the fact that at times we can help, but many times we cannot. When we are faced with suffering, and we cannot fix it, what do we do with that recognition? How do we cultivate acceptance rather than despair, anger, and frustration? Although times are tough, we may have a way of working with hardships, but we cannot always say the same about those we care about. We may struggle and it may not be easy, but we have some degree of control, and when we make mistakes we can learn from them. Having gone through difficulties before, and somehow come through them, we may feel fairly confident that we can once again see our way through. What we have to work with is close at hand: our own mind, our own emotions, our own body, our own blockages and hesitations. We know what we are dealing with, and we can draw on what we have learned by facing similar problems in the past. But we have no control over other people. Although we want the best for our family, for the people we love, we cannot just make it happen. We are helpless. We can be strong for others, but we cannot make others strong.

The struggles of people we care about can be harder to face than our own difficulties. It is not uncommon, for instance, for a dying person who has come to terms with their own mortality to still be in great distress because they are worried that their family or loved ones do not have the inner resources to face what is happening. You recognize that your family is caught up in fear and anguish, pain and confusion—and there is nothing you can do about it. The fact that you are aware of your situation and are dealing with it as best you can does not help. In some ways, it even makes things worse, because you see the contrast. You can work with your own situation but cannot protect the people around you or remove their confusion. And much as you might like to do so, you cannot simply transfer your understanding to others. So in addition to facing the pain of dying, you suffer from the frustration of not being able to help those you love, no matter what you yourself have learned. It is so lonely to know what is going on and be unable to fix it. But you cannot walk the path of another, and another cannot walk the path for you. The reality is that each of us is a traveler, and we travel utterly alone.

This pattern repeats itself in many contexts. In the current economic climate, many people have lost their jobs or are afraid they might. Money is tight and prospects are dim. Savings are disappearing and investments tanking. It is a time of belt-tightening, constriction, doing without, in which many people are cutting back on their expenses—those lucky enough to have expenses beyond the bare necessities. If you have lived through economic booms and busts before, you may be pretty sure that you can weather another round of tightened circumstances and uncertainty. In my own life I have experienced many different economic conditions, and I am grateful for that. I've lived on food stamps and unemployment and I've lived as a middle-class home owner. Because I've experienced both extremes, I know I can adjust to both times of poverty and times of economic well-being.

It is empowering to face poverty and loss and find yourself not destroyed but strengthened by the experience. But even if you are able to weather changes in your health or your economic situation yourself, that is not enough. What about your children? What about your friends? How do you deal with the pain of others? You see so many people struggling just to cover their basic needs and support their families—working to the point of exhaustion, never being able to save a cent, and seeing no end in sight. You see people beaten down by the pressure of trying so hard to succeed but not getting anywhere other than deeper in debt. How do you not feel despair?

You may be worried about your own children, wondering whether they will ever escape from living paycheck to paycheck, barely scraping by. You worry that they may never reach the same standard of living as you have, no matter how diligent and hardworking they may be. The desire to see your children flourish comes up against the harsh reality that you cannot make it happen. You want to help, but your own resources may be limited. And even if you have resources, it can be really hard to know what is truly helpful. It is like the story of a child who comes upon a chrysalis and, touched by the struggling of the moth inside, decides to help it break out. But when the child pulls open the covering, the moth dies. Because the moth did not have to fight to break free, its wings were unable to strengthen and mature, so it could not survive. Blindly trying to solve things may only make them worse.

As you look beyond your own family and friends and your own immediate situation, you see that there are endless problems, endless issues, endless crises. There will always be something to obsess about, always be someone to worry about, always be a reason to give up in the face of the futility of ever making things right. The thought loop of troubles and possible troubles, future troubles and remembered troubles, can take over your mind without interruption or relief. And the more you are captured by such thinking, the more frozen you feel.

Such worrying feeds on itself. It is a self-perpetuating trap. We can become so absorbed in frightening future scenarios that we lose touch with what we are experiencing here and now. Worry can have the perverse quality of making us feel righteous that we care so deeply—and we do not take responsibility for our worrying, but conveniently we blame it on others. Worrying about a person may show them we care, but it also conveys to them our sense of superiority and our lack of trust in their ability to handle their life. With worry, instead of recognizing our frustration at the limits of our power to help, we convert it into an incessant inner mental drone of thinking and anxiety. We are obsessed with all we cannot do, with thoughts of powerlessness. It becomes overwhelming and we do not know how to dig our way out.

Instead of piling up all the problems we cannot solve, one upon the other until we have a giant mountain of impossibility, we could take another approach. In working with people and their problems, we could accept that those problems might not be solved. The other person may or may not be able to deal with their situation, and we may or may not be able to help them. That is the reality and we need to accept that. No amount of worrying is going to change that.

It is difficult to be with a loved one who is unhappy and suffering, and it is tempting to want to save the day and make everything better. We want their pain to go away—and we are uncomfortable with our own pain as well. That ground of mutual pain and rawness is an intensely claustrophobic and forbidding territory to explore. Rather than looking into it, we would like to get out of it, to fix it. But we need to examine that notion of "fixing," particularly the idea of fixing others. We need to question our concepts about how we want things to be and what we want people to become.

If we can let go of some of that, we can see more clearly what we can and cannot do. We can learn not to obsess about all the problems we cannot solve, but to sort through them to find the one or two things we can actually do that might be helpful. It is better to do one small helpful thing than punish yourself for the many things beyond your power and ability to change or affect. Some problems can be solved, some cannot, and some are best left unsolved.

Shantideva, the great Indian teacher of the Mahayana Buddhist tradition, said that if we could do something positive we should just do it. So why worry? He said that if we cannot do something about a problem we should accept that. So why worry? The trick is to keep it simple—either do something or don't.

As we grow and develop and learn from our experience, we are more likely to be able to help people who are struggling more than we are. We can learn when to help and when to step back, and we can see other people grow, as we have, though struggle and hardship. However, although we can prepare ourselves to be able to face tough times, we have no real control over others. We can support the people we love and worry about, but we cannot solve their problems for them—and neither can anyone else solve our problems for us. But we can be together with those we love unsolved. Although each of us must face our own individual journey through life alone, we can travel together, bound by love.

Lack of Money

David Loy

When we understand that money is empty—in the Buddhist sense of having no inherent reality—paradoxically we become much better able to use it wisely. If we don't, like King Midas we will be managed by our money, rather than the other way around.

What is money? Can Buddhism help us understand it? These seem like silly questions. After all, we use money every day, so we must have some basic understanding of what it is . . . but is that really so? Perhaps our familiarity with it has the opposite effect, keeping us from appreciating just how unique and strange money actually is.

Take out a dollar bill and look at it. What do you have in your hands? A piece of paper, obviously. You can't eat it, ride in it, or sleep on it. It can't shelter you when it rains, or warm you when you're cold, or heal you when you're ill, or comfort you when you're lonely. You could burn it, but an old newspaper would be much more useful if you want to start a fire. In itself that dollar bill is less useful than a blank sheet of paper, which at least we could use to write on. In and of itself, it is literally worthless, a nothing.

Yet money is also the most valuable thing in the world, simply because we have collectively agreed to make it so. Money is a social construction that we tend to forget is only a construct—a kind of group fantasy. The anthropologist Weston La Barre called it a psychosis that has become normal, "an institutionalized dream that everyone is having at once." As long as we keep dreaming together it continues to work as the socially agreed-upon means that enables us to convert something (for example, a day's work) into something else (a couple bags of groceries, perhaps).

But, as we know, money always has the potential to turn into a curse. In addition to the usual social problems—in particular, the growing gap between those who have too much and those who have too little—there is a more basic issue. The temptation with money is to sacrifice everything else (the earth becomes "resources," our time becomes "labor," our relationships become "contacts" to be exploited, and so forth) for that "pure means." To some degree that's necessary, of course. Like it or not, we live in a monetized world. The danger is that psychologically we will reverse means and ends, so that the means of life becomes the goal itself. As Arthur Schopenhauer put it, money is abstract happiness, so someone who is no longer capable of concrete happiness sets his whole heart on money. Money ends up becoming "frozen desire"—not desire for anything in particular, but a symbol for desire in general. And what does the Second Noble (or "ennobling") Truth identify as the cause of *dukkha*?

The Greek myth of Midas and his golden touch gives us the classic metaphor for what happens when money becomes an end in itself. Midas was a Lydian king who was offered any reward he wanted for helping the god Dionysus. Although already fabulously wealthy, his greed was unsatisfied, and he asked that whatever he touched might turn to gold. Midas enjoyed transforming everything into gold—until it was dinnertime. He took a bite—ching! It turned to gold. He took a sip of wine—ching! He hugged his daughter—ching! She turned into a golden statue. In despair, Midas asked Dionysus to deliver him from this curse, and fortunately for him the god was kind enough to oblige.

Today this simple yet profound story is even more relevant than it was in ancient Greece, because the world we live in is so much more monetized. Nowadays Midas is socially acceptable—in fact, perhaps there is a bit of Midas in all of us. Living in a world that emphasizes instant convertibility tends to deemphasize our senses and dull our awareness of them, in favor of the magical numbers that appear and disappear in bank accounts. Instead of appreciating fully the sensuous qualities of a glass of wine, often we are more aware of how much it cost and what that implies about us as sophisticated wine-drinkers. Because we live in a society that values those magical numbers as the most important thing of all, most of us are anxious about having enough money, and often enough that anxiety is appropriate. But what is enough, and when does financial planning become the pursuit of abstract happiness? Focusing on an abstraction that has no value in itself, we depreciate our concrete, sensuous life in the world. We end up knowing the price of everything and the value of nothing. Can Buddhism help us understand why such traps are so alluring?

Today money serves at least four functions for us. For better and worse, it is indispensable as our medium of exchange. In effect, as I've said, this makes money more valuable than anything else, since it can transform into almost anything. What's more, because of how our society has agreed to define value, money has come to symbolize pure value.

Inevitably, then, money as a medium of exchange evolved into a second function. It is our storehouse of value. Centuries ago, before money became widely used, one's wealth was measured in cows, full granaries, servants, and children. The advantage of gold and silver—and now bank accounts—is that they are incorruptible, at least in principle, and invulnerable to rats, fire, and disease. Our fascination with gold has much to do with the fact that, unlike silver, it doesn't even tarnish. It is, in effect, immortal. This is quite attractive in a world haunted by impermanence and death.

Capitalism added another little twist, which brings us to the third function of money. It's something we take for granted today but which was suspicious, not to say immoral, to many people in the past. Capitalism is based on capital, which is money used to make more money. Invest your surplus and watch it grow! This encouraged an economic dynamism and growth that we tend to take for granted today yet is really quite extraordinary. It has led to many developments that have been beneficial but there is also a downside, when you keep reinvesting whatever you get to get even more, on the assumption that you can never have too much. Capital can always be used to accumulate more capital. Psychologically, of course, this tends to become the much more insidious problem that you can never have enough. This attitude toward money is in striking contrast with the way that some premodern societies would redistribute wealth when it reached a certain level—for example, the potlatch of native communities in British Columbia. Such societies seem to have been more sensitive to the ways wealth accumulation tends to disrupt social relationships.

The other side of capital investment is debt. A capitalist economy is an economy that runs on debt and requires a society that is comfortable with indebtedness. The debt is at least a little larger than the original loan: those who invest expect to get more back than their original investment. When this is how the whole economy works, the social result is a generalized pressure for continuous growth and expansion, because that is the only way to repay the accumulating debt. This constant pressure for growth is indifferent to other social and ecological consequences. The result is a collective future orientation: the present is never enough but the future will be (or must be) better.

Why do we fall into such obsessions? The *anatta,* "not-self," teaching gives Buddhism a special perspective on our dukkha, which also implies a special take on our hang-ups with money. The problem isn't just that I will someday get sick, grow old, and die. My lack of self means that I feel something is wrong with me right now. I experience the hole at the core of my being as a sense of lack, and in response I become preoccupied with projects that I believe can make me feel more "real." Christianity has an explanation for this lack and offers a religious solution, but many of us don't believe in sin anymore. So what is wrong with us? The most popular explanation in developed, or "economized," societies is that we don't have enough money. That's our contemporary "original sin."

This points to the fourth function of money for us. Beyond its usefulness as a medium of exchange and a storehouse of value and capital for investment, money has become our most important reality symbol. Today money is generally believed to be the best way to secure oneself/one's self, to gain a sense of solid identity, to cope with the gnawing intuition that we do not really exist. Suspecting that the sense of self is groundless, we used to visit temples and churches to ground ourselves in a relationship with God or gods. Now we invest in "securities" and "trust funds" to ground ourselves economically. Financial institutions have become our shrines.

Needless to say, there is a karmic rebound. The more we value money, the more we find it used—and the more we use it ourselves—to evaluate us. Money takes on a life of its own, and we end up being manipulated by the symbol we take so seriously. In this sense, the problem is not that we are too materialistic but that we are not materialistic enough, because we are so preoccupied with the symbolism that we end up devaluing life itself. We are infatuated less with the things that money can buy than with their power and status—not so much with the comfort and power of an expensive car as with what owning a Mercedes-Benz says about me. "I am the kind of guy who drives a Mercedes/owns a condo on Maui/and has a stock portfolio worth a million bucks . . ."

All this is a classic example of "binding ourselves without a rope," to use the Zen metaphor. We become trapped by our ways of thinking about money.

The basic difficulty, from a Buddhist perspective, is that we are trying to resolve a spiritual problem—our "emptiness"—by identifying with something outside ourselves, which can never confer the sense of reality we crave. We work hard to acquire a big bank account and all the things that society teaches us will make us happy, and then we cannot understand why they do not make us happy, why they do not resolve our sense that something is lacking. Is the reason really that we don't have enough yet?

I think that Buddhism gives us the best metaphor to understand money: *shunyata*, the "emptiness" that characterizes all phenomena. The Buddhist philosopher Nagarjuna warns us not to grab this snake by the wrong end, because there is no such thing as shunyata. It is a shorthand way to describe the interdependence of things, how nothing self-exists, because everything is part of everything else. If we misunderstand the concept and cling to shunyata, the cure becomes worse than the disease. Money—also nothing in itself, nothing more than a socially agreed-upon symbol—remains indispensable today. But woe to those who grab this snake by the tail. As the Heart Sutra teaches, all form is empty, yet there is no emptiness apart from form. Preoccupation with money is fixation on something that has no meaning in itself, apart from the forms it takes, forms that we become less and less able to truly appreciate.

Another way to make this point is to say that money is not a thing but a process. Perhaps it's best understood as an energy that is not really mine or yours. Those who understand that it is an empty, socially constructed symbol can use it wisely and compassionately to reduce the world's suffering. Those who use it to become more real end up being used by it, their alienated sense of self clutching a blank check—a promissory note that can never be cashed.

Optimism, Pessimism, and Naivete

Matthieu Ricard

*The Buddhist monk and humanitarian Matthieu Ricard celebrates
the virtues of optimism as the attitude that allows us to move forward
and accomplish our aims in life, despite setbacks and difficulties. While
pessimism convinces us that our problems will last forever and we have
no capability to act, optimism brings hope (the kind that is not simply
the obverse of fear), as well as resolve, adaptability, serenity, and meaning.*

> She loved the rain as much as the sun. Her least thoughts
> had the cheery colors of lovely, hearty flowers, pleasing to
> the eye.
> —ALAIN

One morning in the monastery courtyard, I was looking at a tree
that held a few red flowers and a dozen sparrows. Everything I saw
produced within me a sense of jubilation and of the infinite purity
of phenomena. I forced my mind into a downbeat mood and con-
jured up all sorts of negative feelings. Suddenly the tree looked dusty
to me and the flowers sickly; the chirping of the sparrows began to

irritate me. I wondered which was the right way to look at things, and came to the conclusion that the first had been the correct way because it generated an open, creative, and liberating attitude and led to greater satisfaction. Such an attitude allows us spontaneously to embrace the universe and beings and to tear away any egocentric divide between the self and the world. On the other hand, when we cling to an "impure," negative perception of phenomena, something rings false—we feel "disconnected" from the universe, which comes to seem dull, strange, distant, and sometimes hostile.

The False Process of Optimism

Psychologists have long believed that mildly depressive people are "realistic" in their outlook. Optimists have a tendency to dwell longer on pleasant incidents than on painful situations and to overestimate their past performance and mastery of things.

By these lights, the pessimist would tend to go around with his eyes wide open and to assess situations more lucidly than the optimist. "Reality may not always be a barrel of laughs, but you have to see things the way they are," he might say, whereas the optimist is a genial but incurably naive dreamer. "Life will bring him down to earth soon enough," we think. It so happens that this is not true. Further studies have shown that the pessimist's objective, detached, and wary judgment is inadequate. When it's a question of real situations drawn from daily life, the optimist's approach is in fact more realistic and pragmatic than that of the pessimist. If, for example, a cross section of women who drink coffee are shown a report on the increased risk of breast cancer linked to caffeine, or if a cross section of sunbathers are informed that lying out in the sun increases the risk of skin cancer, a week later the optimists have better recall of the reports' details than the pessimists and have taken them more into account in their behavior. Moreover, they concentrate attentively and selectively on the risks that truly concern them, rather than fretting vainly and ineffectually over everything. In this way, they remain more serene than the pessimists and husband their energies for real threats.

If we observe the way in which people perceive the events of their lives, appreciate the quality of the lived moment, and create their future by overcoming obstacles with an open and creative attitude, we find that the optimists have an undeniable advantage over the pessimists. Many studies show that they do better on exams, in their chosen profession, and in their relationships, live longer and in better health, enjoy a better chance of surviving postoperative shock, and are less prone to depression and suicide. A study was made of more than nine hundred people admitted to an American hospital in 1960. Their degree of optimism and other psychological traits were evaluated in tests and questionnaires. Forty years later, it turns out that the optimists lived 19 percent longer on average than the pessimists— some sixteen years of added life for an octogenarian. Furthermore, Martin Seligman claims that pessimists are up to eight times more likely to become depressed when things go wrong; they do worse at school, sports, and most jobs than their talent would suggest. It was demonstrated that pessimism exacerbates depression and the other difficulties cited, and not the other way around; when such people are taught specifically to overcome pessimism by changing their outlook, they are markedly less subject to depressive relapse. There are definite reasons for this. Indeed psychologists describe pessimism as an "explanatory style" for the world that engenders "learned helplessness."

Two Ways of Seeing the World

An optimist is somebody who considers his problems to be temporary, controllable, and linked to a specific situation. He will say: "There's no reason to make a fuss about it; these things don't last. I'll figure it out; in any case, I usually do." The pessimist, on the other hand, thinks that his problems will last ("It's not the sort of thing that just goes away"), that they jeopardize everything he does and are out of his control ("What do you expect me to do about it?"). He also imagines that he has some basic inner flaw; he tells people, "Whatever I do, it always turns out the same way," and concludes, "I'm just not cut out to be happy."

The sense of insecurity that afflicts so many people today is closely tied to pessimism. The pessimist is constantly anticipating disaster and falls victim to chronic anxiety and doubt. Morose, irritable, and nervous, she has no confidence in the world or in herself and always expects to be bullied, abandoned, and ignored.

Here's a perfect pessimist's parable. One fine summer's day, a driver got a flat in the middle of the countryside. To add insult to injury, he found that he had no jack. The place was practically deserted. There was one solitary house in sight, halfway up a hill. After a few minutes' hesitation, the traveler decided to go borrow a jack. As he climbed toward the house, he began to think, "What if the owner won't lend me a jack? It would be pretty rotten to leave me in a fix." As he slowly neared the house, he became more and more upset. "I would never do that to a stranger. It would be hateful!" Finally, he knocked on the front door, and when the owner opened up, he shouted: "You can keep your jack, you son of a bitch!"

The optimist, however, trusts that it is possible to achieve her goals and that with patience, resolve, and intelligence, she *will ultimately* do so. The fact is, *more often than not*, she does.

In everyday life the pessimist starts out with an attitude of refusal, even where it's totally inappropriate. I remember a Bhutanese official I often had to deal with. Every time I asked him a question, he systematically prefaced his answers with "No, no, no," regardless of what he was going to say afterward, which gave our conversations a comic tone.

"Do you think we'll be able to leave tomorrow morning?"

"No, no, no . . . Be ready to leave at nine a.m."

If pessimism and suffering were as immutable as fingerprints or eye color, it would be more sensitive to avoid trumpeting the benefits of happiness and optimism. But if optimism is a way of looking at life and happiness a condition that can be cultivated, one might as well get down to work without further delay. As Alain has written: "How marvelous human society would be if everyone added his own wood to the fire instead of crying over the ashes!"

Even if we are born with a certain predisposition to look for the silver lining, and even if the influence of those who raise us nudges our outlook toward pessimism or optimism, our interpretation of the world can shift later on, and considerably, because our minds are flexible.

HOPE

For an optimist, it makes no sense to lose hope. We can *always* do better (instead of being devastated, resigned, or disgusted), limit the damage (instead of letting it all go to pot), find an alternative solution (instead of wallowing pitifully in failure), rebuild what has been destroyed (instead of saying, "It's all over!"), take the current situation as a starting point (instead of wasting our time crying over the past and lamenting the present), start from scratch (instead of ending there), understand that sustained *effort* will have to be made in the best apparent direction (instead of being paralyzed by indecision and fatalism), and use every present moment to advance, appreciate, act, and enjoy inner peace (instead of wasting our time brooding over the past and fearing the future).

There are those who say, like the Australian farmer interviewed on the radio during the forest fires of 2001: "I've lost everything, I'll never be able to rebuild my life." And there are people like the navigator Jacques-Yves Le Toumelin, who, as he watched his first ship being torched by the Germans in 1944, paraphrased Rudyard Kipling: "If you can see your life's work destroyed and get straight back to the grindstone, then you will be a man, my son." He immediately built a new boat and circumnavigated the world solo, under sail.

Hope is defined by psychologists as the conviction that one can find the means to attain one's goals and develop the motivation necessary to do so. It is known that hope improves students' test results and athletes' performance, makes illness and agonizing debility more bearable, and makes pain itself (from burns, arthritis, spinal injuries, or blindness, for example) easier to tolerate. It has been demonstrated, for instance, using a method to measure resistance to pain, that people who show a marked tendency to be hopeful are able to tolerate contact with a very cold surface twice as long as those who don't.

Resolve

Resolve is the obverse of laziness. Now, there are many kinds of laziness, but they can all be sorted into three principal types. The first and most vulgar boils down to wanting only to eat well, sleep well, and do as little as possible. The second and most paralyzing leads us to abandon the race before we've even crossed the starting line. We tell ourselves: "Oh, that's not for me, that's well beyond my abilities." The third and most pernicious knows what really matters in life but is constantly putting it off to later, while devoting itself to a thousand other things of lesser importance.

The optimist does not give up quickly. Strengthened by the hope of success, she perseveres and succeeds more often than the pessimist, especially in adverse conditions. The pessimist has a tendency to back away from difficulties, sink into resignation, or turn to temporary distractions that will not solve her problems. The pessimist will demonstrate little resolve, for she doubts everything and everyone, foresees the failure of every undertaking (instead of the potential for growth, development, and fruitfulness), and sees every person as a schemer, an egoist, and a carpetbagger, rather than as a human being who, like all of us, aspires to happiness and dreads suffering. She sees a threat in every new thing and anticipates catastrophe. In a word, when hearing a door creak, the optimist thinks it's opening and the pessimist thinks it's closing.

A few years ago I went to France to discuss ways of undertaking humanitarian projects in Tibet despite the oppressive conditions imposed by the Chinese government. About fifteen minutes into the meeting, someone said, with reference to myself and one of the other participants: "You're talking about the same thing as if it's two different worlds. One of you thinks it'll all end badly, the other thinks everything will turn out fine." The first speaker had said: "To start with, there's little chance that the authorities will put up with you and you'll probably be kicked out right away. And then, how are you going to get permission to build a school? Even if you manage to start building it, you'll get scammed by the contractors, who are in bed with the corrupt local powers. On top of it all, don't forget that you can't force them to teach in Tibetan and classes will end up being held in Chinese." Personally, I found the conversation stifling; my only thought was to get out of there as fast as possible, slip through the net, and get the projects off the ground. Since then, four years ago, in cooperation with an especially enthusiastic friend and the support of generous benefactors, we've built sixteen health centers, eight schools, and twelve bridges. In many cases our local friends asked for permission to build only once the clinic or the school was finished. Thousands of patients and children have been treated and educated in these places. Hesitant at first, the local authorities are thrilled now because they can include these projects in their statistics. From our point of view, the goal we sought—helping those in need—had been accomplished.

Although the optimist may be a little giddy when foreseeing the future, telling himself that it will all work out in the end when that isn't always the case, his attitude is more fruitful, since, in the hope of undertaking a hundred projects, followed up by diligent action, the optimist will end up completing fifty. Conversely, in limiting himself to undertake a mere ten, the pessimist might complete five at best and often fewer, since he'll devote little energy to a task he feels to be doomed from the start.

Most of the people I am constantly meeting in countries where poverty and oppression inspire their assistance are optimists who boldly face up to the extreme disparity between the immensity of the task and the meagerness of their resources. I have a friend, Malcolm McOdell, who has been doing development work in Nepal with his wife for the past thirty years on the basies of the principle of "positive inquiry," an extraordinary practical application of optimism.

"Whenever I arrive in a village," he explains, "people's first re-action is to complain about their problems. I tell them: 'Hold on, it's impossible that all you have is problems. Tell me about the assets and good qualities that are particular to your village and to each one of you.' We get together, sometimes in the evening around a camp-fire. Minds and tongues grow loose and, with a whole new kind of enthusiasm, the villagers make a list of their talents, abilities, and resources. Immediately afterward, I ask them to imagine how they might, all together, put those qualities to work for them. As soon as they've come up with a plan, I ask the final question: 'Who here is prepared, here and now, to take responsibility for such and such aspect of the program?'" Hands shoot up, promises are made, and the work is launched within days. This approach is light-years away from that followed by the problem-listers, who accomplish less, less well and less quickly. McOdell focuses in particular on improving conditions for Nepalese women, some thirty thousand of whom are enjoying the benefits of his initiatives today.

ADAPTABILITY

When difficulties seem insurmountable, optimists react in a more constructive and creative way. They accept the facts with realism, know how to rapidly identify the positive in adversity, draw lessons from it, and come up with an alternative solution or turn to a new project. Pessimists would rather turn away from the problem or adopt escapist strategies—sleep, isolation, drug or alcohol abuse—that diminish their focus on the problem. Instead of confronting them with resolve, they prefer to brood over their misfortunes, nur-ture illusions, dream up "magic" solutions, and accuse the whole world of being against them. They have a hard time drawing lessons from the past, which often leads to the repetition of their problems. They are more fatalistic ("I told you it wouldn't work. It's always the same, no matter what I do") and are quick to see themselves as "mere pawns in the game of life."

SERENITY

Having foreseen and thoroughly tested every possible avenue, the optimist, even when she has temporarily failed, is free of regret and guilt feelings. She knows how to step back and is always ready to imagine a new solution, without bearing the burden of past failures. That is how she maintains her serenity. Her confidence is as solid as the bow of a ship that cleaves through life's waters, be they calm or stormy.

A friend of mine who lives in Nepal told me how he once had to take a plane to give an important lecture in the Netherlands the following day. The sponsors had rented a hall, publicized the event in the newspapers, and expected a thousand attendees. At the airport, he learned that the flight had been canceled and that there was no other way to leave Nepal that night. He told me: "I was deeply sorry for the sponsors, but there was really nothing to be done. A deep calm came over my mind. Behind me, I had just said good-bye to my friends in Kathmandu; ahead of me, my destination had just vanished. I felt delightfully buoyant with freedom. On the sidewalk outside the airport, I sat on my bag and joked around with the porters and street kids who happened to be there. To have been sick with worry would have served absolutely no purpose at all. After about half an hour, I stood up and headed off on foot to Kathmandu with my little bag, enjoying the cool of twilight."

I remember a trip I once took to eastern Tibet. Torrential rains, in combination with the almost total deforestation undertaken by the Chinese, had caused devastating floods. Our ATV had a hard time progressing along a potholed road at the bottom of abyssal gorges, alongside a river that had been transformed into a vast, raging torrent. Glowing in the yellowish light of dusk, the stone ramparts seemed to rise to the sky, echoing the roar of the surge. Most of the bridges had been swept away, and the turbulent waters were rapidly eroding the only navigable road remaining. Every so often, a rock would hurtle down the craggy slopes and smash onto the pavement.

It was a good test of the passengers' optimism. The differences between them was striking. Some were so worried that they wanted to stop, although there was nowhere to take shelter. Others took it all in with composure and wanted to push on and get through as fast as possible. One of us eventually said to the most anxious: "You love action movies. Well, today's your lucky day—you get to be in one." And we all burst out laughing and took heart.

MEANING

There is an even deeper dimension to optimism: that of realizing the potential for transformation that is in every human being, regardless of his or her condition. It is that potential, in the end, that gives meaning to human life. The ultimate pessimism is in thinking that life in general is not worth living. The ultimate optimism lies in understanding that every passing moment is a treasure, in joy as in adversity. These are not subtle nuances, but a fundamental difference in the way of seeing things. This divergence of perspective depends on whether or not we have found within ourselves the fulfillment that alone fuels inner peace and everlasting serenity.

EXERCISE

Experiment with experiencing the same situation through the eyes of optimism and pessimism. Take, for example, an airplane voyage:

Imagine that you are on a long airplane trip en route to a strange city to begin a new job. Suddenly the airplane encounters turbulence. You can see the plane's wings tilting up and down, and you visualize the ensuing disaster. Once the turbulence settles down, you realize your seat is too small. You can't find a comfortable position, and your mind is filled with complaints about the state of airplane travel. You are annoyed that the air hostess is taking forever to bring your drink. When you think ahead to your new job, you feel certain that the people you meet won't like or appreciate you. They will ignore your expertise, keep you away from the most interesting projects, and might even cheat you. You are sure that this trip will be a catastrophe. Why did you ever think you could handle it? You are filled with dread.

Experience the gloomy state of mind such thoughts create.

Then experiment with another way to experience the same situation:

When the plane encounters turbulence, you know that it is part of the journey and vividly feel that every instant that passes by is precious. As the turbulence calms down, you feel grateful and hope that you can use the rest of your life constructively. Although your seat is not particularly comfortable, you find positions that relieve the stiffness of your back and legs. You appreciate how cheerful and helpful the air hostess is, even though she is so busy and has to stand up throughout most of the flight. You are excited by the adventures that await you. You imagine that the people there will be interesting and productive and that you will be given many new opportunities. You are convinced that both your activities and your relationships will flourish and that you have the inner resources to overcome any obstacles that may arise.

Experience this buoyant state of mind that is tuned to the positive.

Appreciate the difference between these two states of mind and understand how they came about simply through the workings of your mind, although the outer situation remained the same.

Acting Effectively in a World of Chaos and Change

James Gimian and Barry Boyce

The ancient Chinese wisdom text The Art of War—*often called "the Sun Tzu," after its legendary author—shares many understandings of the world that are compatible with a Buddhist understanding of effective action in the everyday world. It presents a creative way of dealing with difficulty that we often find reflected in martial arts training as well. Interconnectedness, usually called "interdependence" in Buddhist teachings, is a vital understanding reflected in the Sun Tzu's approach to the world. Appreciating it reorients our responses to chaos and change.*

The recent global financial meltdown, sudden shortages of food-stuffs caused by a shift to biofuel production, and ongoing environmental upheavals easily demonstrate to us how interconnected our world is. A relatively small number of people making some risky decisions about mortgages suddenly causes a cavalcade of effects that results in your neighbor losing his house and his job. It's hard to hang on to the idea that we exist separately and independently, in complete control. And yet that is also good news. We don't have to struggle so hard to be the sole source of every solution to every challenge we face, because the interconnected web that makes up the world brings opportunities we have yet to conceive of.

Interconnectedness and the awe that can be associated with it have almost become clichés, which makes it possible for us to take interconnectedness for granted and think of its implications as trivial. "So what if everything is connected? I still need to finish this report by Friday and get to my daughter's soccer game by six o'clock." From the point of view of the Sun Tzu, interconnectedness, known in Chinese philosophy as "the Tao," is important not because it is mysterious or cosmic; it is important because apprehending things in a linear way is incomplete and ineffective, and the consequences are often harmful. How many managers have focused immense attention on what they want one person to do, only to ignore how that one person fits into the whole system? Rather than working with the system as a whole—the web of interconnectedness that the employee fits into—the manager treats her as an isolated entity, with all the possibilities for alienation and dissatisfaction that such isolation can produce. The same situation occurs often with parents who see their children frozen in space and time and cannot see the whole context that parent and child are sharing. Think of the parent who missed the soccer game, only to find out that the report wasn't really needed so badly by Friday, then learned how the damage to his relationship with his daughter began to hamper his productivity at work.

In a completely linear world, one cause would only have one effect and there would never be unintended consequences, clashing priorities, paradoxes, and dilemmas. However, we know that any time we act, we set off not one isolated reaction but a pattern of chain reactions, and we live within—and to a certain extent, are created by—the chain reactions set off by others. Like a good chess player or a good strategist, we may try to observe and plan for as many of the consequent occurrences as we can, but it is impossible to include them all.

It may seem like a great accomplishment to observe the inter-connectedness of things, perhaps we could even say to "enjoy the Tao," but this is still only a partial victory. We, too, are part of the interconnectedness. While the world changes around us, we are changing right along with it. The mathematician and philosopher Alfred North Whitehead was fond of pointing out that we are not only observers of nature: our very bodies are nature, and they rely for their survival on regular nourishment supplied by the surrounding environment. We are part of the whole that surrounds us.

An important corollary of appreciating interconnectedness—and our place within it—is accepting and appreciating chaos and change, not merely as unpleasant by-products but as vital and even helpful. Conventionally, chaos strikes us as the clustering of myriad details beyond our control that appear to be random and to bear no relation to any pattern. We just seem to be getting hit with one thing after another all over the place. But this definition of chaos takes its meaning only from the point of view of the fixed order that we would like to impose on events, the plan that we hope to carry to fruition unaltered. Events seem random when we cling to limited perspectives that don't allow us to see the greater patterns they may be part of. When a passing acquaintance drops by unexpectedly in the middle of a very busy day, it seems a random act to us, but it is part of a pattern of ordered events in his or her life that led the person to our door. Great movements have been born of seemingly chance meetings and chance occurrences.

From the point of view expressed in the Sun Tzu, chaos is not something to be avoided but is an expression of the power of interconnectedness. It is only frustrating to the extent that we try to *obtain a fixed point outside of it.* Certainly, there are times when we can ride on the plethora of details, and there are times when the details swallow us up, but there is never a time when the mass of details is not there. It is no surprise that "God is in the details" and "the devil is in the details" are both popular sayings.

Resisting change and seeking permanent security seem almost to define what it means to be a human being. And yet they also seem to be based on a fundamental misconception about the way things work and turn out to be very problematic approaches. In general, holding a fixed position denies the reality of change and interconnectedness and thus separates us from the way things actually work. And, in particular, as the Sun Tzu makes clear, fighting solid positions with further solidification is an approach fraught with danger. Martin Luther King Jr. knew that if he attacked the solidly established white power structure head-on with the solid and justified resentment at his disposal, only senseless conflict would ensue. Likewise, trying to change our partner's firmly held opinion by escalating and direct argument only solidifies the resistance. When we face difficulties and resistance, appreciating interconnectedness can allow us to break the momentum of trying to tackle things head-on, to fix and solve them. Appreciating interconnectedness might cause us to pause, stop, and look around.

To become a leader in whatever sphere we find ourselves in at any given time—the sphere of our family, our friends, our colleagues, our nation, our world, our own mind—it can help to consider the teachings of the mandala principle. Geometric designs symbolic of the universe—mandalas—are used in Hinduism and Buddhism as an aid to connecting to reality on a deep level and are also found in the works of Carl Jung and modern artists. The mandala principle teaches us that there is always a center and a fringe, and we are in many centers and fringes. From the point of view of taking action, however, we find ourselves at the center of our personal interconnected system—our mandala—where inner and outer, subject and object, are interconnected, dynamic, and ever-changing, and where apparent chaos gives way to an underlying order apparent from the bigger view.

Change produces daunting chaos if it threatens what we seek to hold on to or to build. When we fear loss or hope for achievement, change may seem a threat. But the same change and chaos can also produce opportunity. Things that were solid and resistant to our efforts can rearrange themselves to produce openings without our discernible direct action. The seemingly monolithic and impenetrable

Soviet bloc dissolved due to internal conditions rather than political or military bombardment from Western powers, but this internal dissolution nonetheless resulted in numerous opportunities for outside influence and development. In our lives, a coincidence such as running into someone at a party can lead to a new job offer that completely alters the predicament we have been preoccupied with for months. When we genuinely see change as being "the way things are"—when we see that situations, conditions, relationships, are always in flux, that no moment is ever exactly like the last one—we can be in a state of relaxed readiness and able to capitalize on openings as they arise. Being part of the interconnectedness and present in the midst of the inevitable change is the first step to being able to take advantage of the unfolding of occurrences.

When we embrace interconnectedness, chaos, and change, taking leadership in our lives is not about controlling and manipulating the environment as if it could be owned. You cannot truly own something that is always changing, but you can be its steward for a while. The effectiveness of the leader, then, comes not from power over other people and things but from *being part* of the interconnectedness, not merely observing it. It's not like being a baby staring at a mobile rotating above the crib. It's being a part of the mobile itself.

The Chinese classic *Tao Te Ching,* by Lao-Tzu (here quoted from the translation by John C. H. Wu), presents the Tao—the totality where all polarities merge and that we find ourselves part of—as a governing principle that is itself ungovernable:

> Man follows the ways of the Earth.
> The Earth follows the ways of Heaven.
> Heaven follows the ways of Tao.
> Tao follows its own ways.

If we limit ourselves to a dualistic view, we are always pitting ourselves against something. Man is pitted against evil, man is pitted against nature, man is pitted against man. Ultimately, however, there is nothing to be against. We cannot enslave the Tao and bend it to our ends. We cannot cleave off a part of it and make it our own wholly protected domain. But by paying close attention to the matters at hand and the context they arise in, we can follow the tendencies, clusters, and patterns. As a result, it is possible to encourage beneficial results within the sphere of our stewardship.

That is what the Sun Tzu suggests we do. It suggests that we can incorporate a view of the world as holistic and see the interconnectedness of the world as an integral part of our sense of being—quite simply because it already is. If we seek to change things to meet a preconceived notion, we will be frustrated, but if we are willing to be part of the change and ride it with attention, we can bring about beneficial action—for ourselves and for others—even in the midst of great chaos and difficulty.

Be What You Need to Be

Thich Nhat Hanh

The bodhisattva, the ultimate master of skillful means, is not limited to one way of doing things, but takes many forms: child, adult, man, woman, artist, politician, musician, teacher, police officer, CEO. In practicing skillful action, Thich Nhat Hanh tells us, we need to be ready to emerge in many guises, able to adapt to whatever the circumstances require.

Buddhism speaks of the four skillful means of a bodhisattva. The first skillful means is making the three kinds of offerings: material gifts, the gift of the dharma, and the gift of non-fear. When you offer good things to people, they have sympathy with you, they regard you favorably, and their hearts are open. Giving someone a book on the dharma, or a CD of some beautiful music that can help them relax—this is the practice of giving, *dana*. But the offerings of a bodhisattva should not be only material things or dharma teachings. The best, most precious gift we can give someone is the gift of non-fear, *abhaya*.

People live in fear of death; they are afraid of losing their self-hood, their identity, afraid of disappearing and becoming nonexistent. So when you offer the kind of teaching, practice, and insight that helps someone touch their ultimate dimension and get free of the fear of being and nonbeing, that is the greatest gift you can offer them.

The second skillful means of the bodhisattva is to practice loving speech. You can be very firm and uncompromising, but you can still use loving speech. You don't have to shout or become hostile to get your idea across. Loving speech can convey your feeling and idea to the other person in a way they are able to hear it and take it in more fully. The third skillful means is to always act to benefit others. You do whatever you can to help the other person in any situation. That is the action of the bodhisattva. The fourth skillful means is the practice of "doing the same thing." This has to do with the bodhisattva's ability to take on the appropriate form in order to be able to approach others and help them. You look like them, dress like them, do exactly what they do; you become one of them so that they will trust and accept you and have the opportunity to learn the path of understanding and love. These are the four skillful means by which the bodhisattva embraces and serves living beings.

The action of Avalokiteshvara, the bodhisattva of compassion, is to be present everywhere at all times and manifest in innumerable forms. In many Asian Buddhist temples, there is a statue of Avalokiteshvara Bodhisattva with a thousand arms. Each arm holds an instrument or object that represents a different sphere of activity in which the bodhisattva can manifest compassion and understanding. In one hand he holds a book—it might be a sutra text or a book on political science. Another hand holds a ritual instrument, such as a bell. Another holds a musical instrument. A modern version of the thousand-armed bodhisattva might hold a computer in one hand. Perhaps the bodhisattva holds a gun in one of its thousand hands. Is it possible to carry a weapon and yet remain deeply a bodhisattva? This is possible. At the gates of temples in Vietnam, you often see two figures: on the left is a statue of a very gentle bodhisattva, smiling, welcoming, while on the right is a figure with a very fierce expression, brandishing a weapon. In Vietnamese the name of this figure means literally "burning-face bodhisattva"—his face is burning, his eyes are burning, fire and smoke are coming out of his nose and mouth. This is the archetype of the fierce, guardian bodhisattva, one who has the capacity to keep the hungry ghosts in check. When we offer ceremonial food and drink to the hungry ghosts, we evoke this bodhisattva to come and help, because the hungry ghosts bring so much noise and disorder with them. We need the burning-face bodhisattva; we need his ferocity to help establish order, because only he can tame the wild hungry ghosts. He is a kind of police chief bodhisattva.

Yet this fierce-looking character is a manifestation of Avalokiteshvara, who takes various forms—as a gentle, motherly bodhisattva, or as a fierce guardian bodhisattva, even as a hungry ghost—in order to better understand and communicate with those he or she has come to help. Some of these manifestations may not look to us like our usual idea of a bodhisattva. If we look for Avalokiteshvara only in a nice, gentle appearance, we may miss him. We have to look deeply in order to recognize the bodhisattva of compassion in his or her many forms—as a child or adult, as a man or woman, as an artist, politician, musician, judge, gardener, police officer, dharma teacher, the head of a big corporation, or a gang member.

In order to approach others to help them transform, you have to become a part of their world so that they will recognize and accept you. Then you can begin to help transform their hearts. This is the fourth skillful means of the bodhisattva, the practice of "doing the same thing." In a gang, you may look, act, and speak like any other gang member, but really you are a bodhisattva. In a prison you manifest yourself as prisoner and become a bodhisattva among prisoners. This is the action of Avalokiteshvara.

Just as burning-face bodhisattva carries a weapon and is a manifestation of the bodhisattva of compassion, when we see someone who carries a gun we cannot automatically say that he or she is evil. Society needs some people to serve as guardians, because there are those who will behave in harmful and destructive ways toward others if there is no one to embody discipline, security, and order. So someone who carries a gun, such as a policeman or prison guard, can also be a bodhisattva. He or she may be very firm, but deep within there is the heart of a bodhisattva. Our task is to help prison guards and policemen, as well as prisoners and gang members, recognize and cultivate their bodhisattva nature.

I have learned a lot from a friend, a police officer who took the mindfulness trainings some years ago, about the suffering of members of the police force in America. It is very difficult for them to do this job. The constant exposure to threat and violence, and the negative way many people react to them, cause the hearts of police officers to harden day by day. They feel isolated, disrespected, and uncared for by society. If police officers do not have skillful means, if they don't have enough understanding and compassion, then a lot of anger, frustration, and despair build up in them. They feel that no one understands how difficult their work is, because they are seen only as oppressors. Communication between the police and the community they are supposed to serve becomes stifled. And in such an atmosphere of hostility and mistrust, some members of the police abuse their authority and actually do become oppressors.

So you can manifest yourself as a policeman or policewoman, and play the role of bodhisattva in order to bring about better communication that will lead to more understanding and compassion. A police bodhisattva might help organize a community meeting and invite people to come and hear what the life of a police officer is like. When officers go to work in the morning, their families do not know if they will return home safely. Their task is to protect others and preserve order, but they know that they might also become the victim of violence. So the job of a police officer is filled with fear and uncertainty, and when you do your job with fear and anger, you cannot do it well. We should understand the immense suffering of members of the police force, prison guards, and others who serve in this capacity. Many people in these professions don't enjoy their jobs, yet they continue. Avalokiteshvara must appear in their midst and try to open their hearts.

A police bodhisattva can work to reestablish communication

between the police and the community, so that they can talk to and listen to one another with understanding and compassion. Communication is possible. Police officers can help non–police officers, and non–police officers can help police officers. There can be collaboration between them. There is a way through any situation, no matter how difficult. And the way that is prescribed by the teaching is to practice deep listening, listening with compassion, and using loving speech, one of the skillful means of the bodhisattva. Once communication is restored we have hope, and suffering will be lessened.

Avalokiteshvara shows us that even if you must be very firm, even when you have to carry a weapon or impose authority, at the same time you can be very compassionate. You can serve as a fierce burning-face bodhisattva with a tender heart and deep understanding. This is how you can be a bodhisattva in that form. But to serve as any kind of bodhisattva—a tender, motherly bodhisattva or a fierce guardian bodhisattva—you have to really *be* a bodhisattva. You can't just act the part, merely appearing to be a bodhisattva outwardly while inwardly your heart is closed. You must have real understanding and compassion in order to be worthy of being called a bodhisattva.

If you look closely at the figure of the thousand-armed bodhisattva, you will see that in the palm of each hand there is an eye. The eye symbolizes the presence of understanding and wisdom, *prajna*. We need both compassion and wisdom to progress on the path. Understanding and wisdom help to bring about love, kindness, and compassion. Avalokiteshvara has so many arms because love needs to express itself in many different forms and through the use of many kinds of instruments. That is why every arm is holding a different instrument, and in every hand there is the eye of wisdom.

Sometimes we may believe that we are acting from love, but if our action is not based in deep understanding, it will bring suffering. You want to make someone happy, and you believe very strongly that you are doing something out of love. But your action may make the other person suffer very much. So even though you believe you are acting from love, you cause your son or daughter, your partner or spouse, your friend or coworker to suffer deeply because you do not have enough understanding of that person. That is why you need the eye of understanding, of wisdom, to be an effective instrument of compassion.

If you don't understand the suffering, the difficulty, the deep aspiration of another person, it's not possible for you to love them. So it's very important to check with them and ask for help. A father should be able to ask his child, "Do I understand you well enough? Do I make you suffer because of my lack of understanding?" A mother should be able to ask her child, "Do you think I understand you? Please tell me so that I can love you properly." That is the language of love. And if you are sincere, your daughter or son will tell you about their suffering. And when you have understood their suffering, you will stop doing things that make him or her suffer, things that you believed you did only for her happiness and well-being. Deep understanding is the substance of which true love is made. The hands of the bodhisattva symbolize action, but our actions must be guided well by the eyes of understanding.

Some of us serve as bodhisattvas with several arms. We take care of our family, and at the same time we are able to participate in the work of protecting the environment and helping others in the world. All of us are capable of being present in many places in the world. You can be here and at the same time, through your compassionate action, you can be in a prison, or in a remote country where the children suffer from malnutrition. You don't have to be present in those other places with your physical body, because you have many transformation bodies that can serve everywhere.

When I write a book, I transform myself into a multitude of forms—the ideas and words in the book—in order to go everywhere. Every book I offer is one of my transformation bodies. I can go into a cloister in the form of a book or inside a prison in the form of an audiotape. Each of us has many transformation bodies, and that is why it is so important to learn to recognize our transformation bodies. Being a bodhisattva is not abstract but is a very concrete practice that we can do—just like Avalokiteshvara, we manifest ourselves in many bodies, many forms, in order to help as many people as possible.

You have to be very awake to recognize the bodhisattva in his various forms. Avalokiteshvara may be very close to you right now. You may be able to touch him just by reaching out your hand. Compassion does exist, understanding does exist. It is possible for us to cultivate the energy of compassion and understanding so that Avalokiteshvara can be with us at all times, in our daily life, and we will be well protected with understanding and compassion.

PART SIX

True Happiness

A Simple Sense of Delight

Sakyong Mipham Rinpoche

Is being happy simply a passing mood based on whether we're having a nice day, week, month, or year? Sakyong Mipham Rinpoche says that being cheerful can be a condition that transcends our circumstances and our station in life, and it can be cultivated through meditation.

I recently asked a Tibetan lama friend, "Who seems happier—the nomads in Tibet or the people you have met in America?" He told me that since America is famous for its wealth and technology, in the beginning he was sure that he would find happier, more cheerful people here. But after the initial phase of simple awe for what the West has accomplished, he began to see people as people, and he had no doubt that the simple nomads of Tibet are happier and more cheerful.

Tibetans do, as a people, seem very cheerful. Is their cheer due to living in a rural culture, or do they owe it to practicing the Buddhist teachings of meditation? In either case, I think their cheerfulness has something to do with simplicity. Simplicity allows us to experience our mind in a raw and naked state. In my own experience, one of the most welcome and important aspects of practicing and studying the Buddhist teachings is that we begin to trust our mind and discover the inherent goodness in it. The result is feeling cheerful.

Most of us think of cheerfulness as a mood that shows up in our life for random reasons—a nice day, a birthday party, or the simple pleasure of being with friends. Even though we don't always experience it as the river running throughout our life, we appreciate cheerfulness and enjoy it when it happens.

Certainly our culture encourages us to put on a cheerful face. It may feel like we are forcing it, which nobody likes. We smear ourselves with cheerfulness and hope that nobody—including ourselves—notices that we aren't happy. Then we crave more. For example, we eat until our stomach hurts, or become so attached to our friend that the relationship falls apart. Because it isn't genuine, this kind of cheerfulness is difficult to maintain, as if we're covering up a deep wound.

On the other hand, sometimes we abstain from cheerfulness. We think that this will save us from feeling tricked or foolish when our cheerfulness comes to its inevitable end. We're convinced that it's better to be on the defense: life will always raise its painful, ugly head. When someone tells us to cheer up and we don't want to cheer up, it just makes us feel angrier.

Under such conditions, and because our moods change constantly, we might not understand that cheerfulness is in fact an inherent quality of mind. Within the meditative tradition, cheerfulness is considered to be the natural, harmonious, and wholesome expression of our truest self. In Tibetan it is known as *dekyi*—blissful, happy energy. Somebody who is cheerful in an unforced way seems to have an air of possibility, a light and fresh approach. This kind of cheerfulness helps the mind to move forward, beyond the distortion and torment of emotions.

Cheerfulness comes naturally with meditation. It is a quality of space created within the mind. When there's space in the mind, the mind relaxes, and we feel a simple sense of delight. We experience the possibility of living a life in which we aren't continuously bombarded by emotions, discursiveness, and concepts about the nature of things.

Lack of genuine cheerfulness is a result of claustrophobia in our mind and heart. There is simply too much going on; we feel overwhelmed and speedy. We were somehow under the impression that life was meant to be happy, and now we're getting the short end of the stick. The harder we try to contort reality into our fantasy of happiness, the less happy we are, and the more chaotic our mind seems.

On the path of meditation we take into account the harshness of life, and perpetually temper that with cheerfulness—not out of ignorance, but out of wisdom. Contemplating the truth of pain and suffering does not lead to depression. Rather, it helps us appreciate what we have, which is buddha-nature. All of us are naturally *buddha*, "awake." Knowing that we are all naturally awake brings delight.

In dark times like these when we feel even more burdened and insecure, we should be contemplating our true nature more than ever. It can cheer us up on any day. Despite all the ups and downs of our life, we are fundamentally awake individuals who have a natural ability to become compassionate and wise. Our nature is to be cheerful. This cheerfulness is deeper than temporary conditions. The day does not have to be sunny for us to be cheerful.

We can depend on random experiences to remind us of these truths, or we can go about it in a systematic way by engaging in a daily meditation practice. When we practice meditation, we are encouraging this natural state of cheerfulness. We don't have to regard meditating as a somber activity; we can think of it as sitting there and being cheerful. We are using a technique to build clarity, strength, and flexibility of mind. In training our mind in pliability and power, we're learning to relax, to loosen up, so that we can change our attitude on a dime. Strength of mind and pliancy are the causes and result of cheerfulness.

When we rise from our meditation seat, we can continue the practice of cheerfulness as we bring it forth into our day. When we're about to sink into a depression or indulge in discursiveness, we can entertain the notion that cheerfulness is an endless possibility, one that gives us the option of moving forward in any situation, instead of being oppressed by it.

"Always maintain only a joyful mind" is a famous slogan by a great Buddhist practitioner named Atisha, who developed many slogans for mind training. Even back in the eleventh century, being cheerful was a meditative path. This path and this training need to be rooted in reality. The reality is that underneath all the flickers of desire and all the dreams we use to fool ourselves into seeking temporary forms of happiness, our mind is clear and cheerful.

It's not that we always need to be cheerful, for there are times when cheerfulness in relationship to what's happening isn't appropriate. Obviously if somebody is hurt or sick, we would be insensitive to respond with cheerfulness.

Nor does cheerfulness require us to be constant cheerleaders. We can delight in just sitting there doing nothing. Going for a walk or eating a piece of fruit can be fulfilling experiences. We do not need to prove our cheerfulness again and again; it arises simply and naturally. We're happy to be alive. Having more money or more food is never going to replace that basic sense of delight.

In Tibet they say, "The joy of a king is no greater than the joy of a beggar." It isn't what we possess—it's what we enjoy. This means the experience of genuine cheerfulness cannot be bought or sold. What makes it genuinely cheerful is that we are free from fixation and attachment. We are free of having to depend on something else to make us happy. We can bask freely in the natural radiance of our mind. This is the equanimity of true cheerfulness—nothing more, nothing less.

It Would Be a Pity to Waste a Good Crisis

John Tarrant

Are we happy even if our map of what we would like to see isn't matching the reality before us? The Zen teacher and psychologist John Tarrant, who teaches using koans and stories, tells us that if we stop and take notice during the height of a crisis, we'll see that indeed we already are happy.

> We're all connected, and we find out how connected we are on days like this. We try to love our neighbors as we would love ourselves, but today we love our neighbors because we realize they are ourselves.
>
> —GOVERNOR DAVID A. PATERSON OF NEW YORK,
> *after the commuter plane crash in Buffalo in February* 2009

Student: "When times of great difficulty visit us, how should we greet them?"
Teacher: "Welcome."

A plane crashing in Buffalo punctuates a time in history in which crashes of all kinds are happening. Houses are worth less than is owed on them, mutual funds that went up in an orderly fashion fall off a precipice, offices lay everyone off with an hour's warning, large chain stores close their doors for good, the busy suburban hairdresser is empty on a Friday, and the hardware store is ominously quiet. Panicked reactions amplify the crisis—the vice president of the semiconductor company stops work on the half-constructed building while the production machinery is in transit on the high seas; the university declares a hiring freeze; and the clinic is threatened with shutting down entirely because it can't replace a receptionist who earns nine dollars an hour. And this all seems to happen very suddenly.

We play with dark fantasies to prepare ourselves for how it might be: "It's going to be hard, very hard, and there will be breadlines, and we will lose all the loot we have accumulated, and we will push shopping carts containing all our belongings, and then we'll die, slowly." Thus I have heard.

But wait a minute: winter is still cold, summer is still warm, bread and cheese and pickled onion is still a plowman's lunch, the sky still has windows of translucent distance at sunset after rain, a wet dog still smells like a wet dog. Perhaps we will be fine. Perhaps we don't have to waste this crisis in wailing and gnashing our teeth.

"You never want a serious crisis to go to waste. And what I mean by that is an opportunity to do things you think you could not do before," says White House Chief of Staff Rahm Emanuel.

The beginning of being fine is noticing how things really are, and in my case this comes from having a practice, from meditating, from noticing life without blame or outrage, or fear, and if there *is* blame or outrage, or fear, noticing *that* without blame, outrage, or fear. With such noticing, compassion enters.

Life Is Uncertain, Surprises Are Likely

Consciousness works by making maps, and there is always a gap between our maps and the territory of our lives. A surprise is a landscape feature that was not on my map. I have an idea I am one kind of person, with, say, a bank account, but it turns out I am another kind of person, without a bank account. Surprises are common and an indication that you are alive. I grew up with people who remembered the First World War; it started in August 1914, and everyone thought it would be over by Christmas. Instead it led to a century of wars. Wars do that. At the time, that was a surprise. After The War, there was the influenza pandemic—another surprise that took millions of lives. There have been positive surprises too. Vaccines were invented, banishing polio, saving my life, and antibiotics, also saving my life.

Our representations are fragile and based on poor data. The mind assigns value to events, saying "this is good" and "this is bad," but the values we give things are usually just arm waving and scrambling about. The world is truly unpredictable in its consequences, and our reactions to events are also unpredictable, even if we have a deep meditation practice.

We can make an ally of surprise. Meditation methods are not intended to make the world predictable, but they provide a space in which we can have our reactions without fighting with ourselves. And in the end, meditation resets the maps and opinions to zero. It overcomes the problem of James Joyce's Mr. Duffy, who "lived at a little distance from his body, regarding his own acts with doubtful side-glances."

Meditation is one thing we know that does work. When we meditate there is nothing else in the world, and whatever we have is enough.

IF YOU ARE ALIVE, THAT'S GOOD—LOWER THE BAR

In any predicament you can notice that you are alive. Considering the vastness of the universe this is an unlikely event, and you can rejoice and take delight in this occurrence, even if times are not hard and no stars are going nova in your neighborhood. Happiness is not really related to having a bank account; if it were, most of the world would be doomed to being unhappy. I have a friend who, for reasons mostly unrelated to foresight, drew her money out before the financial crash. I also have a friend who saw it coming and made money from it. I have another friend whose investment advisor put all his money in Bernard Madoff's Ponzi scheme and presumably lost it. I asked this last friend what the symptoms of money loss were, and he left a voice mail, "Well, I have a previously unsuspected interest in cooking and in fixing up the kitchen. And sometimes I wake in the middle of the night and my left leg is twitching. That's about it." When you really look at what your situation is, it is not what you might have thought. My friend who lost his money is not visibly more unhappy than the other friends. He has also found a more lively and amusing attitude to his work, perhaps because of the thought that he needs to earn replacement money.

The hard bits of life might not be the ones you are dreading. The good bits might be the ones that are always available—a slant of light through the garden and then the rain, running inside to get dry, cooking for friends, the sound of a bird in the early morning when you can't get back to sleep, the act of impulsively giving something away when you have almost nothing. When you are present in your own life, it extends infinitely in every direction.

IN A DARK PLACE YOU STILL HAVE WHAT REALLY COUNTS

The beauty and nobility of your life may be more visible to you if a dark contrast is available. A woman who was meditating with the koan at the head of this piece, the little conversation about hard times and saying "Welcome," was in an unusual situation. Her father was prosecuted for the murder of her mother, a death that happened decades ago and for which no resolution has been found. No one close to the situation believes her father did this. But someone with a grudge, and hearsay evidence, and a relative with dementia, and an eager prosecutor ... if it's a cliché that a prosecutor can get a grand jury to indict a ham sandwich, it becomes personal when you are related to the ham sandwich. The woman with the meditation practice noticed something unexpected though—she is happy, she's not outraged, and although people expect and even want her to be angry with the prosecutor, that is not what she feels. She gave counsel, and sympathy, and money for defense lawyers, but she didn't have to give her own emotional well-being. The intensity of the difficulty actually drove her to deeper practice and the world suddenly became very beautiful, not at an unspecified future date, when the situation will be resolved, but now, when nothing is resolved, or fair, or sensible—now, when it's now. Even the prosecutor's face glowed with light. "No one told me it would be like this," she said. Awakening might happen at any time, perhaps especially when we are convinced that something else is going on. That's a positive surprise, a benign catastrophe.

IF YOU ARE IN A PREDICAMENT, THERE WILL BE A GATE

In the main, koans are predicaments that you can use in case you don't have one lying around in your life. Usually of course you do have a predicament, since being human *is* a predicament. I might think that it's a bad thing to have lost something, but if I start from the current situation there will always be a doorway. When I meditate it's like calling out a spell in a forgotten language. The spell slowly traces the outlines of a door, making the way out visible, even in twilight, even in the darkest, most forgotten prison. When we lose money or get a diagnosis, we might decide that this is a bad thing, but we might be wrong. Uncertainty and the unknown are not things to endure; they are things to rely on. If you don't even consider winning or losing, there will always be a doorway.

When I had cancer, I thought it might be inconvenient or frightening, but it was interesting. It made me a lot less lazy about being present. There was a time when diagnosis, course of treatment, and outcome were all uncertain and, in that condition, my mind reached for certainty over and over again. That quest, being hopeless, brought pain. But when my mind stopped reaching out and fell back into the warm dark of uncertainty, time stretched out infinitely on either side and there was a pool of joy that seemed bottomless—joy in breathing, joy in hearing the birds in the cold before dawn. Having cancer was much more exciting than sitting in an armchair watching the game on Sunday. And everything I looked at had the aspect of tenderness and delicacy. I looked into the checkout clerk's eyes and saw the universe looking back.

What You Need Might Be Given to You

The dark can be warm and beautiful even if you are complicit in your situation. You don't have to be innocent. Lots of people used their houses as ATM machines in a fairly reckless manner—it seemed like a good idea at the time. There is nothing wrong with noticing this; transgression is a known path to wisdom. Taking drugs, clueless love affairs, gambling your money away with Wall Street—losing your grip can empty out your life enough for you to appreciate the kindness at the bottom of things. In the end we have to forgive the universe for the way we live in it, forgive it for the mistakes of our own learning.

We also have to trust our own responses. When I first sat with dying people, I was aware of how ignorant I was and that I didn't know the right thing to say or do. I didn't know whether to say "Go for the light," or to read aloud (as one of my friends does at such times) *The Tibetan Book of the Dead*, or to play Beethoven, or to meditate, or to tell a joke. And this wondering was just the nature of the mind fetching around, trying to find the right map. Actually, a map wasn't needed. I truly didn't know what to say, and if I didn't just make up some nonsense, words would float up out of the black lagoon of uncertainty, words that didn't seem like the sort of thing I could have thought up. And if nothing floated up, I could sit there. The important thing wasn't having the right answer; it was keeping company with a friend when neither of us knew where the journey was headed. That was a deeper meeting than I had planned for.

The True Life Is in between
Winning and Losing

Contradiction is the fully human place to be. The illegal immigrant can't go home because she won't get back into the country if she does. The Republican mayor of a small city who speaks out against illegal immigration gives her a job.

We don't have to pretend not to have our opinions. Mostly we would rather be rich than poor, but also, it isn't usually terrible to have lost our money. We can have a life in between those rather uninteresting discoveries. In between is where humans always are—that's what we have to welcome, a story with an uncertain ending. And this condition is interesting if you inhabit it; it's alive. If I'm facing something that I don't know how to do, the not knowing is what is true and the resources I have, deeply ignorant as I am, will have to be enough.

I have an amusing memory of being in between. I was on a trawler steaming up the coast toward Townsville in North Queensland with a storm starting to come in. It wasn't bad yet; it was three-quarters of a gale but increasing. Visibility was good. We were rolling a lot, but then we always did with a sea running. We were loaded with prawns, and we thought we were rich, rich. So you can see the way the mind swings around: it's good we have prawns, it's bad the storm is coming, it's good the storm isn't here yet, it's bad we are nowhere near port—the whole human story.

We came upon another boat in the fleet. He had taken a wave over the stern, and his cockpit filled and wasn't draining. The boat was now more down at the stern than was really desirable with weather coming in. He was trying to bail, but his stern was low enough that water kept washing in. He could probably solve the problem by throwing his catch overboard, but hell, he wasn't going to do that. He had pawned his guitar and slipped out of port at night ahead of the bailiffs; he wasn't going to surrender those prawns. He was alone, without a deckhand, and there was some discussion on the radio about whether I would swim over to his boat to help out. I wasn't that thrilled at the prospect. Although the water was warm, which was positive, there were sharks, which was probably a negative. But perhaps they weren't tiger sharks, a positive, if true. Also, from his point of view, if I came on board, would he have to pay me a share? And would his boat sink anyway? He was clearly overloaded. The situation looked pretty sketchy.

Then he beached his trawler on a sandbar, where through some peculiarity the wave action wasn't so bad. He was grounded and trying to pump out his cockpit, and it came to me—everybody was completely, deliriously happy. Will he lose his boat? Will I swim over? Are there really sharks? Should I swim over? How much will we get for our catch? How far over will we go on this roll? Everybody was as interested as it is possible to be, as interested as angels would be, watching over the pretty earth. We were delighted to be there wallowing along with our very own predicament. It was funny and it was also a moment of insight—the Buddhist word is *prajna*, the wisdom that cuts through delusions and leads to a natural appreciation and compassion. Not only *can* we be happy in our difficulties, but if we really truly notice, we *are* happy already.

It's important not to discount the idea that in a crisis, you might be having the time of your life.

If You Have Nothing—Give It Away

It rained in the night and I thought I was the rain. When I woke I had many things to do, but I lay there and listened. It was an eternal moment. And when I got up I saw the drops on the deck in the dawn and watched them. The child of the house where I am staying woke up and ran downstairs and jumped into my arms. We kept watching the rain. Nothing else was happening and it was enough.

All of history is here now whatever we are doing. Our minds think we are the rain, and then that we are the little boy, jumping; our minds think we are each other. It's not so hard to give ourselves completely to the world in this way. And when difficulty visits us, perhaps we will see more clearly that we can look after each other, and that, if we have little, we can be more generous than we were when we thought we had a lot. Helping each other might be more fun than guarding our loot.

In Buddhism that is called the bodhisattva path, in which we want everyone to share in the joy of understanding. This path comes from losing things more than from gaining things.

If you lose everything, you may also be lucky enough to lose who you thought you were, along with any fear and despair that goes with that identity. It might be that what we have to learn is to play in the world like someone who really did run away to join the circus when she thought about it as a child. We are part of something vast, and generosity is an effortless consequence of discovering that. We give away in our turn what we have discovered and what we have been given.

Grounded Improvisation

Joan Sutherland

*Over the long haul, says the American Zen teacher Joan Sutherland, we
need to develop binocular vision: one eye aware of how things are coming
and going all the time, the other aware of how they've never moved.*

Something remarkable happened to the national mood in the
United States recently: people have been able to hold two contradic-
tory feelings—elation and sobriety—at the same time. This was un-
mistakable around the time of Barack Obama's inauguration, which
happened just after the collapse of the economy. The general uplift of
one event didn't cover over the anxiety of the other, and the anxiety
didn't cause most people to hedge their bets on the uplift. Equally
remarkable, during inauguration week millions of people moved
spontaneously into public spaces to share the experience together—
not just on the Mall in Washington, where the ceremony took place,
but in city squares, pubs, meditation halls, and friends' living rooms.
Americans who by and large had retreated into their private lives in
recent years were suddenly pouring back into the commons.

These shifts in mood—a capacity to tolerate paradox and a
resurgence of fellow-feeling—coupled with a new administration
that values inquiry, empathy, and reality-based decision-making

are encouraging given the challenges we face. We have a chance to radically change course, together and as individuals. We've apparently decided to value both experience and innovation, and to see what happens when we bring them together. Maybe it's time for a little grounded improvisation.

This isn't the first time we've faced hard times, nor is it likely to be the last. The old philosophical and spiritual teachings are the voices of our elder kin, offering their best advice about what to do when things get tough. Across the generations, they connect us to the vast mystery play of human life, reminding us that people have faced circumstances like this before and have even gotten wisdom out of them. That's the grounded part.

At the same time, and here's where improvisation comes in, some important things have changed over the millennia. In the famous parable of the mustard seed from early Buddhist literature, a woman is overcome with grief at the death of her child. The Buddha says that he will bring the child back to life if she brings him a mustard seed from a house in the village that hasn't experienced loss. Of course, she can't find such a house. From our perspective, those times had a kind of innocence: the world was bounded by the village; if you knew what was happening with your neighbors, you had a whole philosophy of life. Now the images and stories of villagers from all over the world appear in our homes, knocking at our hearts for their share of our concern. And in industrialized nations, it's as if the country were hooked up to a bank of ICU monitors whose readings are beamed instantaneously to every citizen: the state of the stock market and Senate votes are reported in real time on the television screen, news alerts flash across our e-mail and text messages, everyone's got an instant opinion and a media outlet to express it.

We know so much more, in so much greater detail and so much more quickly, about events in our own countries and all around the world than humans ever have, than either our nervous systems or our hearts have evolved to handle. So how do we handle it? How do we draw on the wisdom and the practices that people have been using in difficult times forever, and at the same time acknowledge that there's something different about this time, and make the adaptations we need?

We can begin by recognizing that, under modern conditions, it's natural to feel worried, overwhelmed, outraged, or despairing at such a time. Meditation and similar practices are for moving us deeper into life, to face whatever happens with as clear a mind, open a heart, and willing a pair of hands as possible, and so it would be strange not to feel those things. "I am sick because the whole world is sick," the great lay Buddhist Vimalakirti said a long time ago. Feeling unease in an uneasy world just means you're paying attention; the difficulty comes when you think you shouldn't be feeling that way. Then you're in a fight with life, for being life in all its uncontrollable complexity, and with your own heart-mind for reacting to it. The focus shifts from a direct engagement with the way things are to something more self-centered: how to stop yourself from feeling this way, or how to change the circumstances so they don't make you feel this way.

It's actually helpful to start with accepting the situation as it is. You're more likely to discover a useful response to the situation if you have a less self-centered and therefore more realistic view of things. At times the anger or despair we feel about something is a way of avoiding or taking a break from the fear and sorrow underneath, and so another aspect of having a more realistic view is acknowledging our inner states as well as the outer circumstances. Then sorrow and fear are included as part of the situation and not reasons to turn away from it.

That's the up-close, village view of a crisis—what it's like as it's happening. It helps to have a big, horizon-wide view, too. During the inauguration, Martin Luther King Jr.'s words resounded: "The arc of the moral universe is long, but it bends toward justice." To see that is to be more at ease with the fact that we're not there yet, that the human mystery play is a work in progress. Too often it can break our hearts, how short we fall, but part of the big view is that we're all in this together, all of us awakening together—slowly, sometimes painfully, but on the way. All those smiling and tear-streaked faces on the Mall in January reminded us that a big view is aware of the long arc of things and of how many of us are walking it together. This is what "grounded" means: rooted in history, rooted in each other, rooted in eternity.

The ancestors grappled with how to join the neighborhood view of a crisis and the horizon-wide view of what a big landscape the neighborhood sits in. In mid-eighth-century China, a serious rebellion ushered in a decade of civil war, famine, and disease so devastating that two out of three Chinese died. In the blink of an eye, China went from being one of the greatest empires the world had ever seen to a devastated country whose population had shrunk by two-thirds. A kind of order was eventually restored, but it would be centuries before the nation fully recovered.

The poet Du Fu was trapped in the city where the rebellion took place, and he wrote a poem called "The View This Spring" about what it was like. The poem contains two spare lines that sum it all up:

> The nation is destroyed,
> mountains and rivers remain.

Some Chan (Chinese Zen) practitioners saw what Du Fu saw, from their own perspective: in our world things are always getting broken and mended and broken again, and there is also something that never breaks. Everything rises and falls, and yet in exactly the same moment things are eternal and aren't going anywhere at all. How do we see with a kind of binocular vision, one eye aware of how things are coming and going all the time, the other of how they've never moved? How do we experience this not as two separate ways of seeing, but as one seamless field of vision?

A few Chan innovators had the big-horizon view, but they also recognized that they were facing unprecedented times that cried out for unprecedented, immediate responses. They wanted to leap out of the usual ways of doing things and into new territory—not to escape the catastrophe looming around them, but to more fully meet it. If they were going to be helpful they had to develop, and quickly, flexibility of mind, an easy relationship with the unknown, and a robust willingness to engage with life as they found it. They had to become improvisers.

One of them, Great Master Ma, said that "a person bathing in the great ocean uses all the waters that empty into it." Wherever we find ourselves, whatever we're faced with, that's the Way. There are no detours from the Way; we can't lose our Way. To engage and entangle ourselves with whomever and whatever we meet, to care about them, to throw our lot in with them—that is the Way. Every moment, every circumstance, is another chance to experience things as they are, rather than as we wish or fear them to be.

It's the same with our inner landscapes. Ma famously said that ordinary mind is the Way. We don't reject our thoughts and feelings; even, maybe especially, the mind that doesn't understand is exactly "it." At such a time, maybe not getting it is the most realistic position. Anyone who claims to have an explanation for what's going on, from a metaphysical or conspiratorial or any other perspective, probably doesn't, and is limiting the field out of which improvisation might come. In unprecedented times, no one is an expert yet, and anyone might become one.

It's a good time to be asking questions and to appreciate the ordinary mind's talent for grounding itself in cooking a warm breakfast on a cold day and researching what it would take to become carbon-neutral. It's a good time to turn off the national ICU monitors for an afternoon or a month and read a really old book or go look at some petroglyphs or sit in an old-growth forest. In other words, it's a good time to widen and deepen the field out of which improvisation might come.

There is a unity between our inner lives and the outer world, a continuum that only appears to be separated into factions that are sometimes in conflict. Turn too far toward your own heart-mind and you become self-obsessed; turn too far in the other direction and you burn out. Bring an attitude of warmth and curiosity to both, and the Way begins to open on its own. This is what Ma called living a natural life according to the times. Be part of what's going on around you, and "just wear clothes, eat food, always uphold the way of the bodhisattva." We might think: Oh sure, clothes, food, way of the bodhisattva—nothing to it, right? Just so, according to Shitou, another of the great Chinese teachers of the time. "Your essential mind is absolutely still and completely whole, and its ability to respond to circumstances is limitless."

When we open out into the big view, we rest in this fundamental wholeness, whatever else is going on. From there we're free from the illusion that what we're capable of is determined solely by our individual will. Put that down and things get big and alive. Our essential mind isn't bounded by our skull, and our capacity to respond isn't either. This aspect of realization has everything to do with relationship: We feel more whole and at peace and able to respond because we know we're part of something very large. Remembering this even some of the time can make a huge difference; it can make us bold.

Many people feel that we're entering uncharted waters with our economy and our ecology. As in Ma and Shitou's time, some of what we already know will continue to be helpful, a lot of it won't, and we'll often feel desperately inadequate to the work ahead of us. In eighth-century China, how did people get up every morning and pitch in, knowing that they wouldn't be able to feed the vast majority of starving people or restore most of the ravaged land? The kindly, implacable Ma told them to go out and "benefit what cannot be benefited, do what cannot be done." His words were a particularly Chan form of encouragement: just because something is impossible, don't let that stop you. Put down your despair and your hope, begin from no position at all, and look for what becomes possible when you do.

I have two quotes over my desk: that one from Ma, next to Eleanor Roosevelt's, "Most of the work in the world is done by people who aren't feeling very well that day." These words encourage and console me, reminding me that doing what cannot be done *gets* done by people with all the ordinary human frailties. It gets done by us. For the times when we really get stuck and can't find a way through, Ma suggested that we make ourselves into a raft for others. The old teachers didn't offer any blueprints for constructing such a raft, because it would be different in every situation; we have to improvise. But when we're well and thoroughly stuck, if we help others to discover a way across, they'll bring us along. Eleanor Roosevelt's life of service also turned out to be her way through a desperate personal unhappiness.

One of Ma's heirs said that his teacher taught him two crucial things: First, that each of us is already endowed with the treasure of everything we need. Our enlightenment is already here, as is our kindness and our curiosity and our courage. Second, each of us is free to use that treasure to respond to the life around us. Our freedom to fall willingly into the frightened, blasted, beautiful, tender world, just as it is, is already here. To know for ourselves that we have this treasure and are free to use it, no matter the circumstances—that's grounded improvisation. Ma's heir called it a happy life.

The Natural State of Happiness

Chokyi Nyima Rinpoche

*One of the foremost living exponents of the Buddhist tradition known
as the Great Perfection, or Dzogchen, Chokyi Nyima Rinpoche asks us
to seriously investigate our assumptions about what constitutes happiness.
If we do, he says, we'll come to find "unconditioned suchness," an
effortless state of contentment, compassion, and simple joy.*

We all know, intellectually at least, that the Buddha's dharma is
not merely a topic of study, nor is it simply something to be practiced on our meditation cushions. But as we hurry through our daily
lives, it is easy to forget that the quality of formal practice is inti-
mately tied to the quality of our minds, moment to moment. Practitioners of all levels can benefit from instructions on how to enrich
their own lives and the lives of others by cultivating five noble qualities that are within reach of us all: contentment, rejoicing, forgiveness, good heart, and mindfulness.

The basic nature of our mind is essentially good. The Buddha
taught that all beings are buddhas covered by momentary obscurations; when those obscurations are removed, they are real buddhas.

The true identity of every sentient being, not just human beings, is a state of unconditioned suchness. This is the basic nature as it is, pure and perfect. We have an inherent capacity to care for others and to understand; it's not a product of education or upbringing. To practice the dharma means simply to develop and nurture these intrinsic qualities. That is our task, our responsibility.

According to the Buddhist approach to spirituality, the ability to care includes both loving-kindness and compassion. We aim to cultivate loving-kindness and compassion until they are boundless, totally free from partiality. The ability to understand, when developed to its utmost, is called "the wisdom that realizes egolessness," an insight that sees the fact that the self, or the personal identity, has no real existence.

There are many conventional methods for infinitely expanding our kindness and compassion and realizing the true view. *Contentment*, for instance, the first noble quality, is a valuable asset not only for so-called spiritual people but for everyone. Discontentment ruins every chance for happiness and well-being, but true happiness is immediately present in a moment of feeling content and satisfied. From today on, no matter what, try to appreciate whatever you have: the comfort of your home, the pleasure of your possessions, and the goodness in the people close to you. Happiness is already present and accessible to each and every one of us.

Often when imagining what it takes to make us feel happy, we see some other place or object that we haven't managed to possess: *I'm just about to. I'm on my way there. I can achieve it, I simply haven't yet.* As long as fulfillment is at a distance, we will remain unfulfilled. When we do not get what we want, we are not happy. Ironically, once we do get what we seek, it's not that satisfying and we still are not happy. The grass is always greener on the other side.

We all know that those who have nothing suffer. It is understandable; they are hungry and they have lots of other problems. They may be too hot or too cold. But who is truly happy?

We need to seriously investigate whether people who have fame, power, and wealth are happy and whether those who have nothing are always unhappy. When we look into this, we see that happiness is not based on objects but on one's mental state. For that reason, those who are truly happy are the ones who appreciate what they have. Whenever we are content, in that moment, we are fulfilled. The teachings of the Buddha are common sense.

On one hand, it's very simple: we are all searching for happiness. How do we become happy without a big effort? Whenever we appreciate what we have, we are happy. That effort is an intelligent technique. We might have a very simple life, but still we can think, *This flower is lovely*, or, *This water is good*. If we are too picky, thinking this is wrong and that's wrong, then nothing is ever perfect. We need to learn how to be content so that whatever we have is precious, real, and beautiful. Otherwise, we might be chasing one mirage after another.

The second noble quality is *rejoicing*. Our basic goodness is obscured by negative emotions. The Buddha said that there are eighty-four thousand types of negative emotions, but among these, there are two in particular that often cause problems because they are quite difficult to notice: pride and envy. Envy is one of our biggest, most unnecessary types of mental suffering. If someone else's life is better than ours, we become jealous, angry, and disappointed. It can sometimes make us very uneasy: our food loses its flavor, we have trouble sleeping, and our blood pressure can go up. Rejoicing is the second intelligent remedy to all this useless self-torture. We can mentally share in other people's happiness. Is there any easier way to attain happiness?

The third noble quality is *forgiveness*, which is very important. Pride can be quite powerful. Even in moments when we are loving and caring, if we're not getting along with someone and our heart is saying, "The best thing to do is just forgive," behind that voice there is another one saying, "No, don't. You are right. You did nothing wrong." Pride constantly prevents us from forgiving others, an act that is so healthy and beautiful.

Forgiving and apologizing have the power to completely heal rifts, but we need to understand how and when to apply them. If we try too early, the situation might still be volatile. We need to find the proper moment, and once we've done that, we should be careful about the words we choose, the tone of our voice, and even the physical gestures and facial expressions we make. Each of these has a lot of power, and if one of them is off, we won't be that effective. If, on the other hand, we can express an apology in a heartfelt way, we will always be able to achieve peace, respect, and mutual understanding.

Most important of all is to have a *good heart*, which is the fourth noble quality. Like everything else, in order to have a good heart we need to investigate until we are clear about what true well-being actually is, both in the temporary and long-term sense. Happiness and well-being come not only from loving-kindness and compassion but also from an insight into the true view of reality, because someone who fully recognizes reality becomes a *tathagata*, or fully awakened one. Conversely, the sources of suffering are hate, craving, and closed-mindedness. These three are the roots from which all our troubles grow.

By "true view," I mean knowing the nature of things exactly as they are: the basic, essential nature of "what is." This insight has to do with how we experience things. Everything that appears to us seems real and solid but in fact is only a mere impression of something that occurs as a result of causes and conditions. In and of themselves, things do not possess even a shred of solid existence. This is why the Buddha taught that all phenomena are emptiness while occurring in dependent connection. Hence, it is good to study the twelve links of dependent origination, both external and internal. This will enable us to see that mind is of primary importance; everything depends on it. Whatever is experienced, felt, or perceived is dependent on mind—on an experiencer experiencing something, observing it, knowing it.

Why would the Buddha say that all sentient beings are confused or bewildered? Was it because sentient beings really are confused? It could be that the Buddha was mistaken and that all sentient beings are not confused. We need to investigate this point, because one of the two parties is definitely mistaken. The Buddha also said, "Don't take my words at face value." If they are wrong then we should speak up. We are allowed to examine the Buddha's words for ourselves and to question whether or not he was wrong.

Let's take an example. The Buddha said that all formed things are impermanent and unreal. However, we have the instinctive feeling that things are actually real and permanent. He really challenged us. He said that we haven't bothered to look closely; we haven't questioned our own beliefs. When we do, we discover that things are not really as they seem. Things are re-formed again and again, moment by moment, by causes and circumstances. When we start to carefully investigate and dissect objects, we also see that they are made out of smaller and smaller parts: molecules, atoms, more and more minute particles. If people bothered to explore in this way, they would find that even the atom does not really exist.

In the *Root Verses of the Middle Way*, the great master Nagarjuna wrote that since the formed cannot be found to exist, the unformed couldn't possibly exist either. He also said that samsara is merely our thinking. When we are free of thought, that is real freedom.

The discovery of the unconditioned natural state involves a process of learning, reflection, and meditation training. The most important of these three is meditation. We hear about all different styles of spiritual practice—such as meditating, visualizing, and reciting mantras—but we must understand that there is only one purpose to all these endeavors: improving ourselves. This means allowing our basic goodness to manifest.

To achieve this we need to apply the teachings in daily life. The first step toward developing kindness is *mindfulness*, making our minds as calm and clear as possible, which is the fifth noble quality. This is something we can practice every day, wherever we are, whatever we are doing. We need to be aware each and every moment. What are we saying? What are we thinking? How are we moving about? Be aware moment by moment, before moving the body, before speaking, and also while moving and speaking; then afterward remain aware, asking, what did I say or do?

There are many types of meditation training, but they all fall into one of two categories: the first is deliberate meditation with effort, and the second is practicing being completely effortless, free of conceptual focus. The most profound and truest meditation is the training in complete effortlessness, but it is not our habit to be that way. We are pretty much in the groove of being deliberate, in using effort, whether mental, verbal, or physical. Unconditioned suchness, which is our natural state, transcends every type of mental construct and is effortless. Learning, reflection, and meditation are very important because we need to recognize our true basic state. Through listening and learning we become familiar with the teachings, and through reflection we become convinced of their truth and develop certainty. Learning and reflecting are definitely deliberate and require a lot of effort, but they are essential.

In order to be brought face to face with unconditioned suchness, our basic nature exactly as it is, there are two factors that are very helpful, but they are not easy to acquire. One is boundless love and compassion; whenever love is almost overwhelming, when kindness and compassion are unwavering, there is a moment available for you to realize the unconditioned natural state. The other is sincere devotion to and unshakeable pure perception of the unconditioned natural state. From this spontaneously arises a respect for and pure perception of those who have realized the unconditioned natural state and have the capacity to reveal it to others. This also includes a pure appreciation of anyone who really practices and trains in the Buddhist teachings.

In a nutshell, the real Buddhist practice is to try our best to bring forth in all beings the true sources of happiness and well-being—boundless love and compassion and the unmistaken realization of the natural state, the unconditioned innate nature—while at the same time removing the causes of suffering, which are craving, hate, and closed-mindedness. That is what it really means to have a good heart.

Love and compassion can be expanded until they become boundless, genuine, and impartial, making no distinctions between friend, enemy, and stranger. We must continue in our efforts until we have removed even the slightest obstacle to our love and compassion. Only when our love and compassion have become boundless will they be truly effortless.

Meanwhile, our perseverance should be joyous and spontaneous. Such perseverance springs from our awareness of the unconditioned natural state, therefore it is not merely an admiration, yearning, or longing. As your comprehension of the profound nature becomes stronger and grows deeper, you develop a confident trust. Spontaneous, effortless compassion begins to blossom as you continue to train after having truly recognized the natural state as it actually is. Sincere compassion radiates from the deepest part of your heart. You can't help it; it just naturally springs forth.

Before becoming aware of this natural state, we are bewildered, creating painful states all the time, but by continually training in this, we recognize that beneath everything is an unconditioned natural state. We start to notice that every selfish emotion begins to soften and subside of its own accord. As pain and worry diminish, our confused way of experiencing subsides more and more. Then we begin to really understand how other beings feel. You may ask yourself: What can I do to help them? If I don't help them, who will? This is when real compassion overtakes you and a sincere, unchangeable devotion begins to grow within you. We call this the dawn of irreversible or unshakeable confidence.

True confidence begins with a trust in the instruction that reveals this nature. Once you have experienced firsthand that it works, of course you feel confident. This also is directed to the source of the instructions, the one from whom you received them. You are grateful to him or her, as well as to the entire lineage of transmission through which the instruction came to be passed on to you. That is true devotion. These two, effortless compassion and unchangeable devotion, join forces so that your training quickly grows deeper and deeper. Your practice is strengthened to the point that it is unshakeable, like when a strong gust of wind causes a huge fire with plenty of firewood to blaze even higher.

The great master Atisha wondered what it meant to be really learned and concluded that real wisdom is to understand egolessness. Those with true ethics are those who have tamed or softened their own heart; whenever that is the case and somebody actually cares, is watchful and conscientious, they are demonstrating real ethics. What is the foremost virtue? Atisha said it is to have a profound sense of caring for the benefit and well-being of others. What is the foremost sign of success or accomplishment? Not clairvoyance or miraculous powers but, rather, having fewer selfish emotions. These may sound like just a few simple sentences, but they are very profound and of great benefit when you take them to heart.

Putting Others in the Center

Dzigar Kongtrül Rinpoche

When we put others at the center of our lives, says Dzigar Kongtrül Rinpoche, our natural desire for happiness is liberated from self-centeredness. We discover the open and generous heart of the Buddha.

Our human search for happiness and freedom from suffering expresses itself in everything we do. We emerge from the womb with a primordial instinct to find comfort through suckling our mother's milk. Our instinct for fulfillment drives us—it is not something we need to cultivate. Throughout our countless lifetimes, we have searched for happiness and freedom from pain. We have always been sentient; therefore, we have always had this longing. It lies at the very core of our being.

Animals long for happiness, too. We see it in their propensity to frolic. Play doesn't simply fulfill an evolutionary function; it is an expression of pleasure and joy. As human beings, we understand the joy and freedom that comes from play. We also witness animals' desire for freedom from suffering. Animals fight for survival: their lives consist of trying to protect themselves from predators; they move in herds, hide in their shells, or fly off when afraid. When they are kept in tight cages, mistreated, or face slaughter, animals cry out in pain.

The natural principle that all beings long for happiness and freedom from suffering serves as the basis for generating compassion. The longing that we share with other beings makes empathy possible—it allows us to identify with their pain and their joy. According to the Buddhist view, this natural principle defines positive and negative actions by virtue of how they cause happiness and pain, rather than by morals based on ideas remote from our experience. The path of *bodhichitta*—the wish for others' temporal and ultimate happiness—rests upon this fundamental principle.

A CHANGE OF FOCUS

The longing for happiness and freedom from suffering expresses the great natural potential of mind, which can turn us toward our innate positivity and wisdom. Yet we may wonder why, since we have so much longing for happiness, joy is not a consistent experience. We may wonder why we feel like a victim of our own mind and emotions so much of the time. Why is it we are never able to completely fulfill or meet this longing, no matter what we do?

This longing remains unfulfilled because we try to centralize it—to territorialize it and use it to serve only ourselves. Day in and day out we tend to the self. In countless ways we try to use the world to cherish and protect only ourselves: we want to be liked; we want to be loved, to feel cozy, admired, appreciated, embraced, cherished, stimulated, noticed, respected, saved, rescued. When we centralize our longing for happiness, everything that happens around us happens in relation to *me*. If something good happens to someone else, it is always in relation to *me*. If something bad happens to someone else, it always happens in relation to *me*. Even when we love someone, it is all in relation to *me*.

If happiness could be achieved through self-cherishing, we would certainly be happy by now. But when everything is in reference to "me," we naturally become victims of our own aggression, attachments, and fears. How can we succeed in living our lives according to our preferences in the face of the natural laws of change and unpredictability? Since we truly have so little control in this respect, the only logical result of focusing on "me" is to feel distraught, fearful, and anxious.

Happiness requires that we change our focus. Changing focus doesn't mean we have to get rid of the mind; we don't need to change the basic makeup of the mind at all. We simply need to honor the fundamental principle of putting others in the center by including others in our wish for happiness, rather than focusing solely on ourselves. Self-care is always there. When we balance self-care with care for others, we reduce our fears and anxieties. Self-service is always there; all our wants and "unwants" are always there. Expanding our thinking to include others' wants and others' freedoms, we begin to move toward a happiness that does not rely on the conditions and preferences of self-care.

When we put others in the center, tenderness wells up from within. We feel grateful to others—witnessing their suffering brings us out of the rotten cocoon we sleep in. It makes us a little bit fearless, a little bit accepting, a little bit willing to let go of the constricted sense of self we hold on to. This kind of empathy changes the whole atmosphere of mind. It is the purest form of happiness. The sutras ask, where do the buddhas come from? And the answer in the sutras is, they come from ego. What does this mean? This means that realization comes from our ability to expand our sense of self-care and longing for happiness to include others. This is the business of a bodhisattva.

DECENTRALIZING SELF

The idea of putting others in the center sounds good but, as a practice, may feel contrived. As much as we want to expand our heart to include others, we can't simply leap into a state of compassion and loving-kindness when, in our attempts at self-preservation, we recoil from the experience of our own pain. True happiness cannot be found through the avoidance of pain. We can't decentralize our longing for happiness when we desperately hold on to our own well-being. The tendency to constrict the heart is driven by habit and motivated by fear. It is a deep-rooted and visceral experience. We can feel it in our bodies. It follows us like a shadow.

Shutting out suffering is an extremely dangerous non-dharmic act, because through our aversion we exclude the full experience of mind. We deny impermanence and attempt to keep things in control; we ignore the truth. In short, we can't relax and let things be. In the act of abandoning the truth through rejection, we individuate ourselves from everything around us. In doing so, we don't allow ourselves a bigger, expanded experience that includes our world and the other beings in it.

Ironically, we shrink from a pain that doesn't actually exist. We speak about the *truth* of suffering only in that we experience it. But what is suffering really, when we stop trying to push it away? This kind of questioning needs to be the theme of our lives. We need to take delight in working with our fears. We need to study them and ask ourselves, "What am I so afraid of? Why do I need to protect myself?" We may be afraid to shed our burden because we don't know what will happen. Suffering seems to define our lives. Can we imagine a life without it?

The purpose of all practices on the Buddhist path is to decentralize this notion of a solid, independent "self." This does not mean that we stop functioning as an individual, that we forget our name and wander about aimlessly like a zombie. It means we stop relating to everything in a way that aims only at preserving or cherishing ourselves. When we begin to question the autonomy of "me," the constricted self begins to disperse, which is another way of saying that our ignorance begins to dissolve and we move toward wisdom. Putting others in the center is a powerful method for decentralizing the self. When the self expands to include others, exclusivity is overwhelmed by compassion in the same way that darkness disperses in sunlight.

The practice of putting others in the center is not simply a crusade to do "good." It is a practice based on the understanding that our own happiness is inextricably linked with the happiness of others. We understand that the longing we all have for happiness and freedom from suffering can be a curse or a blessing, depending solely on our focus.

How to Rule

Chögyam Trungpa Rinpoche

In the classic Shambhala: The Sacred Path of the Warrior, *Chögyam Trungpa Rinpoche presented a view of living simply and with great dignity that he inherited from his training in Tibet. In this excerpt, he speaks of the world having a "natural hierarchy" and of finding our place within it, following the rhythms of the seasons of our life—including winters of want and need. Survival and celebration do not need to be in conflict in our life when we appreciate our simple existence as a decent human being. With that realization, we discover that we can live our life as a monarch ruling a kingdom of wealth and richness.*

The warrior's journey of discovering the natural hierarchy of reality and his place in that world is both exalted and very simple. It is simple, because it is so immediate and touching. It is touching your origin—your place in this world, the place you came from and the place you belong. It is as if you were taking a long walk through the woods at twilight. You hear the sounds of birds and catch a glimpse of the fading light in the sky. You see a crescent moon and clusters of stars. You appreciate the freshness of the greenery and the beauty of wild flowers. In the distance dogs are barking, children are crying, and occasionally you hear the sound of a car or truck making its journey on the highway. As the wind begins to blow on your cheeks, you smell the freshness of the woodlands, and perhaps you startle an occasional rabbit or bird as you pass them by. As twilight goes on, memories of your husband, your wife, your children, your grandparents, your world, come back to you. You remember your first schoolroom, where you learned to spell and read and write. You remember tracing the letters *i* and *o, m* and *a.* You are walking in the forest of the *dralas* (the elemental, magical quality of reality that could almost be said to exist as entitities), but still there is a feeling that this woodland is surrounded by other living human beings. Yet, when you listen, you hear only the sound of your own footsteps— right, left, right, left, a crackle when you step on a dry twig.

When you walk into this world of reality, the greater or cosmic world, you will find the way to rule your world—but, at the same time, you will also find a deep sense of aloneness. It is possible that this world could become a palace or a kingdom to you, but as its king or queen, you will be a monarch with a broken heart. It is not a bad thing to be, by any means. In fact, it is the way to be a decent human being— and beyond that a glorious human being who can help others.

This kind of aloneness is painful, but at the same time, it is beautiful and real. Out of such painful sadness, a longing and a willingness to work with others will come naturally. You realize that you are unique. You see that there is something good about being you as yourself. Because you care for yourself, you begin to care for others who have nurtured your existence or have made their own journey of warriorship, paving the way for you to travel this path. Therefore, you feel dedication and devotion to the lineage of warriors, brave people, whoever they have been, who have made this same journey. And at the same time, you begin to care for all those who have yet to take this path. Because you have seen that it is possible for you, you realize that you can help others to do the same.

You begin to see that there are seasons in your life in the same way as there are seasons in nature. There are times to cultivate and create, when you nurture your world and give birth to new ideas and ventures. There are times of flourishing and abundance, when life feels in full bloom, energized and expanding. And there are times of fruition, when things come to an end. They have reached their climax and must be harvested before they begin to fade. And finally, of course, there are times that are cold and cutting and empty, times when the spring of new beginnings seems like a distant dream. Those rhythms in life are natural events. They weave into one another as day follows night, bringing, not messages of hope and fear, but messages of how things *are.* If you realize that each phase of your life is a natural occurrence, then you need not be swayed, pushed up and down by the changes in circumstance and mood that life brings. You find that you have an opportunity to be fully in the world at all times and to show yourself as a brave and proud individual in any circumstance.

Normally, there appears to be a conflict between survival and celebration. Survival, taking care of your basic needs, is based on pragmatism, exertion, and often drudgery. Celebration, on the other hand, is often connected with extravagance and doing something beyond your means. The notion of ruling your world is that you can live in a dignified and disciplined way, without frivolity, and at the same time enjoy your life. You can combine survival and celebration. The kingdom that you are ruling is your own life: it is a householder's kingdom. Whether or not you have a husband or wife and children, still there is a structure and pattern to your daily life. Many people feel that the regularity of life is a constant imposition. They would like to have a different life, or a different menu, every second, at every meal. It is necessary to settle down somewhere and work at having a regular, disciplined life. The more discipline that occurs, however, the more joyous life can be. So the pattern of your life can be a joyous one, a celebration, rather than obligation alone. That is what it means to rule the kingdom of your life.

The notion of kingdom here is that your life is potentially wealthy and good. There is a great deal of misunderstanding about wealth. Generally being wealthy is viewed as meaning that you have lots of money, but the real meaning of wealth is knowing how to create a goldlike situation in your life. That is to say, you may have only twenty dollars in your bank account, but you can still manifest richness in your world.

Interestingly, if you are lost in the desert, without food and water, even if you have lots of gold in your pack, you can't eat it and you can't drink it, so you are still starved and parched. That is analogous to what happens to many people who have money. They have no idea how to eat it and how to drink it. Once I heard a story about an Indian chief who struck oil on his property and became rich. He decided to buy twenty basins and bath taps at once as a sign of his wealth. People can spend thousands of dollars and still be dissatisfied and in tremendous pain. Even with all that supposed wealth, they may still be unable to enjoy a simple meal.

True wealth does not come about automatically. It has to be cultivated; you have to earn it. Otherwise, even if you have lots of money, you will still be starved. So if you want to rule your world, please don't think that means you have to spend a great deal of money. Rather, true wealth comes from using manpower, individual power. If your suit has lots of lint, don't send it to the cleaners right away— clean it yourself. That is much less expensive, and also more dignified. You put your own energy and effort into caring for your world. The key to wealth, or the golden key, is appreciating that you can be poor—or I should say, unmoneyed—and still feel good, because you have a sense of wealthiness in any case, already. That is the wonderful key to richness and the first step in ruling: appreciating that wealth and richness come from being a basically decent human being. You do not have to be jealous of those who have more, in an economic sense, than you do. You can be rich even if you are poor.

That twist is a very interesting one and very powerful in terms of how to deal with world problems. Too often the politics of this world are based on poverty. If people are poor, they want to take money or resources away from those who have more. And if people are wealthy—in the sense of having money—then they want to hold on to what they have, because they think that giving up some of their money will make them impoverished. With that mentality on both sides, it is difficult to imagine any fundamental change taking place.

Or if it does take place, it is based on tremendous hatred and violence, because both sides are hanging on so tightly to what they think is important.

Of course, if you are starving, then what you want is food. In fact, food is what you need. But the genuine desires of those who are in need can be ruthlessly manipulated. War based on grasping has happened over and over again in this world. People with money have been willing to sacrifice thousands of human lives to hold on to their wealth, and on the other side, people in need have been willing to massacre their fellows for a grain of rice, a hope for a penny in their pocket.

Mahatma Gandhi asked the Indian people to embrace nonviolence and to renounce clinging to foreign ways, which they associated with wealth and prosperity. Since most Indians wore cloth that was British-made, he asked them to give up wearing British cloth and weave their own. This proclamation of self-sufficiency was one way, and a powerful one, of promoting dignity based not on material possessions but on one's inherent state of being. But at the same time, with every respect for Gandhi's vision of nonaggression, which he called *satyagraha*, or "seizing the truth," we should not confuse his message with extreme asceticism. In order to find one's inherent wealth, it is not necessary to renounce all material possessions and worldly pursuits. If a society is to have a sense of command and being ruled, then someone has to wear the three-piece suit at the negotiating tables; someone has to wear a uniform to keep the peace.

The basic message of the Shambhala teachings is that the best of human life can be realized under ordinary circumstances. That is the basic wisdom of Shambhala: that in this world, as it is, we can find a good and meaningful human life that will also serve others. That is our true richness. At a time when the world faces the threat of nuclear destruction and the reality of mass starvation and poverty, ruling our lives means committing ourselves to live in this world as ordinary but fully human beings. The image of the warrior in the world is indeed, precisely, this.

The basic practice of richness is learning to project the goodness that exists in your being, so that a sense of goodness shines out. That goodness can be reflected in the way your hair is combed, the way your suit fits, the way your living room looks—in whatever there is in your immediate world. Then it is possible to go further and experience greater richness by developing what are called the seven riches of the universal monarch. These are very ancient categories first used in India to describe the qualities of a ruler. In this case, we are talking about developing these qualities individually, personally.

The first richness of the ruler is to have a queen. The queen—or we could say wife or husband, if you like—represents the principle of decency in your household. When you live with someone with whom you can share your life, both your wisdom and your negativities, it encourages you to open up your personality. You don't bottle things up. However, a Shambhala person does not have to be married. There is always room for bachelors. Bachelors are friends to themselves as well as having a circle of friends. The basic principle is to develop decency and reasonability in your relationships.

The second richness of the universal monarch is the minister. The principle of the minister is having a counselor. You have your spouse who promotes your decency, and then you have friends who provide counsel and advice. It is said that the ministers should be inscrutable. The sense of inscrutability here is not that your friends are devious or difficult to figure out but that they do not have a project or goal in mind that clouds their friendship with you. Their advice or help is open-ended.

The third richness is the general, who represents fearlessness and protection. The general is also a friend, a friend who is fearless because he or she has no resistance to protecting you and helping you out, doing whatever is needed in a situation. The general is a friend who will actually care for you, as opposed to one who provides counsel.

The fourth richness is the steed, or horse. The steed represents industriousness, working hard and exerting yourself in situations. You don't get trapped in laziness, but you constantly go forward and work with situations in your life.

The fifth richness is the elephant, which represents steadiness.

266   Chögyam Trungpa Rinpoche

You are not swayed by the winds of deception or confusion. You are steady like an elephant. At the same time, an elephant is not rooted like a tree trunk—it walks and moves. So you can walk and move forward with steadiness, as though riding an elephant.

The sixth richness of the ruler is the wish-granting jewel, which is connected with generosity. You don't just hold on to the richness that you achieve by applying the previous principles, but you let go and give—by being hospitable, open, and humorous.

Number seven is the wheel. Traditionally, the ruler of the entire universe holds a gold wheel, while the monarch who rules this earth alone receives an iron wheel. The rulers of Shambhala are said to have held the iron wheel, because they ruled on this earth. On a personal level, the wheel represents command over your world. You take your seat properly and fully in your life, so that all of the previous principles can work together to promote richness and dignity in your life.

By applying these seven principles of richness, you can actually handle your family life properly. You have a wife or husband, which promotes decency; you have close friends, who are your advisers; and you have your guardians, or companions, who are fearless in loving you. Then you have exertion in your journey, in your work, which is represented by the horse. You ride on your energy all the time; you never give up on any of the problems in your life. But at the same time, you have to be earthy, steady, like an elephant. Then, having all those, you don't just feel self-satisfied, but you become generous to others, like the wish-granting gem. Because of that, you rule your household completely; you hold the wheel of command. That is the vision of how to run your household in an enlightened fashion.

Having done that, you feel that your life is established properly and fully. You feel that a golden rain is continuously descending. It feels solid, simple, and straightforward. Then, you also have a feeling of gentleness and openness, as though an exquisite flower has bloomed auspiciously in your life. In whatever action you perform, whether accepting or rejecting, you begin to open yourself to the treasury of Shambhala wisdom. The point is that, when there is harmony, then there is also fundamental wealth. Although at that particular point you might be penniless, there is no problem. You are suddenly, eternally rich.

If you want to solve the world's problems, you have to put your own household, your own individual life, in order first. That is somewhat of a paradox. People have a genuine desire to go beyond their individual, cramped lives to benefit the world. But if you do not start at home, then you have no hope of helping the world. So the first step in learning how to rule is learning to rule your household, your immediate world. There is no doubt that, if you do so, then the next step will come naturally. If you fail to do so, then your contribution to this world will be further chaos.

Contributors

EZRA BAYDA has been practicing meditation since 1970. He originally trained in the Gurdjieff tradition, and began formal Zen practice in 1978, receiving dharma transmission in 1998. He now lives, writes, and teaches at Zen Center San Diego. He is the author of *Saying Yes to Life—Even the Hard Parts* and *Zen Heart*.

SYLVIA BOORSTEIN, PHD, is a cofounding teacher at Spirit Rock Meditation Center. She is the author of many best-selling books—including *Happiness Is an Inside Job*—and a frequent contributor to the *Shambhala Sun*. She lives in both California and France—with her husband of fifty-five years, Seymour—and travels widely teaching meditation and loving-kindness.

BARRY BOYCE is senior editor of the *Shambhala Sun* and *Buddhadharma* magazines. He is also a freelance writer and writing teacher, and a member of the Denma Translation Group, which produced a critically acclaimed and best-selling translation of *The Art of War* by Sun Tzu. He is co-author of *The Rules of Victory: How to Transform Chaos and Conflict—Strategies from* The Art of War (excerpted here).

MICHAEL CARROLL is an authorized teacher in the lineage of the renowned Tibetan meditation master Chögyam Trungpa Rinpoche and a consultant and business coach for many large firms and non-profit organizations. He is the author of *Awake at Work* (excerpted here) and *The Mindful Leader*.

PEMA CHÖDRÖN is one of America's leading Buddhist teachers and the author of many best-selling books, including *The Places That Scare You*, *When Things Fall Apart* (excerpted here), and *Start Where You Are*. Born Deirdre Blomfield-Brown in 1936, she raised a family and taught elementary school before becoming ordained as a nun in 1981. Pema Chödrön's root teacher was Chögyam Trungpa Rinpoche, who appointed her abbess of the monastery he founded in Cape Breton, Nova Scotia, Canada. Since his death in 1987, she has studied with Trungpa Rinpoche's son, Sakyong Mipham Rinpoche, and her current principal teacher, Dzigar Kongtrül Rinpoche.

CHOKYI NYIMA RINPOCHE is the abbot of one of the largest Buddhist monasteries in Nepal, Ka-Nying Shedrub Ling, and the founder of the Rangjung Yeshe Institute for Buddhist Studies and Rangjung Yeshe Publications. He is the eldest son of the late Tulku Urgyen Rinpoche, one of the preeminent teachers in the Great Perfection (Dzogchen) tradition of Tibetan Buddhism. He is the author of *Present Fresh Wakefulness* and *The Union of Mahamudra and Dzogchen*.

JOHN DAIDO LOORI ROSHI—one of the heirs to the revered Zen master Maezumi Roshi—is the founder of the Mountains and River Order and the abbot of Zen Mountain Monastery in Mount Tremper, New York. He has written books on koans, art, photography, and basic Zen, including *Mountain Record of Zen Talks* (excerpted here) and *The Way of Mountains and Rivers*.

HIS HOLINESS THE DALAI LAMA, Tenzin Gyatso, is the spiritual and temporal leader of the Tibetan people and a winner of the Nobel Peace Prize. He is also a profound Buddhist teacher who is the author of many best-selling books, including *Worlds in Harmony: Compassionate Action for a Better World* (excerpted here) and *In My Own Words: An Introduction to My Teaching and Philosophy*.

ZOKETSU NORMAN FISCHER is a Soto Zen priest in the Suzuki Roshi lineage and a well-known writer and poet. A former abbot of the San Francisco Zen Center, he is founder of the Everyday Zen Foundation. His many books include *Sailing Home: Using Homer's Odyssey to Navigate Life's Perils and Pitfalls* (prose) and *I Was Blown Back* (poetry).

CAROLYN ROSE GIMIAN is an author and editor living in Halifax, Nova Scotia, and a regular contributor to the *Shambhala Sun*. She is the editor for many of the books of Chögyam Trungpa, including his *Collected Works* and *Smile at Fear: Awakening the True Heart of Bravery*. She is also the founding director of the Shambhala Archives, dedicated to the collection and preservation of the teachings and artifacts of Trungpa Rinpoche and associated teachers.

JAMES GIMIAN is the publisher of the *Shambhala Sun* magazine and the codirector of the Denma Translation Group, which produced a critically acclaimed and best-selling translation of *The Art of War* by Sun Tzu. He has offered seminars, corporate retreats, and leadership programs that teach how to effectively apply the strategies and principles of *The Art of War* in a wide range of contexts. He is co-author of *The Rules of Victory: How to Transform Chaos and Conflict—Strategies from* The Art of War (excerpted here).

JOSEPH GOLDSTEIN is a guiding teacher and cofounder of the Insight Meditation Society in Barre, Massachusetts. He lectures and leads retreats around the world, and is author of *One Dharma: The Emerging Western Buddhism*, *The Experience of Insight*, and *A Heart Full of Peace* (excerpted here).

THICH NHAT HANH is a renowned Vietnamese Zen master, poet, peace advocate, and founder of the Engaged Buddhist movement. The author of more than forty books, including *The Miracle of Mindfulness*; *Peaceful Action, Open Heart: Lessons from the Lotus Sutra* (excerpted here); and *You Are Here* (also excerpted here). He resides at practice centers in France and the United States.

Jon Kabat-Zinn, PhD, is a scientist, writer, and meditation teacher engaged in bringing mindfulness into the mainstream of medicine and society. He was the founding executive director of the Center for Mindfulness in Medicine, Health Care, and Society at the University of Massachusetts Medical School, and the founder and former director of its world-renowned Stress Reduction Clinic. He is the author of several best-selling books, including *Full Catastrophe Living*; *Wherever You Go, There You Are*; and *Coming to Our Senses: Healing Ourselves and the World through Mindfulness* (excerpted here).

Dzigar Kongtrül Rinpoche is the founder of Longchen Jigmé Samten Ling, a mountain retreat center in Crestone, Colorado, where he lives with his wife. He is the author of *It's Up to You: The Practice of Self-Reflection on the Buddhist Path* and *Light Comes Through: Buddhist Teachings on Awakening to Our Natural Intelligence* (both excerpted here).

Jack Kornfield, PhD, trained as a Buddhist monk in Thailand, Burma, and India. He is a cofounder of the Insight Meditation Society in Barre, Massachusetts, and of the Spirit Rock Center in Northern California. He is the author of *A Path with Heart*; *After the Ecstasy, the Laundry*; and *The Wise Heart: A Guide to the Universal Teachings of Buddhist Psychology* (excerpted here).

Judy Lief is an *acharya* (senior teacher) in Shambhala International as well as one of the principal editors of the work of Chögyam Trungpa Rinpoche. She is the author of *Making Friends with Death: A Buddhist Guide to Encountering Mortality*. Lief has taught extensively on working with Buddhist practice in the context of caregiving. She lives with her husband in Vermont.

DAVID LOY is the Besl Professor of Ethics/Religion and Society at Xavier University and a Zen teacher in the lineage of Koun Yamada. His books include *A Buddhist History of the West: Studies in Lack*; *The Great Awakening: A Buddhist Social Theory*; and *Money, Sex, War, Karma: Notes for a Buddhist Revolution* (excerpted here). He spent the early part of 2009 in Jerusalem, contributing as a Buddhist scholar to a research project on Jewish mysticism in comparative perspective.

SAKYONG MIPHAM RINPOCHE is the spiritual leader of Shambhala, an international network of Buddhist meditation and retreat centers. He teaches throughout North America, Europe, and Asia and is a regular contributor to the *Shambhala Sun*. He is the author of *Turning the Mind into an Ally* and *Ruling Your World*.

PHILLIP MOFFITT, former chief executive and editor-in-chief of *Esquire* magazine, is founder and president of the Life Balance Institute, a nonprofit organization devoted to the study and practice of spiritual values in daily life. He is a member of the Spirit Rock Meditation Center Teachers' Council and teaches *vipassana* meditation at retreat centers around the country. He also holds a weekly meditation class in Marin County, California. He is the author of *Dancing with Life: Buddhist Insights for Finding Meaning and Joy in the Face of Suffering* (excerpted here).

THE DZOGCHEN PONLOP RINPOCHE is a meditation master and scholar in the Kagyu and Nyingma schools of Tibetan Buddhism. He is the president of Nalandabodhi, a network of meditation centers, and founder of the Nitartha Institute, a course of Buddhist study for Western students. He is a frequent contributor to the *Shambhala Sun* and a recurring panel member for *Buddhadharma* "Forum," a discussion among teachers of various Buddhist traditions. He is the author of *Wild Awakening* and *Mind beyond Death*.

Matthieu Ricard was translator and senior student of Dilgo Khyentse Rinpoche, the twentieth century's foremost teacher of the Great Perfection (Dzogchen) tradition of Tibetan Buddhism. He is a participant in current scientific research on the effects that meditation has on the brain. He is the author of *The Monk and the Philosopher*, *The Quantum and the Lotus*, and *Happiness: A Guide to Developing Life's Most Important Skill* (excerpted here).

Sharon Salzberg is a renowned teacher of insight meditation and the cultivation of compassion. She is a cofounder of the Insight Meditation Society in Barre, Massachusetts, and of the Barre Center for Buddhist Studies. Salzberg has released *The Kindness Handbook* and *Unplug*, an interactive audio kit published by Sounds True. She is the author of *Faith: Trusting Your Own Deepest Experience* (excerpted here).

Joan Sutherland is the founding teacher of The Open Source, a network of Zen communities in the western United States that is part of the Pacific Zen School. She is a frequent contributor to the *Shambhala Sun* and *Buddhadharma* magazines. She recently moved to Santa Fe, New Mexico, where she is establishing a center for the koan way.

Shunryu Suzuki Roshi (1904–1971) was founder of the San Francisco Zen Center and a pivotal figure in the transmission of Buddhism to the West. His teachings have been published in the classic *Zen Mind, Beginner's Mind* (excerpted here), *Branching Streams Flow in the Darkness: Zen Talks on the Sandokai,* and *Not Always So.*

John Tarrant Roshi is director of the Pacific Zen Institute, where he works with students using koans, storytelling, and artistic process. He has a PhD in psychology and teaches at Duke Integrative Medicine at Duke University Medical School. He is the author of *Bring Me the Rhinoceros* and *The Light inside the Dark.*

CHÖGYAM TRUNGPA RINPOCHE (1940–1987) escaped his native Tibet in 1949, eventually moving to North America, where he founded Vajradhatu, a worldwide network of meditation centers. A prolific writer, poet, calligrapher, and artist, he became one of the most influential Buddhist teachers to come to the West. He was the author of such classics as *Cutting through Spiritual Materialism, The Myth of Freedom, Born in Tibet, Training the Mind* (excerpted here), and *Shambhala: The Sacred Path of the Warrior* (also excerpted here).

TSOKNYI RINPOCHE is the son of Tulku Urgyen Rinpoche, one of the preeminent teachers of the Great Perfection (Dzogchen) tradition of Tibetan Buddhism. He is the founder of the Pundarika Foundation, which has retreat centers in both Asia and North America. He teaches extensively in the West. He is the author of *Carefree Dignity* and *Fearless Simplicity* (excerpted here).

POLLY YOUNG-EISENDRATH, PHD, a Jungian psychoanalyst, is clinical associate professor of psychiatry and clinical associate professor of psychology at the University of Vermont and clinical supervisor and consultant on leadership development at Norwich University. A longtime Buddhist practitioner, she is the author of over a dozen books, including *The Self-Esteem Trap: Raising Confident and Compassionate Kids in an Age of Self-Importance.*

Credits

James Gimian and Barry Boyce, "Acting Effectively Amidst Chaos and Change." Adapted from *The Rules of Victory* by James Gimian and Barry Boyce, © 2008 by James Gimian. Reprinted by arrangement with Shambhala Publications Inc., Boston, MA. www.shambhala.com.

Joseph Goldstein, "The Practice of Loving-Kindness for All." © Joseph Goldstein, 2007. Reprinted from *A Heart Full of Peace,* with permission from Wisdom Publications, 199 Elm St., Somerville, MA. 02144. wisdompubs.org.

Thich Nhat Hanh, "Be What You Need to Be." Reprinted from *Peaceful Action, Open Heart: Lessons from the Lotus Sutra* (rev. ed., 2008) by Thich Nhat Hanh with permission of Parallax Press, Berkeley, California, www.parallax.org.

Thich Nhat Hanh, "Healing Pain and Dressing Wounds." From *You Are Here* by Thich Nhat Hanh, © 2001 Éditions Dangles, Saint-Jean-de-Braye (France) and © 2001 by Unified Buddhist Church, Inc. Reprinted by arrangement with Shambhala Publications Inc., Boston, MA. www.shambhala.com.

Jon Kabat-Zinn, "Dharma." From *Coming to Our Senses* by Jon Kabat-Zinn. Copyright © 2005 Jon Kabat-Zinn, PhD. Reprinted by permission of Hyperion. All rights reserved.

Dzigar Kongtrül Rinpoche, "Have Courage and a Sense of Humor." From *It's Up to You* by Dzigar Kongtrül, © 2005 by by Dzigar Kongtrül Rinpoche. Reprinted by arrangement with Shambhala Publications, Inc., Boston, MA. www.shambhala.com.

Dzigar Kongtrül Rinpoche, "Putting Others in the Center." From *Light Comes Through* by Dzigar Kongtrül, © 2008 by Dzigar Kongtrül. Reprinted by arrangement with Shambhala Publications Inc., Boston, MA. www.shambhala.com.

Jack Kornfield, "The Transformation of Desire into Abundance." From *The Wise Heart: A Guide to the Universal Teachings of Buddhist Psychology*, © 2008 by Jack Kornfield. Used by permission of Bantam Books, a division of Random House, Inc.

David Loy, "Lack of Money." © David R. Loy, 2008. Reprinted from *Money, Sex, War, Karma: Notes for a Buddhist Revolution* with permission from Wisdom Publications, 199 Elm St., Somerville, MA. 02144. wisdompubs.org.

Sakyong Mipham Rinpoche, "How Will I Use This Day?" From the March 2009 issue of the *Shambhala Sun*.

Sakyong Mipham Rinpoche, "A Simple Sense of Delight." From the November 2003 issue of the *Shambhala Sun*.

Phillip Moffitt, "Mindfulness and Compassion: Tools for Transforming Suffering into Joy." Reprinted from: *Dancing with Life* by Phillip Moffitt. Copyright © 2008 by Phillip Moffitt. Permission granted by Rodale, Inc., Emmaus, PA 18098.

Matthieu Ricard, "Optimism, Pessimism, and Naivete." From *Happiness* by Matthieu Ricard. Copyright © 2003 by Nil editions, Paris; Translation copyright © 2006 by Jesse Browner. By permission of Little, Brown & Company.

Sharon Salzberg, "Faith: Trusting Your Own Deepest Experience." From the chapter "Faith and Fear," adapted from *Faith: Trusting Your Own Deepest Experience* by Sharon Salzberg, copyright © 2001 by Sharon Salzberg. Used by permission of Riverhead Books, an imprint of Penguin Group (USA) Inc. ("Autumn" by Rainer Maria Rilke, translated and copyright © Jonathon Cott, reprinted by permission of the translator.)

Shunryu Suzuki Roshi, "Transiency." From *Zen Mind, Beginner's Mind* by Shunryu Suzuki; protected under the terms of the International